In the midst of a society th... is gro... ...ed, narcissism, and abuse, we n... ...p... ...solutions in order to walk safely through the "minefields" before us. *The Becoming*, by Hope Zins, is a book that shares her personal journey filled with pain and seemingly impossible situations throughout abusive patterns but ends in victory with secured identity and purpose established in her life. *The Becoming* is a book for this hour.

Patricia King
Patricia King Ministries
Minister; Television Host
Author of A Prophetic Manifesto for the New Era:
20 Prophetic Words for the 2020s
patriciakingministries.com

Full of truth and inspiration, *The Becoming* was not just your run-of-the-mill feel-good read, but it reached down deep to uncover lies and deception, pulled them out, and lovingly replaced them with the truth of God's love and grace. It was an easy read. It was risky, vulnerable, and absolutely genuine. Like having a conversation with my dearest friend, this book brought me in close to reveal to me and remind me who I really am and who my Creator made me to be—absolutely, wonderfully, uniquely, and fearfully made. I wholeheartedly recommend this book to all who are longing for true healing and deeper relationship with Jesus.

Dr. Alexandria Crumble
Singing Prophet and Founder of
Surrendered Hearts Collective Ministries
Author of *Dear Worshipper, Do the HeartWork*
alexandriacrumble.com

Hope Zins, author of *The Becoming*, is a bright beacon in this unprincipled world—igniting our paths to righteousness. *The Becoming* reflects the anointing of God that rests on Hope's life to esteem others higher than herself. This book will capture and saturate your heart with love and bold truths as unapologetically shared by Hope. The evidence of her faith will catapult you to study the Word and establish a closer walk with God. What an anointed compass for purposeful living! After reading *The Becoming*, lives will be challenged and inspired to fulfill their God-given purpose. Oh, what a blessing!

Sandra Rutledge Kitwana
Vocalist; Author; Motivational Speaker
Founder of Positive Images of Ohio, Inc.
Youth Leadership Program

The Becoming captured me from the very first word, and I could not put it down. Hope's style of writing, sincerity, and vulnerability she presents through the pages is nothing short of healing from the hand of God. She uses her life's mistakes to allow her readers to connect to God's truth of their value. You will not be the same after reading *The Becoming*. You will experience a mirror of identity transformation right before your eyes. This is a must read for anyone who has yet to walk in the truth that God is for them and not against them.

Debra Lynn Hayes
Chief Admissions Officer,
Igniting Souls Publishing Agency
Author of *RISE...*
What To Do When Hell Won't Back Off
debralynnhayes.com

There were so many people who came to mind as I read this book, including myself! Hope's transparency and the way she weaves scripture throughout her story was so inspiring, encouraging, and faith-building! I don't know how anyone could not feel some sort of healing and deliverance in their soul after going through every chapter of this book! One of my favorite statements from *The Becoming* was a pinnacle moment—a revelation from the Lord, "The world needs what *I* designed *you* to give in the way I created you to give it." This foundational statement is reiterated throughout every chapter of the book!

Pamela Wantz
Senior Pastor, Linden Avenue Baptist Church

In the pages of her book, Hope Zins brings us into a powerful encounter with Jesus and His love, grace, and transforming goodness. Her honest and transparent testimony opens the doors for "the becoming" of God's plan for every reader to manifest.

Jackie Murray
Co-pastor, Living Word Church

Holy Spirit has truly anointed our dear sister-in-Christ, Hope Zins, to write this encouraging and inspiring book. Abba Father has blessed her with the uncanny ability to be super-transparent, which aids in her enthusiasm to help others become who He created them to be. There is a God-sized void in everyone that she confronts and gives biblical as well as practical solutions. These truths that have transformed her life are in the pages of this "must read" book. We highly recommend this book for believers and non-believers!

Bishop John and Overseer Tina Jennings
Pastors, Kingdom Authority Ministries International, Inc.

The Becoming is an open book to the heart of this dear sister. Not only did this bring the revelation of truth through revealing the lies and proclaiming who we are in Christ, but it took you into the depths of her heart through personal experiences of healing, restoration, forgiveness, and love. A story of redemption through the heart of a Savior. It takes courage, strength, vulnerability, boldness, and fearlessness to dig deep into the wells of your soul and unlock your true value and identity in Christ, and this is exactly what Hope accomplished. A fearless warrior proclaiming truth. We highly recommend this book to all. It has been an honor to know this dear sister and we fully support what the Lord is doing in her life! What an honor to be a partaker of what the Lord will do through this great piece of work.

John and Linda Martin
Ministers; Founders of Warrior House Ministries

Hope Zins shares insights that will help us overcome the wounds and failures of our own choices and the lies of our manipulative enemy, the accuser. The wonderful victory and resilience she found in the Lord as He led her through a season of dark night experiences to increasing freedom is found in these pages.

Karen Haupt
Minister; Intercessor;
Founder of Dayton House of Prayer

In my career, I have the privilege of enjoying a variety of books and genres. But something about Hope's book, *The Becoming*, stuck with me. It was like we were having a cup of tea, and her story made me cry, laugh, and ponder. I know Hope wants God to receive all the glory through her story, and I stand with her in agreement on that. She doesn't merely tell a story, but she invites the reader to hear *her* story and how they can overcome. I pray you find freedom in God's truth when reading this.

Felicity Fox
Editor; Ghostwriter; Author of *Where the Holidays Go*
www.thefelicityfoxhouse.com

What Readers Are Saying About The Becoming

"I'm not much of a book reader, but *The Becoming* captured my attention right away. I couldn't put it down once I read the first chapter. I wanted to keep reading to see what happened next! As I read, I was able to tell that Hope not only really cared about me, but she could really relate to me. At times, it felt like just the two of us were having a conversation because I could intimately relate to her experience and emotions as if I were walking in her shoes. Other times, she was so relating to me that it felt like she was taking a page right out of my own life! I'm not sure how she was able to bring humor out of such hard situations, but she did, I even found myself chuckling several times as I read. When you're walking through difficulty in life and relationships, you can feel so isolated and lonely. After reading *The Becoming* and the God-given message of hope God has given Hope, I feel stronger knowing I'm not alone. He is with me."

Sandy F.

"This book is an open window to the Father's heart. Everyone can find themselves in Hope's story as she bares her heart with such graceful vulnerability. It's an invitation to a safe place with God as He reveals His nature through her life. I kept having to put the book down to process what was happening in my own heart! As the story progressed, so did my own healing journey. This book is a genuine expression of the goodness of our God, empowering the reader to co-labor with our Heavenly Father to break the chains of bondage and soar into new realms of freedom. I felt refreshed after drinking from the rivers of living water that flow from this amazing woman's surrendered heart."

Carmen R.

"Hope is a God-lover. He is her First Love. I believe her testimony of salvation, deliverance, and healing will set many, who have been stuck by their past, free. Hope helps the reader by revealing who they really are in Christ Jesus our Lord. I've known Hope since before she could walk and now seeing her run in Jesus causes me to rejoice! So keep running, Hopey, run! And I pray that all who read *The Becoming* are also propelled to run in Jesus by the power of the Holy Spirit for such a time as this."

Tammy K.

"*The Becoming* is the story of how Hope found hope in the midst of her shattered life. This book is passionately written and has rich nuggets of wisdom and truth woven throughout. It is a work obviously penned by the Holy Spirit through the writer!"

Cherri T.

"Having keys gives you access to things preciously locked away, specifically for someone who sees the value of what is behind closed doors. When every door seems closed and every road a dead end, it's God who provides the keys to His goodness and love. He wants to give you *all-access* but to receive it, we must be willing to know Him better—to know His heart. *The Becoming* is like an all-access key.

Hope reveals how the things she felt she had to lock away and hide became the key to her finding her identity in Christ, giving her access to *all* of God's heart and promises. God doesn't want you to hide but receive this key as a tool to reveal who you are to become. With an open heart, read *The Becoming* and start a journey of healing and inspiration, where, through the words shared, the Holy Spirit becomes your guide to experience the true healing available to you!"

Jennelle B.

"Have you ever felt like you were lost in a sea of hurt, pain, and confusion? Have you ever wondered if you will be able to heal and move past that brokenness? If so, *The Becoming* by Hope Zins is for you. In this book she is raw and vulnerable. She meets you in your brokenness and walks with you into a place of healing and security. Through these pages she effortlessly leads you down a path of soul deep forgiveness and will help you rediscover the beautiful peace that comes from having our identity rest in Christ. This book is an inspiring, true story of overcoming pain and adversity, and embracing the love that can be waiting on the other side. *The Becoming* is a needed book for this time."

Kelley R.

The Becoming

The Becoming

Discover Your Value.
Find True Confidence.
Embrace Your Freedom.

HOPE ZINS

AUTHOR ACADEMY elite

Please note that the name satan is intentionally not capitalized, I choose not to give him the credit of proper literary rules. The words Heaven and Kingdom (of God) are capitalized in honor, reverence, and love to my Lord Jesus, Father God, and Precious Holy Spirit—the beautiful perichoresis teaching us to dance the dance of unity and love.

Published by Author Academy Elite
PO Box 43, Powell, OH 43065
www.AuthorAcademyElite.com

Identifiers:
LCCN: 2021905648
ISBN: 978-1-64746-749-4 (paperback)
ISBN: 978-1-64746-750-0 (hardback)
ISBN: 978-1-64746-751-7 (ebook)
Available in paperback, hardback, e-book, and audiobook

Any Internet addresses and websites printed in this book are offered as a resource. They are not intended in any way to be or imply an endorsement by Author Academy Elite, nor does Author Academy Elite vouch for the content of these sites and numbers for the life of this book.

Some names and identifying details have been changed to protect the privacy of individuals.

Dedication

I dedicate this book to all who are searching for value, meaning, and fulfillment in life. I've seen your faces and felt your heart as I wrote these words. *You* are the reason I wouldn't give up writing, even after suffering a traumatic brain injury that left me unable to walk or talk for a time. You matter, dear one; the years I've invested into this book proves it. You matter so much to me that I refused to quit, and you matter so much to God that He wouldn't let me! To those of you who are longing for the "more" in life, this book is for you. I pray the words on the page become the words on your heart. Even on your darkest days please don't forget—you matter and you're a person of value, dignity, and worth—God and I agree. You are about to embark upon an adventure of a lifetime to the center of God's heart and it holds pure love, joy, and delight for you. Happy reading, my friend! Happy becoming …

Contents

Foreword
(Words from a Mother's Heart)

I have had the honor and God-given privilege of knowing this author personally since the time I gave birth to her. I can authenticate her life-encounters as she sits down with you to reenact some of her hardest tests and trials as well as victories. Her transparency will make you feel like she is sitting across the coffee table from you, as a friend speaks openly and honestly with another friend.

Her gift of writing and communication will captivate you and draw you into her journey, as though you're walking alongside her. Her greatest goal is *you*. You, seeing how your life can be transformed, as hers was by the amazing love of the Father.

Every chapter has a unique and clever title that gives you an idea of what she will be talking about next as her story unfolds. We all have a story to tell, and Hope desires that you will have many stories of triumph to share from your own life as you read this very encouraging book. Life's experience is one of our best teachers, and it is greatly beneficial to look at our hearts as God takes each of us through our own transformation of *becoming*.

Candy Poland
RN; Hope's mom, friend, counselor, and prayer warrior

Acknowledgments

There are not enough words, ink, or pages to thank all the people I want to honor. So, to those of you who have supported me in this project, in any way—big and small, from the bottom of my heart, I thank you and praise God for you.

To my loving, supportive, successful, hunky husband, Alan Frederick Zins, who inspired me with the idea to write this book in the first place, the words "thank you" do not feel like nearly enough. The way you love me and bring out the best in me is beautiful. Truly, God joined us together for such a time as this. Wherever you are is home, my love. Out of all the people in the world, I'm so thankful the Lord led our hearts to each other. Our love is a living testimony of how God so graciously heals and brings beauty out of brokenness. I would choose you again in a heartbeat, honey. Thank you for being an example of Jesus' love and protection for me as His bride. You make my faith stronger because of how you love me.

To my amazing, loving, supportive parents, Harold and Candy Poland, it would be impossible for me to tell this story without you. I'm so thankful at how God used your wisdom and prayers to pull me out of such dark times. You raised us with beautiful, living examples of what love, wisdom, and integrity look like—and I don't dare take that or you for granted. The way you live greatly influences others in more ways than you know, and it will not return to you void. Thank you for making a lifelong investment into eternity through your family. I love you and am over-the-moon grateful for you.

To those who financially contributed to this project because you believed in me and my message and wanted to plant a seed into the Kingdom of God, I couldn't have done this without you, with all sincerity and gratitude, I thank you. In alphabetical order: Amanda Harman; Charity Vargas; Craig and Shelia Barnes; Harold and Candy Poland; Jacquelyn and Rich Olivieri; Jahn and Debby Luke; Jeff and Dee Landis; Jeff and Henny Thomas; Joel and Amber Peña; Pete and Kathy Avnaim; Ron and Angie Cross; Sean and Rachel Garrison; Shawn Patrick; Tim and Tammy Kingery; Tim Francis. I'm so thankful for your eternal investment and support. God bless your generosity and may seven times as much be granted to you and your descendants forever.

To my editor and now friend, Felicity Fox. You were such an amazing support full of wisdom and grace through the emotional process of deeply diving into the heart of the matter and bringing out the gold without changing my voice or message. It takes a person who sincerely cares about bringing out the best in others to tenderly and supportively do what you do, how you do it. Thank you, my friend.

To the team at AAE, thank you for making this project possible. I am grateful for the God-connections that led me to you. I am so thankful for this opportunity and pray it's the first of many.

Above all, thank you Jesus, my Lord and Savior, my Best Friend, Comforter, Counselor, Editor, Wisdom, Bridegroom, and Beloved. Without you, none of this would be possible—no story, no book, no restoration, no message. I found the One Thing worth living for, and it's you, my precious Jesus. There is no language in the words of man that can describe the depths of love, gratitude, and adoration I feel for you. You can have my heart, my message, and my life, for I finally found freedom in living for an audience of One. This is for you, my Love, this is for you.

Introduction
(You're Worth the Fight!)

The sensation came from behind and sent shockwaves down my spine to the tips of my toes and back up to my brain again. I sat stunned, unable to understand what had just happened. The look of horror on my friends' faces was undeniable. I tried to ask what was going on, but when I heard myself speak, I didn't recognize my own voice. It sounded jumbled, like my words were running together and not making any sense. My eyes scanned all around me, searching for an answer, and as I looked, the whole world seemed to turn topsy-turvy, and I felt as if I were falling. I steadied myself in my seat as I heard one of the girls sitting beside me exclaim, "Oh my gosh! She just hit you!"

Out of the corner of my eye, I saw a young lady walking past our table with her arms up, holding a stack of chairs in the air. Suddenly, it dawned on me; the sensation I felt was her accidentally hitting me on the head with the chairs.

I had so much to say, but as I tried to get the words out, it felt as if my tongue and mouth were working independently of my brain. I stood up to get some air and was so overcome by a dizzying wave of nausea that I fell back into my seat. The look of concern on my friends' faces was growing worse ...

Hours later, I found myself being wheeled into the emergency room, soon to face more tests and scans than I'd had in all my thirty plus years combined. Words like "stroke" and "cranial hemorrhaging" were being tossed back and forth between the physicians attending to me, and I could tell by their faces that they were concerned. I tried focusing my eyes so I could find my husband, Alan, but everything was so blurry and bright that I could hardly see. Suddenly, as if he knew I was searching for him, I felt his hand take mine and as he did, I could sense God's grace washing over him.

And right there, in the midst of absolute pandemonium, the peaceful words of Jesus fell on my ears clearer than I'd ever heard before, "I am with you, even until the end of the age. What the devil meant for your destruction; I will use for good in every area of your life."

The next three days went by like a blur as I was examined, monitored, poked, and prodded. Thankfully, the report was no stroke, no cranial hemorrhaging, but a traumatic brain injury (TBI) resulting from something called a "whole brain concussion with hematoma." Because I was hit from behind and because I was sitting down at the time, the blow to my head caused my brain to "scramble" in my skull, affecting all the lobes in my brain instead of just one or two as it would in a typical concussion.

Side effects of the brain injury included: constant migraines; tremors; whiplash; hypersensitivity to sound and light; processing disorders; and severe vertigo. In addition to the whole brain concussion, I sustained a vestibular concussion, which left me unable to stand or walk on my own and with significant impairment to my speech.

After three days, I was permitted to go home, provided that around-the-clock care was arranged for the upcoming weeks and follow-up therapies and doctors' appointments were scheduled. Before I was discharged from the hospital, my attending neurologists told us that recovery from a TBI could be unpredictable, but they were hoping I would recover within a month. As time went on, they hoped I would recover in three months ... then six ... nine ... then a year, and hopefully not longer.

Little did I know that I was about to head down a *lo-ong* road to recovery, which was eventually reported to last the rest of my life ... But I have a promise from God—He promised to heal me *completely*, not just partially. And a promise from God is greater than any report from any person, no matter their level of expertise.

Since I was unable to walk or move around on my own, I was completely dependent upon my husband for almost everything for the first couple of months. After starting my therapies, I slowly transitioned from a wheelchair to a walker and was eventually able to independently do things such as sit up, bathe, and get dressed. But I was still a long way from walking without assistance or tolerating even the slightest noise or light, and driving was absolutely out of the question since simply riding in cars threw me into severe vertigo attacks.

The therapies were tremendously difficult. I can't explain to you how surreal it is to think you can pick up your feet and simply walk to the other side of the room and yet not be able to hardly move when you try. It's like my brain and my body were on different wavelengths, and the therapy was there to help them effectively communicate together again. (I don't take any steps for granted now.) The types of therapies I received throughout my recovery were several: vestibular; physical; osteopathy; cognitive; speech; psychological; emotional; and more. But the message was always the same—if you give up here and now and refuse to fight, you will cognitively and physically remain at that place for the rest of your life.

To be honest, there were many times I wanted to give up. So many times, I lay in bed, and my husband held me as we wept together. But I always came back to the truth that I had *so* much to fight for—my husband, my family, my friends, my future, *you—yes you!* You, living a free and fulfilled life in Christ was a significant focal point in my fight.

See, before my injury I had written the book you are now reading. I was just getting into the publishing process when I was hit on the head and *everything* in my life came to a screeching halt, including this book. I could hardly put one foot in front of the other, let alone one word. Suddenly, my life was silent. Everything stopped—coffee with friends, date nights with my husband, running and working out, driving, reading, listening to music, cooking, cleaning, posting on social media, walking around the house—I mean *everything*. All I could do for months on end was stay in bed and pray. I'll tell you what, friend, when everything is stripped away, what really matters comes into focus really fast.

While I would never want to go through that painful process again, I can honestly say it was one of the most spiritually strengthening experiences I've had. Now, I didn't always recognize this was the case as I was going through it. I just knew I had a choice. I could get angry at God and blame Him for causing or allowing the injury to happen, as others around me had sometimes suggested. Or I could hold onto the revelation of His goodness and believe that He is who *He* says He is—the Father of mercy, the God of all comfort, the One who heals the broken and holds us together. I chose to believe *Him*.

Often, others around me were looking for answers to why the injury happened, and sometimes, I would hear them working through their thoughts and emotions. And while I understood their process, I knew I couldn't let it be mine. I couldn't get stuck on the *why*. For the sake of my faith and my fight, I had to keep my focus on the *Who*. Who had promised to bring me through? Who had promised to heal me and make me whole? Jesus. And a promise from God trumps every problem, process, and report. Period.

I know it might sound crazy, but some of the sweetest moments I've ever encountered with Jesus came out of this time. From the outside looking in, it was hard to see how something so beautiful could come out of something so horrible. But while I was going through it, unexplainable peace washed over me in wave after wave. If you've ever walked through a life-changing difficulty with Jesus, I'm sure you can relate.

Before my injury, I'd always felt like I had to earn God's love and goodness toward me. But after the incident, there was nothing—and I mean absolutely *nothing* I could do to even attempt to earn anything from Him. Yet I had never known His love in such profound and real ways. I'd physically feel His arms holding me, comforting me as I rested in bed. The tender whispers of His loving voice rose up like soft caresses in my heart, "I'm here, baby. I'm right here with you. I'm in this with you; we're walking through it together."

And there, in that quiet place, the Lord made it clear that my love for Him originates from His love for me. In other words, it takes God to love God. Those were no longer just words on a page in Holy Scripture for me; they became a living and breathing revelation of who God is for me and who I am in Him. The words on the page became the words on my heart, the fabric of my being.

As I lay there for hours on end, it would feel like mere minutes had passed as I was caught up in the mysterious and amazing revelation of His love. As I lingered in that secret place, Jesus taught me the art of exchange. I discovered that He loves to hear what's on my heart, but He also longs to reveal to us what's on His. And as I listened to His heart, I was amazed at the levels of love and affection, approval, and passion I found there.

And this was only the beginning. I was embarking upon a lifelong journey of discovering the Father's heart reflected in the life of Jesus and the power of the Holy Spirit. It's the greatest of adventures we're all invited to discover.

At the time of this writing, it's been almost four years since my injury, and to be honest, I'm still not one hundred percent. But I will be—and I refuse to stop fighting. I have determined to stubbornly refuse to change the subject off the goodness of God and His ability and willingness to heal. Because I've experienced His miraculous power for myself, yet there's still *so* much more of Him I greatly desire to discover. I believe you do too. Otherwise, you wouldn't have started reading this book.

I need you to understand, dear one, that what you hold in your hands isn't just a book—it's a *miracle*, a promise fulfilled. Throughout my healing journey, I encountered many instances where I was told, "I can't ..." But *God* told me I *can*. And as I said earlier, *His* word trumps every other voice. Through *Him*, we can do *all* things. He doesn't need our extraordinary abilities or fancy degrees; He just needs our "yes." Our resounding yes will carry us farther than any endorsement, equipping, or qualification ever could. You know why? Because *He* gets to take the lead—and He'll never lead us where He won't go.

Is there more to this story? Oh, my goodness, *so* much more, but that's for another time. Right now, what I want you to turn your attention to as we approach our time together is this: you'll get out of this journey what you put into it.

If you give up along the way and refuse to fight the good fight of faith for your freedom and your future, you are susceptible to remaining in that place of stagnancy. Until you resolutely decide to not let fear or distractions talk you out of your breakthrough, you will settle for less than the best for your life and the lives of those you impact.

You are worth fighting for, my friend. I truly believe that I hope you do too. You can do this, dear one. I'm right here with you, cheering you along, reminding you that your freedom is worth the fight. What's more, God is walking this road with you, relentlessly wooing you with His love and drawing you into the *much more* He has in store for those who simply ask. He'll never give up on you or withhold His best from you—He never has. He said you were worth His very best, and you know what, He still does!

I'm excited to get started on the road with you, my friend. I'm sure you'd like to know what you can expect on our journey together. Or maybe you're that person who's wondering if this book is for you. Let me satisfy your curiosity by saying this book is for anyone who wants to be freed from the feeling of being stuck. Stuck in the cycle of unhealthy relationships. Stuck in self-sabotage and destructive decisions. Stuck in people-pleasing. Stuck in settling for less. Stuck in past hurts and repetitive patterns. Stuck in toxic soul ties and emotional wounds. Stuck in disorder and apathy.

This book is for anyone who wants to discover the *much more* God has in store for them and especially for those who feel like they can never get to it. As if your breakthroughs and blessings seem to vanish as soon as you start to get a glimpse of them. If this describes you, your life, and your longings, this book is for you.

I'll be honest, I spent hours working and then reworking, writing, and then rewriting the material I had prior to my brain injury. When I was finally able to start reading again, I remember revisiting my book and thinking, *Wow, my message has totally changed because my perspective has totally changed.* I'm not looking through the lens of religious lies anymore; I'm looking through the lens of God's love. And friend, looking through the lens of His love is where we find the truth and it's where we find the faith and strength for the fight.

So, if you're wondering whether you have the strength to fight for the freedom and fullness God has in store for you, let me just take the pressure off. All the faith and strength for the fight is found in the power of God's love. The heart of this book is truly about finding the heart of God and what His heart holds for you. I promise: His heart holds more love, kindness, and affection for you than you've ever dared to dream. He's really *that* good.

It's high time to stop letting fear be louder than love and the only way to do that is to find and fill up with the endless love God holds for you. It's the most exciting adventure you'll ever discover—because it's the adventure you were created for! That's right—God not only created you to love, but He also created you to be loved. You were made to discover His heart for you. Then, and only then, you'll be able to love others in the safe, healthy, and reciprocal ways you've always wanted.

So when you're ready, turn the page, and let's get going. And you'd better hold on tight, baby, because we're in for a fun, wild ride!

CHAPTER ONE

Hand Crafted by Design
(You Are Not an Accident)

There are no ordinary people.
—C.S. Lewis, Weight of Glory

I was crying.

In a wide-open room, full of all sorts of people, I found myself weeping. Keenly aware of how loud my sobbing had become, yet completely unable to control it.

The icy walls that had long held my heart hostage were finally thawing, melting like so many drops of rain—cleansing the dirt, softening the soil, and preparing for new growth in the garden of my soul.

It was unmistakable. God had brought me to this place. This room, filled with other broken, hurting people for one simple purpose. Healing. Deep healing poured out from God's pure love.

Years of hurt were healed in this one monumental, life-changing moment. A moment that would later prove to be of pinnacle importance in my life.

1

Have you ever had one of those: a pinnacle, monumental, life-changing moment? A moment where time seems to stand still and nothing and no one exists—except you and the awesome God who created you.

In this moment of brokenness and abandon, the Lord reassuringly whispered to my heart: "Never before and never again will there be another you. So be the best 'you,' you can be. Because the world needs what *I* designed *you* to give in the way I created you to give it."

Like salve, God's words soothed my soul, "You may not have been considered a worthy bride, but *I* consider you worthy. Your value is not found in what *others* have said, but in what *I* say. And I tell you, I have loved you with an everlasting love; with unfailing love, I have drawn you to myself and called you mine. You may have been mistreated and neglected, but I will never leave you or forsake you. Take My hand and let Me dance you through this life. Lean your head on My chest and trust Me to protect you against the obstacles and fears spinning around you. Trust Me when I tell you, you are *not* a mistake—I don't make mistakes. You are exactly as I designed, according to My desire and My delight."

Maybe like me, you have allowed what others said or did to define you, your value, your worth, and perhaps even your dignity. But I'm here to tell you—*you* alone are the one who gets to decide who you are and what you do, dear one.

Not them.

And the *only* thing you should be using to define your created value is God's view of you. Because God sees you, my friend. You aren't beyond His scope. He hasn't lost sight of you. He sees all we are and everything we do.

Do those words bring you peace? Or do they make you cringe and run for cover?

Maybe you view God as a ruthless dictator Who weighs every wrong move and balances every bad decision. One Who totals up your tallies, preparing to pull out your punishment at a moment's notice. Over the years, God has gotten a pretty bad rap as we've learned to wrongly attribute the hurts others have caused onto Him and His perfectly good, loving nature.

When God sees you, friend, He sees you not as you are but as He *created* you to be. He doesn't look at what you've done, but what's been done *for* you. He only ever views us through the lens of love.

His love.

If we've allowed anything or anyone to determine who we are and how we see ourselves, that's contrary to His truth, it needs to go.

Plain and simple.

It's high time we take back our dignity and freedom to choose and believe God's truth—His Word—His love laid out for us in written form—over what others say and do.

I realize that sometimes this is easier said than done especially when the lies are THIS CLOSE. So close, we can't seem to see past them in either direction. Like when someone you thought you could trust tells you one thing, but your insides are screaming something else altogether.

With this, I can absolutely identify. This person, we'll call him "Manny," knew all the right things to say. When I met him, I was in a far more impressionable place than I wanted to admit. You see, I'd always been such a strong-willed person who wasn't afraid to speak her mind. This got me in quite a bit of trouble as a kid—just ask my parents! Even in grade school, though I was often bullied, I stood up for the other kids who were also bullied. This made me more of a target in the end, but even back then, I had this driving force within me to stand up for what was *right*.

3

But when I met Manny, I was full of confusion, uncertain about myself and my beliefs. I'd recently returned from living out of state where I was involved in something that was supposed to be God-honoring. However, it ended up being anything but God-honoring. The experience, which was supposed to be spiritually strengthening, turned out to be more like a waking nightmare when the safety and sanctity of several of us were violated.

So, there I was back at home, confused and searching for truth, and in walked Manny. Or, in this instance, we'll call him, "Mr. Right-Words" because he certainly knew what to say to catch my attention. While there were warnings in my heart, and my gut said to get going, his words felt so validating—so soothing.

Psalm 55:21 (NLT) says, "His words are as smooth as butter...his words are as soothing as lotion, but underneath are daggers!" I couldn't have said it any better myself. His words made me feel so pretty, so captivating, so safe ... at first. And while I don't think his intention was to become a manipulator, the darkness he so often entertained wouldn't have wanted it any other way.

Up until then, I'd never had anyone pursue me the way he did. It seemed the more unsure I was about him, the more he stepped up and assured me he was sincere in his intentions. Whether it was taking the time to hear my heart, meet my family, make me dinner, or send me flowers, there was nothing subtle about his pursuit.

When we first started dating, we laughed a lot and had quite a bit of fun. It was simple and easy. When we first confessed our love for each other, I was inclined to think he was the one, but still something kept nagging me on the inside. There was no sign of passion or love for God in his life. Sure, he was *intellectually* interested in God and attended the same church I did, so I thought that would be enough. Certainly, it'd turn into something deeper than a desire for head knowledge, and his heart would catch up, right? I had *never* been so wrong.

Several months into our relationship, he suddenly stopped calling or coming around as often, but he always seemed to have some reasonable excuses for his absence. These excuses always worked to manipulate my emotions. Such as, "I'm taking the weekend to seek God about our future," or "I'm not able to call as often because I'm running low on my minutes." (Yes, this was *way* back in the stone ages when you only got so many minutes with your mobile provider plan.)

I was so giddy to hear he was taking time with God and so empathetic of his needs that common sense often eluded me. For example, why not simply use your landline if you maxed out your minutes? Or do you need the *whole* weekend, *every* weekend to soul search, and shouldn't *I* be included in that "future" discussion? I may not have directly asked him (or myself) these questions, but in my gut, I knew something was wrong.

So yeah, my friend, I get having your gut say one thing and having the one you love say another.

I wish I would've tuned into truth when the deceptions were suffocating me and the lies were closing in. When my insides were screaming their warnings, but my loved one was whispering his sincerity. Now I know that even when it is painful and even when I don't feel like it, there is only one thing to do when I want the truth. I must turn to the One Who *is* Truth.

Why?

The only thing able to shatter the deceptions that destroy our value, self-worth, freedom, and dignity is God's truth.

That bears repeating: *God's* truth is the only thing that renders the enemy's destructive lies, powerless. No matter how dark and deep the pit goes, it cannot overshadow the light of God's truth. John 1:5 (NLT) says, "The light shines in the darkness, and the darkness can never extinguish it." And Luke 8:17 (NLT) says, "For all that is secret will eventually be brought into the open, and everything that is concealed will be brought to light and made known to all."

So, let's start at the beginning and let's begin with the truth. And, dear one, the truth is you do not need to wait around for that certain someone to validate you or your value. The only one who can truly validate you is *you* and *Jesus*. Now, to make sure you're really getting me, let me say it in the way God got *my* attention: *Never before and never again will there be another you. So, be the best you, you can be.*

Hand-Crafted, Skillfully Designed

Okay, so maybe at this point, you're thinking, blah, blah, blah, I've heard it all before, but I'm just like everybody else. Well, honestly, to some degree, you would be right. Most of us have two eyes, two ears, one nose, a mouth, and four limbs.

But the thing is, there is something deep inside you— something special. And even though you may feel ordinary, this ... ooh, buddy ... *this* makes you extraordinary!

What is it? Well, you're just going to have to wait a second. I'll get to that in a minute.

Right now, what I really want you to get is this: when God made you, He didn't just throw a bunch of leftovers in a pot and hope for the best. No! You've been hand-crafted and skillfully designed by your Maker!

You haven't been mass-produced like toys on an assembly line, my friend. From the lilt of your laugh, to the muscles in your calves. The size of your nose, to the distance between your first and second toes. The beat of your heart, to the way you pronounce your R's. All of it has been custom made and masterfully designed like a rare and precious diamond. Those freckles on your nose. That mole on your chin. The birthmark that covers your left shoulder. God put those there intentionally! They aren't mistakes in your makeup. They're evidence that you've been handmade by your Creator to make you, well, *you!*

He knew what He was doing, and He knew what He was getting when He made you. After He was done, He stood up, dusted Himself off, and stepped back to admire His handiwork. God, your Creator, rejoiced and took great delight when He fashioned you, and you know what—He still does (see Zephaniah 3:17).

Well, I promised we'd get back to what takes you from ordinary to *extraordinary*, so here we go. Do us both a favor, okay? Grab a mirror. It doesn't matter what size.

Got it?

Okay, now look closely. Closer ... a little bit closer ... *There!* Did you see it? That flash? That glimmer? That sparkle in your eyes? That's it: Hope! That's what takes you from ordinary to extraordinary—hope!

Hope that everything I'm telling you is true.

Hope that God really did make you unique.

Hope that your life really isn't just some big cosmic accident.

Hope that no one else will ever think, talk, or act like only *you* can.

Hope that God made you on purpose, with a purpose, for a purpose!

So, why should you care? Care about your life? About whether God made you, *you* for a reason? Because you only get *one time* around at this thing.

You get *one* chance, *one* life to decide who you want to be. See, we don't get a do-over. Our lives are a one and done kind of thing. You can literally think of it as a once in a lifetime opportunity. Hebrews 9:27 tells us God has destined every person to die one time. And Job 14:5 (NLT) says God alone knows "…how many months we will live, and we are not given a minute longer."

How, then, do you make the *most* of your life? How do you become the person you *want* to be? We become who we *want* to be by embracing the person we were *created* to be. I know that might sound a bit cheesy, but stick with me here, okay? Because it's true. When we accept who God has created us to be, we're well on our way to becoming who we want to be.

Ephesians 2:10 tells us we are God's workmanship. His masterpiece. Created new in Christ Jesus to become the person and achieve the purposes and passions He planned for us, long before we were born.

So, how do we know who we were created to be? Well, to know more about who we were *created* to be, we first need to know more about our *Creator* and His Father's heart for us.

Our Story

Regardless of what others may have said to you or about you, your existence is *no* accident. Speaking of the Lord, Psalm 139:13 (NLT) says, "You made all the delicate, inner parts of my body and knit me together in my mother's womb."

Your life is the intentional, intricate handiwork of an amazing Creator. Do you know He marvels over you and made you in His own likeness (see Genesis 1:26)? He's a *perfectly* good Father with a heart more than big enough to hold and welcome us *all* into His divine, wondrous love story.

The story is the same for me as it is for you. God, according to His pleasure and delight, made us for intimacy and unity with Him and His beautiful body of believers. His story has no room for filters or fakeness. No pressure or performance. Just amazing, relentless, irresistible love. This is the story He's writing on your heart and mine.

We *all* write stories about our lives. There's an ongoing monologue, a voice-over of sorts, that we all say to ourselves as we go about our days. For a long time, I thought my own monologue depended upon what others had to say about me. This kind of thinking caught up with me, and eventually, I found myself lost in Manny's story. As my relationship with him progressed, I realized I didn't even know who I was anymore.

I was so lost in his plot, it scared me. But instead of scaring me out of the relationship, I buried myself deeper into it; doing whatever I could to make and *keep* him happy with me. As long as he was happy with me, my world was alright.

If I'd known what would evolve from this relationship, I'd like to think I would've run the other way. Suddenly, missed phone calls and weekends turned into whole *weeks* without seeing or hearing from him. And of course, it always came with excuses he knew I'd accept. "I'm working lots of extra hours right now, so I can save for our future." Or "I'm taking some much-needed time to evaluate my life and where it's going and I need to not be distracted by someone I love so much." (Oh, brother.)

I mean, *come on!* How did I not see through that? But I didn't. Because I only heard what I *wanted* to hear—and he knew it. In fact, after a while, *everyone* knew it. And a while after that, I started getting really bizarre phone calls from my friends telling me they saw him in places he shouldn't have been, with people he shouldn't have been with, and doing things he shouldn't have been doing. And of course, whenever I discussed it with him, he denied it, and I believed him—because I *wanted* to believe him.

I wanted to believe he was the guy who had worked so hard to get my attention and put so much effort into pursuing me. I wanted to believe he was the guy, *he* wanted me to believe he was for me. Unfortunately, this was only the beginning of him showing his true colors, but instead of choosing to see the truth, I chose to be color blind.

Have you ever found yourself lost in someone or something? Have you ever felt you were too far gone in your mess for God to find you?

The wonderful truth is, we're never lost from God. He's promised never to leave us, and nothing and no one can separate us from His love (see Hebrews 13:5, Romans 8:38, 39). No matter how lost we feel, friend, God calls us *found*.

No matter how much we think we've messed up our story, God doesn't call us a mess; He calls us much loved. Even the messiest stories bring Him glory because that's how He's designed it. He's promised to work all things out for our good, and His goodness is His glory.

No matter the messes we've made or what life throws our way, we get to decree and declare God's good plans and promises over our lives. We get to feed from this place because God is *greater*. He's greater than our stories. Greater than our problems. Greater than our messes. Greater than our hearts (1 John 3:20).

We never have to wonder if what we've done, our background, or our story would make God withhold from us. He never holds out on us; it's not in His nature (John 3:16, Romans 8:32). In fact, He takes personal the good plans and purposes He has for us because He personally backs all of His promises.

If you're looking for the proof in His promises, my friend, you don't have to look any further than *Jesus*.

The Found

He left the peace, perfection, and majesty of Heaven (Philippians 2:5–8). He made Himself vulnerable to our human experience. He encountered every human emotion and hardship—and then He overcame them (Hebrews 4:15, John 16:33). He only did what He saw the Father doing and only said what He heard the Father saying (John 5:19, John 12:49). He healed all who came to Him for healing and brought deliverance to every demonized, tormented individual He ever encountered (Matthew 8:16, Luke 6:19, Acts 10:38). He did so many miracles that if they were written down, the world could not contain them (John 21:25). Jesus provided a *perfect* picture of what the Father is like (Hebrews 1:3).

He gave His life as a ransom for ours (Matthew 20:28). His broken body makes ours whole (Isaiah 53:5). The blood He shed overcame all sin, sickness, and shame, deficiency, and pain (1 Peter 2:24, Romans 8:34, 37). He knew sorrow so we might have joy (Isaiah 53:3, Isaiah 61:1-3). He became poor that we might become rich (2 Corinthians 8:9). He bore and broke every curse, so we might bear His name and break every chain (Galatians 3:13, Galatians 5:1). He defeated death, so we might have everlasting life (John 11:25, John 3:16, 1 Corinthians 15:57). He triumphed over sin, hell, and the grave to make us righteous, restore what was lost, and reconcile our relationship with the Father (1 Corinthians 15:55–57, 2 Corinthians 5:18-21, Luke 19:10).

Jesus gave it *all*. He painted a perfect picture of our perfect Heavenly Father, and it's not in *His* heart to withhold from us any more than it is *Jesus'*. You may expect God to hold out on you because it's the way you've been treated; maybe it's the way you've been treating yourself. But can I just speak reassurance of the Father's love over you, my friend? He treats us better than anyone else—even better than we treat ourselves.

For years, I've struggled with feeling like everything has to look perfect, sound perfect, and be perfect. Let me tell you something, friend, I've never won that struggle. But I'm so grateful and oh so relieved that I don't have to. I simply have to surrender that struggle to my Savior because He's the only One who's perfect. And He perfectly meets me in the middle of my imperfection.

Psalm 138:8 (NKJV) tells us that "The Lord will perfect that which concerns me…" So please don't wait until you've "got it all together" to cry out and come to Christ Jesus. You'll be wasting precious time on something that's not going to happen *apart* from Him, like I did. It's needless and pointless to live under the pressure of performance-based approval because He's *already* put His stamp of approval upon us. He knows us best and loves us anyway. Aren't you so glad? I know I am!

There's no way I could ever deserve this kind of love. I've messed up way too many times, taken way too many wrong turns. I've wrecked relationships, compromised on purity and power. I've traded my peace for self-pity, sought self-indulgence over surrender, and made pleasing-people a priority over pleasing God.

Despite all my dumb decisions, God draws me close. His greatest desire is for me to come to Him. His desire for you is the same, dear one.

It always amazes me that the King of Glory gave it all so we might know His goodness. And all it takes is a willing heart and faith to believe He is love, and He is mighty to save. In our searching, we find His salvation—the salvation of Jesus Christ who came to seek and save the lost.

The cheaters.

The liars.

The sloppy.

The sordid.

The scared.

The broken.

The abuser.

The abused.

The lost.

Because we all get lost and afraid sometimes. That's why He came to seek us. To save us. *All* of us (Luke 19:10).

To all who believe in and receive Him, He's given the right to become the children of God (John 1:12). Jesus died a sinner's death so we might live and have everlasting life. Because of Him, we're no longer the lost—we're the found!

Why would Jesus put Himself through such torment? Such heartache and pain when He could have cried out to His Father to send twelve thousand angels to release Him (Matthew 26:53)? One word: love. Because He loves us. He loved us *then* and He loves us *now.* His language is love, and He loved us enough to follow through with what He said He would do.

In love, He saw beyond the cross ... beyond the grave ... beyond the empty tomb.

Looking beyond, what did He see?

You. Yes, you, living in a sin-stained, hopeless world, wrought with worry, pain, and weakness.

He looked past the blood-stained cross and said *you're worth it*. Worth the spilled blood. Worth the nail scars.

Worth the writhing pain. Worth the humiliation. He said you're worth the rescue. Worth the mission. Worth the follow-through.

If facing death meant saving you—He, my dear one, said *you* are worth it.

Words Matter

There might be people who tell you that "You're no good. You're a waste of time. You won't amount to anything. You're a mistake. You'll never succeed. You're not pretty enough. Not smart enough. Not strong enough."

My dear, *I'm* here to tell you those people are *wrong!*

I'm super grateful to be able to say my siblings and I were raised by two really wonderful parents who went above and beyond to make sure we knew we were loved. Their words of validation and affirmation blessed us and pointed us to the love of our Heavenly Father and His always good love.

You can imagine then what a shock and sad surprise it was for me when I encountered words of hatred and harassment at school. It seemed the popular pastime for my peers was to line up only to knock me down. As the years went on, this was something that grew increasingly worse.

At school, the words I heard were filled with hate and made me feel horrible. Even though the words I most often heard at home were full of love and affirmation, my school experience made my mom and dad's words hard to believe. As time went on, the carefree, cheerful child I used to be was replaced with someone much moodier and withdrawn.

Words are powerful, aren't they?

With words, we build-up, and with words, we tear down. It's easy to be affected by what others say, even when we don't want to be. Words change our environments—both internal and external. Sometimes, we even find ourselves molding into the person *others* say we are. At the same time, we will also mold to whatever *we* speak out of our own mouths. Either way, depending upon the words used, this can be a good thing or a bad thing.

It's easy to fall into the temptation of trying to make everyone around us happy. When we try to become someone other than the person God made us to be—whether to prevent hurtful words others use against us or assuage self-imposed perfection—we'll find ourselves collapsing under a heavy load of pressure we were never made to carry.

The truth is, there's such freedom in living for an audience of *One*. God's words about you are only good, and they never change. He doesn't love you one minute and hate you the next. He's *always* on your side. Thinking that He's for us one second and out to get us the next is inconsistent with the way Jesus lived and the perfect picture He provided us of our Father.

Sometimes, we can get so caught up in what others say that *their* words become bigger and more important to us than *God's*. I've definitely done this, and it made me feel miserable. I got so caught up in allowing others' words to define me that I lost myself in the process.

I lost myself in the words the kids at school used against me. I lost myself in trying to live up to what Manny wanted. For a time, I even found myself lost in religious standards. Standards someone told me I should follow if I wanted to be considered righteous. Now, all I want is to follow after my sweet Jesus, who came to find me—and you.

Friend, even when others fill our heads with flattery or a sense of self-importance, it's essential to know who we are and what we bring to the table. Not because of what someone else says, not even because of what we say since our emotions can sometimes drive our words, but because of what *God* says.

Otherwise, we put ourselves—and our hearts at risk for all sorts of hurt because no one else can ever come close to encouraging us the way our Heavenly Father can. He knows our hearts better than anyone, and only *He* knows how to help us discover the passions, purposes, and plans He's hidden in them.

Passions, Purposes, and Plans

It started several months into our relationship. It seemed like I was losing Manny's interest, and the pressure to compromise my purity was often implied. While I held my ground in some areas, if I had to do it again (thank God I don't), I'd tell him to take a hike!

With this pressure came a great deal of insecurity on my end and aggressive independence on his. It's hard to believe I didn't make the correlation between the two, but rather than seeing what was right in front of me, I chose to set my sights on what *could* be. This wasn't a conscious decision, mind you. Still, the daily choices we make build the framework of our thought-life, and our thought-life establishes the framework of our everyday life.

Whenever Manny and I were together, we argued. Whenever he called, we argued even more. At this point, God was giving me all sorts of signs to sever the relationship. I had countless people telling me to end it. Obviously, unwarranted advice is the worst kind, but they certainly had a point and only said what they did because they cared. Several friends told me they saw him out with other women, and I even had a friend confess that the two of them had been physically involved.

Needless to say, I was gutted. But did I leave? No! Every time, he convinced me the others were lying and trying to come between our love. (Oh, brother.) Did I believe it? You bet I did. Why? You already know the answer: because I *wanted* to, and the framework for these thoughts was already in place, making it much easier to fix my focus in that direction.

What this sort of whiplashed relationship does to a girl's self-esteem is disastrous. I actually had several men express their interest in me during the long periods of time I didn't see Manny, but I told myself they weren't serious. No one would ever really be interested in me. Manny was the best I could get, so I was better off simply settling for what I had with him. What a lie!

The more I settled, the more he seemed *un*settled. The more unsettled he seemed, the more I did whatever I could to make (and keep) him happy. Right around this time, I started to struggle with deep depression and eating disorders. It's also when I started getting really sick with cysts, stomach ulcers, and all sorts of digestive issues and ended up in the hospital for emergency care and tests several times. Unfortunately, Manny was still widely unavailable, even in this, and yet I always found a way to make excuses for him. Making him sound better to anyone who would listen—*including myself.* Looking back, it's no wonder my parents were so concerned.

Maybe you can relate. It might seem normal to feel depressed and bad about yourself, to expect others to let you down and live life with walls up.

The truth is negativity *isn't* normal. Not at all. We were made in the image of God, and He's the most positive, sunny person we'll ever know. The truth is, we have a choice in what we align with, and whatever we set our hearts and minds on the most is what our lives will manifest. This is why God tells us in Romans 12:2 to be transformed by the renewing of our minds, rather than conforming to what the world says is normal. When we start to believe that God really does love us purely for who we are—the person He's made us to be—we begin to change. To transform. (More on this in upcoming chapters.)

It's vital that we step into His love. Not only for our sake but for the world around us because we have a *purpose*. We bring something to the world in a way that only *we* can, according to the design and delight of our Maker which will also be our delight. *His* design is *our* delight; that's how He designed it (see Ephesians 2:10; Ephesians 1:5, 6). We're important to Him, dear friend. He didn't design our purpose only with *others* in mind; He did so with *us* in mind.

God's purposes and plans are always for our good, to give us an abundant, hope-filled future (see Jeremiah 29:11, John 10:10). He didn't randomly reach into a hat and pull out each of our purposes. No, we'll find His purposes and plans naturally fill us with passion—they will make our hearts *burn*.

But how will we ever get to His good plans when we're stuck in the muck of self-set limitations or in what others have said or done? We won't. Not in the way or to the capacity He designed if we don't let go of all the junk of unbelief.

You want to hear something astonishing? We can't earn God's purposes or equip ourselves enough for them either. They're founded and grounded in His goodness and grace. That's not to say we shouldn't set time aside to steward and stir up what He's provided and prepared for us. But He doesn't call us because we're qualified. He calls us because He's a good Father who wants to see His children succeed even more than they do!

I would never succeed as a surgeon. I know it's not something I was called to do. I'd be passed out right beside the patient—that's not exactly what you want in a steady-handed surgeon! But I am called, as surely as you are, although my calling won't look like yours or anyone else's.

It's beautiful the way the Father fits us all together. He creates our callings to *compliment*—not *compete* with each other. When we get into the whole competition, comparison thing, we take away from what God has placed within us.

We're not called to compete; we're just called to come. Come because God doesn't need our fancy words or first-rate resumes or even our list of accomplishments. All He needs for His plans to succeed—the only thing He asks us to bring—is a willing heart.

Even if we don't feel confident, it's okay because as we grow in Him, His confidence becomes our confidence (see Jeremiah 17:7). I realize it sounds too good to be true, but it is! Amazing? Yes. Astounding? Always. True? Absolutely.

You might be thinking right about now: *But Hope, you don't know where I've come from or what I've done.* Honestly, honey, I don't need to. In the world's eyes, my background would definitely disqualify me from being used for God's holy purposes. But it's funny because our backgrounds often become the building materials that construct and condition us for our callings.

From this perspective, can you see how the pressure is absolutely off? God's purposes and plans for us have nothing to do with our performance. Quite the opposite, actually. They're far less about our giftings and so much more about His goodness.

More

My passion is to reach those of you who want *more*. More out of life. More out of your marriage. More for your family and relationships. More results. More drive. More passion. More purpose.

But I'm certainly not the only one who's passionate about you finding your more. God is *far more* passionate about you finding your more than I am! Jesus said in Matthew 7:9–11 that even though we've been born into a sinful nature, we know how to give good gifts to our children. So how *much more* will your Father in Heaven give good things to those who ask Him?

God cares about you finding your more, my friend. The thing is, we'll never find our more until we leave our *less*.

For years, I wanted more out of my life but was afraid to leave the less I'd been settling for; it's what I was familiar with. It was what I knew. I knew *less*. I didn't know *more*. I may not have known what my more looked like, but I knew it would take leaving my less. I really wanted more, but I wasn't ready to leave my less.

Isn't it crazy how we become so accustomed to settling for something—even if that something isn't so great—that we fight for it? That's what I did. For years, I fought against my more. I refused to loosen my grip on what really needed to go, and yet I wanted to receive something new at the same time.

It doesn't work this way. It can't. I can't white-knuckle the steering wheel and tell God to drive. This is a contradiction that got me going nowhere, but in circles, for years. Repeating the same conversations, the same issues, the same insecurities and wearing everyone out—including me. But you know who never grew tired of all my ramblings and wanderings? God. Friend, He's *so* faithful!

I mean, He'll walk with us *all* the way. Until we're ready to lay that thing down, He's right there with us. Drawing us. Pursuing us. Constantly assuring and *re*assuring us that we can rest it all in His loving hands and trust Him through the process. His plans for us are better than ours, but we won't find them until we lay ours down.

It took me over eight years, a lot of abuse, and ultimately realizing that I wasn't responsible for Manny's life or decisions to leave—and finally *stay* gone. Praise God for praying parents. I know they were faithfully praying for my safety and sanity the whole time, and I needed their prayers. It was their prayers that helped open my eyes to see the truth.

The truth that God was always with me, loving me, saving me. Even in the middle of my mess, when I was on the floor in a puddle of tears, God was *with* me. Even when destruction was all I could see, and I felt totally worthless and invisible, God was *loving* me. And even when I would fantasize about ending my life and write suicide letters to my family, God was *saving* me. He held me right there in the midst of the pain and the battle. And because He's such a wonderful Father, He *refused* to let me go or leave me alone.

He does the same for you, friend. He holds you like the Father you've always wanted, the friend you never had. No one wears out their welcome with Him. He's always reaching, always walking into our less and our mess and beckoning us into His more.

It's so much easier with Him than I ever knew. I had assumed that when I did finally leave my less, it would be such a gut-wrenchingly awful experience—so terrifying and painful—I wouldn't live through it. Yet when I was truly ready to walk away from my less, what I found was surprisingly and refreshingly the opposite.

Instead of a heavy burden of heartache, I found joy. Instead of loneliness, I found real love. Instead of fear, I found faith. Instead of hopelessness, God greeted me every morning with His more for me.

I'm not saying it was never hard or that I didn't experience heartache. I did. I grieved for what I lost, but once I was out, I realized I never really had what I thought I did in the first place. Then, I grieved for spending so much time on something that wasn't what I thought it was. I grieved for being in love with an *idea* rather than what was *real*. But you know what? The grief of leaving my less was only a drop in the bucket compared to experiencing the joy of discovering my more.

The truth is, I didn't really need to know what my more looked like because God did. I only needed to trust Him to help me out of my less and into His more.

God's more for us will always look like more than we've ever expected. Remember at the beginning of this chapter, when I said I was crying uncontrollably in a room full of other hurting people? Well, this was a women's healing retreat I attended, which helped me to release the loss of my less to the Lord, so I could start to step into His more for me.

I had never experienced the healing love of Jesus like that before. It was like all that time He was waiting for *me* and once I was ready—I mean *truly* ready to give Him what He knew was causing me such heartache and pain—He took it. I came insecure, broken, torn down, and truly ready for a change. God came with the fullness of power and presence; He came ready to bring change. He's never put off by our troubles, quite the opposite; His strength is made perfect in our weakness. What a relief!

The second night of the retreat I brought it all before him at the altar. I remember this beautiful exchange took place. Like every attachment I'd ever had with Manny, in an *instant*, was gone, totally removed. In its place arose a piercing, bright white light that washed over me, and I felt so clean, so free that I thought my heart would *explode!*

I couldn't stop crying. Not because I was sad, but because I had never felt so loved and validated in all my life. There are no words in the human language that can describe this amazing encounter. It was as if God took His holy eraser and removed all those years of abuse, neglect, codependency, and chaos from my mental and emotional memory bank. Talk about receiving *more* than I expected!

God is so faithful, friend. Aren't you so glad? I know I am! I definitely couldn't have done it without Him.

Even if we're the one who made the mess in the first place, He's faithful and doesn't hold it against us. Even when we feel like we don't deserve His help, He doesn't hold out on us. He's so much better than we think He is. His goodness and love can't be measured; they go so far beyond our comprehension and on and on forever!

We can trust that *His* more is always bigger than the more *we* have in mind—and it's a million times better than any kind of less we're living in. That's why it's so important to ask Him to help us think His thoughts and dream His dreams. To pray what He prays and see what He sees.

If we want to experience the fullness that God has for us, we'll have to be willing to leave some lesser things behind, such as fear, lies, denial, and complacency. We are invited and given permission to lay these lesser things down, so we can pick up and run with God's promises.

Permission

Permission is powerful. Whatever we give permission will impact, not only our lives, but the lives of others all around us. I deceived myself into giving someone permission to run my life for a long time; someone who proved to be totally unworthy of my trust, let alone my permission. While I finally did leave and get help, it took me over eight years to get there. Those are eight years I'll never get back. And honestly, before I finally found the bravery to break it off, things got *way* worse before they got any better.

This doesn't have to be your story, dear one. With everything that's in me, I don't want it to be. I'd much rather you walk around the pit than fall into it. I'm sure your future self would wholeheartedly agree.

That's why I'm committing to you here and now, my friend. I commit to being beside you, working right along with you in every process we explore. I commit to being authentic with you, real and honest. I commit to making myself vulnerable in our time together because vulnerability brings breakthrough and breaks off bondage. I want to see abundant breakthroughs in my lifetime; I believe you do too. Otherwise, you wouldn't still be hanging here with me. So, let's be real with each other. Let's also be real with ourselves. Most importantly, let's be real with the One who already knows and loves us best.

Unless we're willing to be honest with ourselves throughout this process, it's not going to work. At least not in the way, and to the capacity it could, if we committed to giving ourselves permission.

Permission to be vulnerable to whatever the Lord reveals to you. Permission to see yourself through His eyes. Permission to pursue the promptings He puts on your heart. How will you recognize His prompting? His promptings always lead us deeper into His love and freedom. Even when they lead us to uncover what we've worked so hard to cover up. In His love, the Lord never leaves us to the makings of our own misery, and so often, what we keep hidden keeps us miserable. He's kind enough to help us out of the bondage and into the breakthroughs. And when we believe Him to be the Bondage Breaker, we *break through* to our breakthroughs.

We have so much to explore in our time together, friend, and I'm so honored and excited to be taking this journey with you. While we're cruising down the road together, I'm going to ask you to do us both a favor and truly permit yourself to see your value through the lens of the Father's love and refuse to give up on yourself throughout the process. Pursue God's perspective of you and posture your heart in a place to receive from the One who will never stop pursuing you.

Please make yourself vulnerable and available to God, even if it is something you've never done before. Even if it feels like a foreign experience or a bunch of bologna, I'm asking you to please allow the One who loves you best to lead you best. Give yourself permission to explore the truth of His amazing love for you.

The Creator of the universe and everything in it wants to confirm His existence and goodness to you in greater ways than you could ever imagine! He's been wanting to. But He's a gentle Father who will not forcefully push His way into our lives. He waits for us to let Him. So, I encourage you—even if it's just to see what happens—give Him permission. You'll be glad you did.

CHAPTER TWO

Coloring Outside the Lines
(Finding Christ-Centered Confidence to Be Yourself)

Let no one ask a stronger mark of an excellent love to God, than that we are insensible to our own reputation.

—Madame Jeanne Guyon

Friend, have you ever found yourself doing and saying things you normally wouldn't simply to feel like you fit in with the people around you? Of course, you have. I mean, we've all done some pretty foolish things to feel like we fit. (I know I have.) But for a lot of my life, I didn't feel like I fit in anywhere.

Growing up in a school where you're known as the girl nobody wants to be around was tough, and unfortunately, it was just a small county building that housed all grades from kindergarten to twelfth under one roof. So instead of having a chance to start fresh every couple of years,

I had to endure the same classmates—from elementary through senior high—who incessantly told me everything they thought was wrong with me.

Like how I stuttered and had to take in-school speech therapy (that certainly didn't help). And how skinny and scrawny I was with big, bucked teeth and frizzy, fried hair. I'd beg my mom to give me one of those home perms (remember those? oh my goodness!), and a few days later, I'd brush it out. I mean, what was that about? I honestly don't know why I did that! But the end result was *disastrous!*

I didn't have any real friends, so I hung out a lot by myself, talking to Jesus, reading books, or daydreaming my own stories. When you spend so much time by yourself, you get quite good at imagining things. I'd be sitting in class or walking down the halls imagining I was off on some grand adventure. I probably looked somewhat strange to anyone who was watching, which is pretty funny when I stop to think about it. It's a good thing I can laugh at myself!

My hard-working parents didn't have a lot of extra spending money back then, so wearing name brands like Levi's and Nike was a rarity. Instead, I sported my Jordache jeans and L.A. Gear sneakers. (I see you shaking your head and smiling, I bet you rocked a pair or two of these in your time too!) So, yeah, I was a really strange looking kid, without any fashion sense, and a *wild* imagination.

The few so-called friends I did have only wanted to hang out after school. They didn't want to risk their reputation by being seen with me while *at* school. Talk about a self-esteem crusher. But when you're desperate, you'll settle for anything.

When I look back at pictures, I can't help but laugh—along with all my nieces and nephews. The only ones who say I was cute are my parents and my hunky hubby, Alan. Although I've caught him chuckling a time or two when he thought I wasn't watching! So, yes, it's totally okay to laugh, friend. I'm used to it! It's healthy to laugh at ourselves in a lighthearted, loving way. It keeps us from taking ourselves too seriously.

I may have been an awkward kind of a kid, but the bullying still hurt. When you get bullied, it makes you question what's wrong with you. But when the bullying is relentless, it makes you question your actual existence. Eventually, you find yourself attempting anything and everything to make it stop, and if that doesn't work, you look for ways to make your *life* stop.

This is right where I found myself at age seventeen. Friendless and caught in a cycle of deep depression and self-destruction, fantasizing about death and eventually attempting to take my own life. What I really needed was a true friend who would validate me and tell me that my life really was worth living. What I really needed was *Jesus*.

Maybe you're feeling the same way, dear one. Let me just tell you, Jesus is here for you, as sure as He was there for me. He held me together, brought healing to my heart, and restored my soul. He'll do the same for you, honey.

He wants to be our *Best* Friend!

Our Best Friend

I'm talking to you right now, my dear, and I'm telling you, you deserve better than settling for scraps of attention. You deserve someone who will walk through the trenches of life with you and relentlessly hold your hand. That Someone is always right here for you, and His name is Jesus. If you don't know Him, I encourage you to invite Him to do life with you right here and now before we go any further.

Ask Him to come and breathe His life upon your heart because we're not truly living until we let Him in. You and me—*all* of us were made to know and experience the love He has for us. *His* heart makes *ours* whole. We'll always feel an emptiness until we let Him fill us up with His love. Sex, drugs, fortune, and fame won't fill that place. Until we call upon His name, we'll always feel like something is missing. That something is actually Someone, and He's right here waiting for you, my precious friend.

God isn't distant or removed. He's given His very best to reach you. He so loved you that He sent Jesus, His one and only Son, to save you. Because no matter how good any of us try to be, we simply can't save ourselves. That's why we need a Savior, and that's why Jesus came—to seek and save us all.

When we surrender to Him, we're giving up our right to run life *our* way, which is wonderful because we tend to make a mess of things. When we surrender our rights to Him, as Lord and Savior, He shares *His* rights with us. Rights to freedom, joy, and peace. Rights to grace, power, and strength. We receive the right to live in and from *love* rather than *fear*. In fact, living from His love makes fear run and hide!

You'll never have a friend better than Him, my dear. He's the *best* decision and the *best* friend you'll ever make. Take it from someone who lived quite friendless for the first seventeen years of her life.

Lasting Impressions

Did you know that in the 1970s, the average person was exposed to about 500 advertisements a day? But according to a study done by CBS News, that number has increased to 5,000[1]! Want to know what's crazier? That study was done in 2006! There's no doubt we're now living in a time of absolute advertisement oppression.

You know what's so sad about all these ads, aside from the obvious inconvenience they cause? The message they predominantly portray is, "You're not okay unless ..."

You're not okay unless you have the latest gadgets, hippest trends, and look like you've just stepped out of a fashion photoshoot. You know what else is sad about their messages? More often than not, we're influenced by them.

Now before you go getting all defensive on me, let me ask you, why do you wear the clothes you do? And guys, don't give me that, "because my wife picks them out" excuse. I mean, even if what you wear looks like you don't care, you cared enough to pick it out. My point is, impervious as we like to think ourselves to be, we can all be impressionable at times. I'm saying, what we put before our eyes and ears absolutely impacts our real lives.

My husband, Alan, and I recently started watching The Great British Baking Show. So, guess what we've found ourselves doing lately? You guessed it. Baking! But not just baking, we've been buying and taste-testing desserts and breads in our best Paul and Mary impersonations. "Oh, great lamination on that pastry." Or, "That cake seems quite close textured." As if we actually know what we're talking about! But it has been *smashing* good fun!

We've read and researched more recipes on breads and brûlées, pies and patisseries than we could ever pull out of our oven! While it's all been enjoyable and quite interesting, it goes to show that whatever we put in really will come out. (And I'm not just talking about our ovens!)

Advertisement companies know this. That's why they spend countless dollars researching which angle best promotes their products or elicits an emotional response from the public. They don't simply throw ads our way and hope they'll work (well, maybe they do that too). They know if they can get us to identify with their product, we're far more likely to want it to be part of our image.

To the world, it's all about image. So Jesus told us to be all about innocence and wisdom (see Matthew 10:16), for He knows that what we put in is what will come out.

You know who knew this long before the advertising execs ever did? The Holy Spirit. That's why He says, "Watch over your heart with all diligence, for from it flow the springs of life" (Proverbs 4:23, NASB). We have to be careful with what we do with our hearts because our heart affects our entire life.

How will we recognize if we're being influenced by something that's not of God, whether it's a relationship or what we entertain? Well, for one thing, it'll ruthlessly wear us out without filling us back up. For another, it'll take us down roads where we'll find ourselves doing and saying things we swore in a million years we never would.

Stuck

I thought I knew how to have fun, and I thought we agreed on what fun was. That is until Manny said I didn't know how to have fun anymore. Several months into our relationship, he said I was too uptight and needed to learn how to relax. But wasn't fun supposed to be easy-going and light-hearted and not make me feel sick to my stomach? As our ideas of fun grew farther apart, I found myself growing farther from the girl I used to be. Doing things I shouldn't have been doing, in places, I shouldn't have been.

While these things certainly helped me gain more approval with Manny, they made me feel all anxious inside as I was increasingly compromising my morals and values. I remember thinking, *This isn't right. I shouldn't be compromising who I am for another person.* But then, I'd quickly hear another voice, a *manipulated* memory of my mom saying something like, love is about compromise and commitment. And while she was right, she meant for her words to be applied to a *healthy* relationship full of trust and integrity.

You know, satan isn't worthy of our conversation, yet we still have to find a way to be real about him without going on a witch hunt or denying his existence. Either one of those options gives him too much credit, and he definitely doesn't deserve it. What we do need to know about him is that he's a manipulator. He's been one since the beginning—just ask Adam and Eve. As a manipulator, he works hard to twist the truth and blur the boundaries God has set for our safekeeping (we'll talk more about this in chapter six).

As a manipulator, he'll use any amount of material he can find to try to confuse and contort the way we translate God's truth into our everyday decisions. He takes what we remember or what we've watched or read or heard and puts a spin on it. So, what was once outright wrong now seems alright somehow, and what was once wholly right now seems sort of wrong. This is how we find ourselves doing things we said we never would.

Isn't it good to know that while the enemy works hard to influence us through fear and intimidation, God has given us the gift to choose whether or not we allow him access to our thoughts and attention? satan is a defeated foe, and the only power he has is the power *we* give him.

When I remembered my mom's words, I didn't realize they were a warning, a lifeline to what real love looks like. But because I wasn't feeding my thoughts and feelings from a healthy place, I took it as permission to *keep* compromising. My thought was since all relationships take compromise; some must simply take *more* compromise than others.

I was full of so much confusion, and as I continued to give into unhealthy compromises of my morals and values, that confusion only increased. I know now that God is never the One who fills us with confusion (see 1 Corinthians 14:33). Confusion only comes from the enemy.

In spite of what my instincts said, I started saying yes to things I never thought I would. I mean, at first it felt good to feel like I was keeping his attention, like maybe I was finally going to be enough for him. But you know, once you start compromising your core values to satisfy someone else, even if it's only a little, you'll end up compromising an awful lot.

When I say yes to something today, that I would have said no to yesterday, it's only a matter of time until I'm saying yes to *another* compromise tomorrow. Let me stop here for a minute, friend, and say, no one is worth selling off little bits and pieces of your soul and if they ask, it's not out of love or respect. Love and respect would never ask in the first place. Quite frankly, it's out of selfishness, and to see how far they can get you to give in, it's a challenge— one where no one wins.

> *Let me stop here for a minute, friend, and say, no one is worth selling off little bits and pieces of your soul and if they ask, it's not out of love or respect. Love and respect would never ask in the first place.*

Right around this time, I remember more than once looking in the mirror and not even recognizing my own reflection. My eyes, which used to shine so bright, had since grown dim, replaced with a gaunt look of hunger and despair. But the hunger I felt was from far more than the eating disorders I'd started months before. I was hungry for a sense of belonging and longing for the security of knowing I was loved. For a real sense of confidence rather than exhaustingly acting like everything was okay. In my exhaustion, I remember asking God how much longer the storms would last. Not knowing I was actually the maker of my own tempest.

Maybe you can relate. Maybe you know what it feels like to fool yourself into thinking you'll fit in if you compromise here and give in there. Only now, you're not so sure you know (or like) who you are anymore. And like me, maybe this is where you've found yourself living for a while—stuck and wondering how long the storms will last.

The Full Life

Ahh, the full life.

Even the sound of it is like a drink of cold water on a hot summer day. Refreshing. Right? God has a full life planned for you, my friend. Believe it? If you're not *living* it, it might just be because you're not *believing* it.

Back then, I would've called my life anything but full. Miserable was more like it. I'm almost embarrassed to say I kept attributing it to not feeling like I was enough for Manny. He became the gauge by which I graded my life, the standard by which I set my status. If he gave me attention, I was in a good mood, having a great day. If not, my day and I were both ruined. I find it hard to believe how he couldn't have known this about me because I'm pretty sure it was obvious to everyone else: I was desperate.

You know, there's a kind of desperation that's okay, healthy even. One which spurs us on to run after God and the good plans He has purposed for us. This wasn't that kind. Plain and simple, the desperation I felt was fueled by fear. It was the kind of desperation that makes you feel like you have to measure up to what *they* want. Otherwise, you're not worth that much.

He wanted me to allow him to have control over my emotions, and I was inclined to allow him that control, but this put a lot of pressure on us both. On him because no one should be expected to live under the responsibility of being another person's reason for living. On me because no one should be expected to live under the pressure of performance-based affection (if you do this and that, *then* I'll love you). On our relationship because no relationship can be expected to withstand the ongoing weight of putting *all* their hopes for *everything* in each other.

The truth is, it's never okay to measure ourselves by someone else's standards. Thank goodness our worth isn't found that way; it's only found in what God has to say. But I didn't know that then. I mean, I knew it, but I didn't *know* it. You know what I mean? I knew it like you know two plus two equals four or like you know your home address. I knew it with my *head*. I didn't know it with my *heart*.

"God loves you, Hope, and He has good plans for you!" I heard this my entire life. But hearing it and believing it are two totally different things, aren't they? If God had such good plans for me, why was my life so miserable and full of problems, pain, and sorrow? I realize now that most of the pain and problems I experienced could've been avoided if I'd decided to step out of my less and into the much more—the full life—my Father promised me.

I'm not saying every issue that occurred throughout the course of that time was solely due to my own decisions, but I certainly had a lot more say in them than I realized. And even though a lot of the pain and problems I experienced could have been prevented by my own choices, God still provided for me. For every problem I encountered, even when they were of my own making, He provided His promises and provision throughout the entire process.

Stepping into the Full Life

Sometimes we get so focused on our problems that we can't see the promises and provision He's given us *for* the problem. We want what He's promised to provide, but we have a hard time stepping past the problem to what's waiting on the other side. What would be the point of God's promises and provision if we never experienced any problems? The provision He promises us is *because* we encounter problems. He has given us exceedingly great and precious promises to redirect our perspective *off* the problems and *onto* Him and His provision as a perfectly good Father.

When we have a hard time seeing past the problem and stepping into God's promised provision, I believe it's because we're living by our emotions. We want to *feel* the faith for what we're stepping into *before* we step into it. If we don't feel like we have the faith to step into His promises, we find it more difficult to trust Him to provide. But the truth is, God's promises are equally as real whether we *feel* they are or not.

Our feelings are completely irrelevant to the reliability of God's promises. His promises are true. Period. And the deeper we go with God, the more we find this to be true. We think less about what we *feel* and more about what He *said*.

He said He'd never break His promises. He said He'd never lie. He said every word He speaks, He will also complete. When we take Him at His Word, we can step out knowing He's faithful no matter what we feel. We don't even need to examine our emotions or try to find out what we're feeling. Faith doesn't operate in the realm of feelings. Faith operates in what is *unseen*.

God Himself is a faith-filled God. Hebrews 11:3 tells us God created that which is *seen* out of that which is *unseen*. He spoke, "Let there be..." and it was so (see Genesis 1:3, 26). He brought forth what was in His heart into the natural realm by *speaking*. We were created in His very own image (Genesis 1:26), which means we have the same life-giving power in *our* words. That is why faith *speaks*.

Faith speaks and faith sees. Faith hears and faith responds. Regardless of what we're feeling, faith responds with action and rest. We act on what God says and we rest in His promises. Often, God will ask us to step out in faith, *then* our feelings will follow. Faith steps out, feelings follow.

Stepping out in faith means we believe *before* we see the breakthrough. Faith is our connector to what is unseen. Through faith, we connect to and pull on the promises of God in the *spiritual* realm, so the provision we've been praying for will manifest in the *natural*.

Faith prophetically acts upon what is revealed by the Spirit. We put our faith into action by doing, decreeing, and declaring as the Spirit of God leads—connecting our faith to the truth of *His* promises and pulling them into *our* possession.

This is why faith celebrates, for it *sees* what is yet unseen. With perseverance and persistence, faith rests in what God says. It does not become anxious or fearful, but overflows with hope even while we're still waiting on our miracle. Faith knows God never fails and stands on His promises. It knows with all certainty that His Word is a sure foundation. Yes, even when problems persist, faith enables us to praise because God is always faithful.

I want to be clear. We don't praise God for the problem itself. We praise Him for the opportunity to learn and grow from the problem. While problems are not in His heart for us—there were no problems in His original design—learning and growing from our problems is.

Back then, I felt like my life was all about problems. Now, I realize life is *less* about problems and *more* about the way I respond to them.

Faith affects the way we respond to issues and problems, and our *response* affects our lives and the lives of those around us. What I'm saying is, like it or not, the fullness of our lives is linked to the fullness of our faith. Faith is essential to experiencing a full life. The good news is, faith is also a *gift*.

Ephesians 2:8,9 (NKJV) says, "For by grace you have been saved *through faith, and that not of yourselves; it is the gift of God*, not of works, lest anyone should boast" (emphasis added). All the pressure is off, friend. There's no need to *measure* our faith. In fact, I've found faith increases not from assessing how much I *feel* like I have, but rather turning my eyes on Jesus, the Author and Finisher of our faith. Faith is a *gift* and He is the Giver. So, if I want more faith, the answer isn't to look at *myself*, but at the *One* who gave it to me in the first place. Faith doesn't come by *force*; faith comes by *rest*. Galatians 5:6 (TPT) tells us that love activates faith. If I want greater faith, I must fall more in love with Jesus and *rest* in His love for me. He truly has designed it to be a delight for us. Amazing. What an intimately intentional Father.

Since we need to not go by our feelings, how will we know when we've moved into faith for what we're asking for? We'll know because we'll be able to celebrate with a sense of certainty, as if we've already received what we asked for, even while we're still waiting for it to appear. We'll refuse to let fear talk us out of living life fully alive, wide awake, and with a sense of expectation in the goodness of God. We'll choose to see every issue from God's perspective, and in *His* perspective, He's already won!

It's not like we're manipulating God with our praise or hyping ourselves up to believe it. Our sense of celebration comes out of our certainty that God is faithful and will faithfully provide. Just as Jesus told His disciples in Mark 11:24 (NKJV), "Therefore I say to you, whatever things you ask when you pray, believe that you receive them, and you will have them."

Our ability to celebrate despite circumstances along the way is actually part of our maturity process—one that's meant to be full of discovery, excitement, and joy! It's a process we need. One that enables us to receive His answers with a *yielded*, rather than a *resistant* heart. So, when we finally receive His promise, we'll have the faith, confidence, and character to carry it. For God doesn't only want us to *receive*, He wants us to *sustain* what we receive.

A Confidence Boost: Seeing from God's Perspective

Perspective is a powerful thing.

Perspective doesn't only determine how we view ourselves; it determines how we view the world around us. Perspective determines what kind of friend we are and the way we think about our neighbors. It highlights how we see the homeless and the marginalized. Perspective also exposes the priority we place on people and things around us and even affects the way we respond when we run into rough news.

The perspective I have now of my past is completely different from what it was while I was in it. But I'm sure we've all run into some people who seem utterly incapable of moving on from what happened years ago. You see them five, ten, fifteen years later, and they still have the same old problems. From their perspective, it's almost like five *days* have passed—not five *years*.

They mentally live with their focus behind them; therefore, they can never move ahead. Keeping our perspective on our past, especially if it was traumatic, puts our brain and body in a constant state of stress. All this backward focus keeps us from ever truly entering into productive sleep or rest, which can easily translate into a lifestyle of addiction and overstimulation.

This is, in part, why it's difficult to leave an abusive relationship. You're not only leaving the person and the dreams you had with that person, you're also leaving an overstimulated, stressful lifestyle which becomes strangely addictive.

So, if we want to leave our overstimulated, addictive lifestyle behind, we must learn how to replace our old, panic-filled perspective and embrace one full of life and peace.

I used to lie awake at night and dream about a calm life without Manny. I imagined what it'd be like to go through a day without something traumatic or dramatic happening and how it'd feel to experience the peace I knew as a child. But every morning for eight years, I'd wake up and think, *who am I kidding?* There's no way I could ever leave him. I don't even know who I am without him. So, I stayed. Because by that point, I was already addicted to an overstimulated lifestyle and in my perspective (I'm sorry to say), life was all about him.

Looking back now, those mid-night heartfelt glimpses full of hope and a future weren't merely random wires getting crossed in my brain. God was pursuing me and showing me what could be if only I would step out and trust Him. If only I would change my perspective. Because perspective is a powerful thing.

With the right perspective, kingdoms rise, but with the wrong perspective, they fall (see Proverbs 11:10; 29:2). But the most important kingdom perspective is God's Kingdom perspective. Unlike us, God's Kingdom perspective is eternal—He sees the ending from the beginning, and He's not surprised by a single thing in the middle. Since this is His perspective, *He's* the One who knows the promises we need to hear in the present to propel us into the favorable future He has planned for us.

So if we're not seeing from God's perspective, it's possible that He's releasing bounties of blessings to us, but we don't even know it because they haven't come packaged according to *our* preconceptions.

When we're seeing from God's perspective, we'll see delays differently than we did before—less about the do's and don'ts and more about the *discovery*. Proverbs 25:2 (BSB) puts it this way, "It is the glory of God to conceal a matter and the glory of kings to search it out." God hides revelation in mystery not to be cruel, but for our glorious discoveries. He doesn't hide treasures *from* us but *for* us. When this is our perspective, everything becomes a joy and a treasure worth celebrating. And the treasures we haven't yet found, look far less frustrating and more like delights we still get to discover.

Jesus told us, "Everything I have is yours," (Luke 15:31, John 16:13–15). So, what if God is waiting for us to take Him at His Word? What if, instead of *us* waiting on *Him*, He's waiting on us? Waiting for us to turn our petitions into proclamations. Our pouting into praise? To pray *with* Him rather than *at* Him. Because as much as He wants us to share our hearts—He also wants us to hear His. Listening is half our conversation with Him.

What if those trials we've been trudging through lead us to our greatest triumphs? Isn't it possible that the sorrows we've been experiencing are sowing our strongest seeds of faith? Preparing us for the now-made-possible impossibilities of tomorrow. Because what is impossible with man is made easily possible with God (Luke 1:37).

Friend, isn't it possible that through your difficulties, God is showing you, it's your Father's delight to fight for you and that He's a Mighty King who cannot lose? Could it be, He's training you to turn your complete attention onto Him so He can show you how to release His power everywhere you go? He's put the exact same Spirit that was inside His Son, inside of you (see Romans 8:11). And sometimes, He wants to fight not just *for* you, He wants to fight *with* and *through* you.

Sometimes, I can get so focused on the fight and doing all I know to do; but it's like nothing is working. It can feel like I've been pressing against a wall with all my might, and no matter how hard I push and persist—though my faith is being built in the process—that wall doesn't budge an inch. At these times, I've found God is asking me to simply surrender to Him and trust *Him* to knock it down for me.

Other times, I've been on my knees for days and that thing isn't going anywhere. That's when God, with a twinkle in His eye, puts a sledgehammer in my hand and says, "Let's do this one together."

So how do we know which one we're supposed to do, sledgehammer or surrender?

Jesus told His disciples in John 15:15, "No longer do I call you servants, for a servant does not know what his master is doing; but I have called you friends, for all things that I heard from My Father I have made known to you." Jesus didn't call just anybody His friends, only the ones who dedicated their lives to Him. Jesus didn't tell just anyone that it was given to them to know the mysteries of Heaven. He said this to a handful of men who were willing to be lay-down-lovers for the Kingdom of God.

My point is, we'll know what we're supposed to do by spending time with Him. When we get away with Jesus and come to know His voice and ways, we'll not only discover what to do, we'll discover how good He is. When we discover how good He is, we make the easy decision to become lay-down-lovers, and He calls us His friends. When we're His friends, all things He hears from His Father He makes known unto us, and it is given unto us to know the mysteries of the Kingdom of Heaven.

Seeing our identity and authority in the light of His perspective helps us reconsider the way we look at ourselves, others, and every circumstance we'll ever face. God's perspective helps us see that our conditions are creating in us stronger Christ-centered confidence and faith than we've ever had before. His perspective fills us with the Christ-centered confidence that causes us to boldly think outside the box, see beyond the circumstances, and even color outside the lines.

1. https://www.cbsnews.com/news/cutting-through-advertising-clutter/

CHAPTER THREE

How Do You *Love* Me?
(Our Need for Love Redefined)

He died not for men, but for each man.
If each man had been the only man made,
He would have done no less.

—C.S. Lewis

I find people-watching really entertaining. And I don't mean the creepy kind that requires me to carry around a pair of binoculars in my back pocket.

No. *Definitely* not that kind.

It's interesting to watch the way people interact with each other. Their laughter brings a smile to my lips; their tears make me cry. When we watch the way children interact with their parents, anyone can see we were created with a need to know we are loved. Loved. Safe. And secured.

No one needs to tell us to want to be wanted. No one needs to tell us about our need for love. No one needs to portray to us the pain that comes from being unprotected. These basics have been built into our DNA and hardwired in our hearts. They rise up within us and scream to be satisfied.

God knew what He was doing when He knit us together with these needs. He didn't do it to be cruel. He did it because He knew our deepest needs would only ever truly be satisfied by His deep love for us. If we were to walk around self-satisfied all the time, we'd never know there's something—*Someone*—so much better at satiating our needs than ourselves.

Our hunger for love is actually healthy, when we look to the Father to fill it *first*. When we don't, it leads to disastrous relationships and self-sabotaging cycles. But before we get into any of that, let's first learn about what love *is* and the way love is *learned*.

What Is Love? Love's Covenant.

Many consider love to be a feeling. Something that is satisfied in our emotions when we acquire the right connections. I would agree with that to a certain extent, but love is also a commitment. A choice. A *covenant*.

There's love according to the world, and then there's love according to God. Love, according to the world, is usually based on self-gain. How can you satisfy me? It's a contract. One that says, as long as you make me happy and do these things which I have requested, I will remain with you. It's not that everyone in the world is always so selfish; it's simply that the world, in essence, is self-consumed.

We're all born into a self-consumed nature until we surrender our lives to Christ. Then, that nature dies, and God's love transfers us into a new nature of righteousness, peace, and joy and helps us live from that place of newness. God's love isn't a contract; God's love is a covenant.

Covenant isn't a word we hear too often anymore. When God makes a covenant with us, He's essentially making us a vow, an unwavering, never-ending promise that can never be broken. This is seen in Scripture when God swears by Himself since there's no one and nothing greater for Him to swear by (see Genesis 22:16, Isaiah 45:23, Hebrews 6:13). Even when we're faithless, God remains faithful because He cannot deny Himself or His own Word (2 Timothy 2:13). Isaiah 55:11 says it this way, God's Word—His covenantal promises—will never return to Him empty without first accomplishing and succeeding in the matter for which He sent it.

The word covenant in the Hebrew is *karath*, and it means to cut in the flesh, to cut a covenant, or to make a blood covenant. God did this with us; He cut a covenant and signed it with His Son's own blood at the cross. He showed us what true love looks like through the cross. For it was at the cross, Jesus' blood was spilled, forever sealing His covenant with us.

Because of Jesus, we now live in a new covenant where love conquers all and we come to the Father by grace, rather than by what we do. Jesus didn't come to nullify the old covenant of living by the letter of the law; He came to *fulfill* it. He satisfied what we in our sinful nature could never do—live a perfect life. He did this for us so right relationship with the Father could be restore and righteousness and love could reign within us once again (Colossians 1:19, 20).

When we receive Him, we're made new and we live out of His love, and when we live out of His love, we no longer want to do the things we used to do. When we walk in the newness of who we are in His love, we live devoted to Him, not because we *have* to, but because we *want* to.

47

And the more we surrender to God's love, the more His love becomes our motivation in everything we do.

This is the beauty of the covenant God cut with us through the cross. Now every single one of His promises are yes and amen through Christ Jesus and the covenant He made with us through Him. This is a covenant Father God will never break. He's proved this to us through the cutting of Jesus' flesh on the cross, through the gift of His Holy Spirit, and through His Holy Word. It's hard to fathom that God could love us this much, but He does. He proved it.

What Is Love? Love's Character.

God will *never* quit loving us, even if we walk out on Him, our actions do not alter His affection toward us. He's constant. He doesn't change, no matter how much we do, His love is faithful and longsuffering. That means it bears with us. His love is patient and kind, even when we're not. Even when we don't believe in Him, He believes in us because His love sees and brings out the best in us.

Sometimes, we run into situations that seem hopeless, but God's love is never without hope. First Peter 1:3 tells us we've been born into His living hope. This means His hope is alive and breathing and with us all the time, in every moment and every situation.

Other times, we run into situations that make us feel fearful, but God's love is perfect. First John 4:18 (NLT) tells us, "...perfect love expels all fear. If we are afraid, it is for fear of punishment, and this shows that we have not fully experienced his perfect love." As the Scripture says, once we fully experience His perfect love, we have nothing to be afraid of because nothing is bigger, greater, or stronger than His love.

God isn't out to get us (as in punish us), He's out to *get* us (as in draw us closer to Him). He's not a grumpy old man who's always in a bad mood. If we see Him this way, it simply means we haven't yet come to know His heart as much as He's invited us to. God has the sunniest disposition of us all, and that's never going to change! He's always joyful and full of laughter and cheerfulness. And when we encounter His heart for us, we can't help but be filled with joy and laughter too (see Nehemiah 8:10, 12)!

When we see Him as some big, bad punisher of all our blunders, we have the wrong perspective of our Father. I realize this perspective is often perpetrated in religious circles, but religion cannot capture and assimilate the heart of the Father the way only relationship with Him can. This negative perspective of the Father can also be attributed to what our parents or those who raised us did or didn't do; but please don't confuse the two. He's not your mom or your dad. He's not the relative who raised you or the foster parents who placed you.

His love is perfect, and He loves you perfectly. He'll never hurt, misuse, or abuse you. When we feel like He's hurt our feelings, it's only because we've been guarding our heart against Him. We'll get into this more in a bit.

If we're picturing God as the grumpy old man upstairs, we've got the wrong picture. We wouldn't even be able to experience love if it weren't for Him; for love comes from God. He *is* love as First John 4:7–8 tells us; we can only love Him because He *first* loved us (see verse 19).

The Passion Translation gives us a great perspective regarding the Greek definition of God's love:

> The Greek word is agapē, which describes the highest form of love. It is the love God has for his people. It is an intense affection that must be demonstrated. It is a

loyal, endless, and unconditional commitment of love. Feelings are attached to this love. It is not abstract, but devoted to demonstrating the inward feelings of love toward another with acts of kindness and benevolence.[1]

God's love is kind. He's the kindest, most caring person we'll ever know. Psalm 36:7–8 says His lovingkindness is precious and in Him we take refuge and drink our fill of abundance from His house, from the river of His delights. His love isn't only kind, it's enduring. His love hasn't only suffered *for* us, it suffers *with* us. What I mean is, His is a love that mourns when we mourn and weeps when we weep.

His is a love that suffers long by patiently putting up with our stupidity without making us feel foolish for what we've done. But in His love, God doesn't leave us in our mess, either. His love overcomes us and causes us to triumph over anything that tries to overwhelm us. Whether it's our own stupidity or snares of the enemy, God's love leads us into victory. The way to win any war is to stand in His love, and fight *from* His victory, for "His *demonstrated* love is our glorious victory over *everything*" (Romans 8:37, TPT, emphasis added).

God's love doesn't hold out on us; it doesn't give up either. It doesn't rejoice when we're up against hardships, and it doesn't delight in darkness. God's love lives in the light; it rejoices in what's bright and best. His love is patient. He doesn't care how many times we get it wrong, He'll still be right here, waiting on us, wrestling with our hearts. He doesn't count how many times we fall down, but how many times we get back up. This is who He is—for you, for me, and everyone in between.

What Is Love? Love's Goodness.

God's love is good. He's a Father who wants more and dreams bigger for us than we do! Sometimes, the spirit of religion comes in and steals our awareness of His goodness through theologies set up by traditions of men that aren't at all reflected in the life of Jesus.

In the seventeenth chapter of John, we see Jesus in the Garden of Gethsemane pouring out His heart in prayer. Now, keep in mind this was *right* before He was betrayed and abandoned by those He was closest to. *Right* before he was arrested, falsely accused, and withstood trial. It was *right* before He was brutally beaten and mocked, and a crown of the sharpest Jerusalem thorns was shoved into His skull. This was *right* before He was savagely flogged with a whip embedded with pieces of bone and metal; a whip that snagged so deep it tore His flesh right off the bone, and according to biblical history, even exposed His inner organs. It was *right* before He was forced to carry an extremely heavy wooden beam, immediately after his body was ripped to shreds and his lifeblood was spilling out everywhere. He prayed this prayer *right* before He was nailed to the cross and crucified. *Right* before He carried and ultimately overcame every curse and sin, all death, sickness, and disease from the beginning of time, to its end. And right before all these horrific things happened to Him, what was on His heart? *You.* You and me. *All* His believers.

His love is *that* good. He wasn't only praying for the unity and strength of those who were His disciples then, He was praying for all who would one day believe in Him through their message—which was *His* message (see John 17:20). How did He finish His heartfelt, powerful prayer? With these words, "I have revealed to them who you are *and I will continue to make you even more real to them, so that they may experience the same endless love that you have for me, for your love will now live in them, even as I live in them"* (John 17: 26–27, TPT, emphasis added).

Because His love is so good, God not only sent Jesus to the cross to overcome every curse, sin, death, and the grave for all time, but He sent Him to be our model and reveal to us what the Father is like. That's why Jesus only did what He saw His Father doing, and only said what He heard His Father saying. Jesus isn't only our Great Intercessor, praying on our behalf as Romans 8:34 tells us, He's our model. So, if Jesus didn't do it or say it, why would we?

Our problem is sometimes we forget how good His love is, and we get stuck thinking we're somehow still responsible for saving ourselves. Yet, the entire old testament proves this is impossible. So why are we still trying? The Apostle Paul put it this way in Galatian 3:3 (TPT), "Your new life in the Anointed One [Jesus] began with the Holy Spirit giving you a new birth. Why then would you so foolishly turn from living in the Spirit by trying to finish by your own works?" Jesus Himself said, "Until John the Baptist, the law of Moses and the messages of the prophets were your guides. But now the Good News of the Kingdom of God is preached, and everyone is eager to get in" (Luke 16:16, NLT).

When we encounter God's goodness (when we know it by *experience*) and watch Him work His awesome ways throughout our lives, we realize we really don't have anything to worry about. Our Father owns it all, and He's always good! Every good and perfect gift comes from Him, so why waste our time worrying about today or borrowing worries from tomorrow?

Because God's love is good, He's given us access to all of Heaven's resources by the same Spirit that was inside of Jesus. This same Holy Spirit that was in Jesus is now—*always in the present-tense*—living inside of us! It's an extraordinary life when we allow ourselves to truly encounter God's always good love.

What Is Love? Love Is Family.

God's love looks like family. All who believe in and have received Jesus have been given the right to be called the children of God. Ephesians 2:19 and Galatians 6:10 remind us that we are members of the household of God and faith. And in John 13:35, Jesus said everyone would know we are His disciples if we love one another.

Remember back in John chapter seventeen, when Jesus was praying for us? Part of His prayer was, "I pray for them all to be *joined together as one* even as you and I, Father, are joined together as one. I pray for them to become one with us *so that the world will recognize that you sent me.* For the very glory you have given to me I have given them *so that they will be joined together as one and experience the same unity that we enjoy.* You live fully in me and now I live fully in them *so that they will experience perfect unity,* and the world will be *convinced* that you have sent me, *for they will see that you love each one of them with the same passionate love that you have for me*" (verses 21–23, TPT, emphasis added).

Isn't it amazing that we can actually *convince* the world of God's love simply by how we love each other? That's a *big* deal! So, if the world isn't convinced of God's love, it seems to me, we need to do a better job of loving each other.

1 Corinthians 13:1–2 tells us that we could speak with all the eloquent languages of Heaven and earth, but if our words are without love, what we're saying is reduced to raucous. We could have great faith and possess supernatural

knowledge to understand the secrets of God, we could foretell and forth-tell the future through prophecy, but if we don't know how to love, we're nothing.

It sounds like learning how to love is a pretty serious issue to our Poppa God. So, how do we? It certainly isn't something that comes from our own willpower or resolve. I'm certain every single one of our lives proves this to be true. I know mine sure does!

Love for God and love for each other is actually the result of experiencing God's love for us. Our hearts are set on fire with His furious love. Therefore, we can't help but spread the sparks around. And the more we're filled with the fire of His love, the more we become a living flame.

The Passion Translation has this to say about what love means in Aramaic (Aramaic was the common language spoken in Israel when Jesus walked the earth):

> The Aramaic word for love is hooba, and it is a homonym that also means "to set on fire." It is difficult to fully express the meaning of the word and translate it into English. You could say the Aramaic concept is "burning with love" or "fiery love," coming from the inner depths of the heart as an eternal energy, *an active power of bonding hearts and lives in secure relationships* (emphasis added).[2]

Did you catch the end there? "*An active power of bonding hearts and lives in secure relationships*" (emphasis added). Love is learned in *secure* relationships. So, it seems fitting for us to discover what love looks like, in relationship, by going back to the very first relationship any of us would have ever established.

How Love Is Learned

Most of us learned about love from those who raised us, who coddled us, and kept us fed, warm, and dry. When we were little, their silly faces and soothing inflections became real life lessons on what love looks like. First words and first steps. First day of school, first time we scored a goal. First kisses and first stitches. They were there through it all, marking our measurements and milestones along the wall.

But what if this doesn't describe the way it was when you were little? What if the way you were raised wasn't quite so caring?

Maybe you never knew nighttime tuck-ins or backyard barbeques. Maybe family field trips and mommy-and-me moments weren't a part of your past. What if you found yourself floating in and out of foster homes, dreaming of a family you could one day call your own.

What if your parents were too involved in their own lives to trouble themselves with yours? Or what if they simply weren't around because *somebody* had to keep food in the fridge and a roof over your head?

Maybe the home in which you were raised wasn't so safe and sound. Maybe it was downright dangerous. Perhaps one of your parents tried to overcompensate for the lack of love or interest of the other? What kind of mixed messages were sent and *stayed* with you because of this?

If the signals we received from those who raised us were all mixed up and messed up because our love and value were somehow tied to our performance or fluctuated from one parent to the other, it causes us to seriously question our worth and where it comes from.

On the other hand, their messages could have been crystal clear, and they may have said it all day every day, but unless we *believed* and *received* what they were saying, it's like their words were never spoken. Until we receive love and believe we are someone worth loving, their words—as wonderful as they were—will not make their mark.

We will not let others love us beyond the degree that we love ourselves.

Incidentally, this is the way it works in other relationships as well. Whoever it is, we will not let others love us beyond the degree that we love ourselves.

If we view ourselves as unlovable, we will sabotage every relationship we ever build with this lie. And oftentimes, we don't even know we're doing it. I've found this lie is rooted in self-worth, which is something we learn at a young age. If we aren't taught—or if we're talked out of believing—we're valuable, we don't or won't believe we're worth loving.

But here's the thing, and I *really* want you to hear me now, Jesus told us to love others *as* we love ourselves. So, if we want to experience love through healthy relationships, we must first learn how to love *ourselves*. And we absolutely can, when we let God's love overwhelm us and any lies that are attached to our self-worth. We'll continue to expand upon this subject as we travel throughout our time together, for now, let's return to our conversation at hand.

We reinforce whatever we believe, and whatever we reinforce will greatly affect our lives and relationships. If the ones who raised us were unable to clearly and consistently convey unconditional love *or* if we refuse to believe and receive their love, our human tendency is to look for it in someone or something else. Either way, this is how life can get quite messy.

Trust me, I know.

Love Lost

For all the loving, life-giving words my parents spoke over me, the words *I* chose to recollect, repeat, and ruminate on were the ones that said I'd never be enough. So, when Manny started saying the same thing—even after I'd compromised my morals and values for him, my passions, pursuits, and purity—it only worked to reinforce the lies I'd already been believing.

"You're really not enough, and you never will be." The lies screamed in my ears even as I worked harder and harder to prove them wrong. It was a never-ending battle. But little did I know that if I kept fighting it on the *enemy's* terms, it was a battle I was never going to win ...

I was losing him. The little bit of grip I had on Manny—the one I never should have had in the first place—because real love doesn't white knuckle the one they're with. Real love willingly rests them in the hands of the One who loves them best. Real love trusts because real love is reliable.

Obviously, I didn't know what real love was since my version of love wasn't trusting, and Manny's version of love wasn't reliable. When love has to be controlled, it's no longer love. It's something else altogether and it's not only unhealthy, it won't last, unless you *make* it last, which is absolutely exhausting. And that's right where I was, trying to make something last that I really should have let go a long time ago. Instead, I was desperate to get back to how our relationship had been at first—fun, happy, easy—now it was *none* of those things. I had hoped that if I kept holding on, we'd eventually return to how we were and how I imagined us to be, even if I had to beg, bleed, and borrow to get there.

Right around this time, Manny grew even more evasive than he already was, and when I *did* see him, he was abusive. I began dreading conversations with friends and family because almost all of them ended in examples and arguments as to why I should leave or how they'd seen him at certain establishments not fit for someone with a steady girlfriend.

I started getting even sicker and was rapidly losing weight and interest in life. I knew it wasn't wise to stay with him much longer, and that summer, we finally split.

I told myself it was a good thing, but the truth is, I was a mess. You'd think I'd have been relieved, but when you've allowed someone to have *that* much control over your life and they're suddenly not in your life anymore, in some twisted way, it feels like life's no longer worth living. On some level, you know it's not okay to feel this way, yet escaping these feelings seems impossible. You're caught between two extremes, and it's like no matter what you choose, you lose.

I sent him so many letters and messages throughout this time, thinking if I could only find the right words, it'd bring him back, and everything would work itself out. Later, I learned I was operating in what mental health professionals call "magical thinking" or "bargaining."

What I know now that I didn't have the confidence to know back then was the battle for my worth had *already* been won. *I* wasn't responsible for helping him to recognize my worth. So why waste my time trying to remind him? The truth is people who don't value *themselves* have a hard time recognizing the worth of *others*. And while we're called to love them with *God's* love, they don't make safe or healthy candidates for life-relationships.

If Manny didn't already know my worth, then he wasn't the man for me. And quite frankly, he didn't *deserve* to be.

The Voice of Love

It had been impressed upon me, or I somehow concluded that if I were entangled in sin, I would no longer be able to hear God's voice. My sin would have stopped me from hearing what He had to say to me. I know now this is definitely a deception. Of course, it is! That's like saying sin is stronger than the power and presence of Almighty God. We all know this isn't true because Jesus defeated and utterly overcame sin at the cross. The devil tries to deceive us into thinking God disconnects Himself from us if we're doing or saying sinful things, but if we look at the life of Jesus, this is not at all how He interacted with others.

Jesus was constantly connecting with those who made all kinds of messes. The women caught in adultery (John 8:1–11). Zacchaeus, the tax collector and thief (Luke 19:1–10). Simon, the sexist and self-righteous religious leader (Luke 7:36–50). The woman at the well living outside of the safe parameters of marriage (John 4:4–42). Nicodemus, the pharisee who wasn't even brave enough to openly interact with Jesus during the day (John 3:1–3). Mary Magdalene, out of whom He cast seven demons (Mark 16:9).

If Jesus didn't withhold His love from these folks, who, until His arrival, were living under the old covenant, then He certainly wouldn't withhold His love from those of us who are now living in the *new* covenant. The *better* covenant we just talked about a bit earlier in this chapter. We've been redeemed from living under the curse of the law (the old covenant) because Christ became a curse for us, so we might inherit the blessings of Abraham, and the promise of His Spirit through faith (Galatians 3:13, 14).

Jesus *is* the Word of God (John 1:1, 14). We should really think it strange for Him *not* to have something to say. If I'm not hearing Him, it's either because I'm not listening,

I'm entertaining other voices, or He's already spoken what I needed to hear, and He wants me to remember and revisit His words.

I know now that what Jesus said in John 10:4–5 is true. He is the Good Shepherd, and His sheep recognize and are familiar with His voice, but they will run away from the voice of a stranger. But I didn't know that then. And because I didn't know the voice of Love, I lived without knowing what love really was, so I listened to other voices that opposed true love.

God's love absolutely amazes me. Sometimes we feel like we have to earn it, otherwise, we don't think we deserve it. The truth is we don't deserve it, and there's nothing we can do to earn it. It's *one hundred percent* based upon God's goodness. And you know what, sometimes we find God's goodness in the strangest places. I know I did. I found it right there, in the midst of my messy breakup and a broken heart.

I remember waking up to His words working their way into my heart, bringing me comfort and a sense of calm I hadn't had in a long time. Even when my prayers revolved around Manny or when they were frantic and full of fear and anger, God's response was never reprimanding or steeped in shame. When His conviction came, it came with His kindness. When lessons were to be learned, He delivered them with love.

I was amazed at how well I could hear His voice. I mean, if anyone *deserved* to hear His voice, it *definitely* wasn't me. I'd made way too many compromises in my life, so I assumed I had to stand at a distance and watch while my Heavenly Father feasted with His *real* family.

The truth is, the only one who held me at a distance was *me*.

We decide where we draw the line with God and how deep we go into intimacy with Him. With intimacy comes friendship, and with friendship comes clear communication.

The truth is our ability to hear God's voice is actually encoded into our DNA and when we accept Christ as our Savior, that ability is activated. Are there things I can do to activate that ability even more? Sure. Of course. We'll talk more about these and how to put them into practice as we go further along in our journey together, friend.

You know what the beautiful thing is about hearing God's voice? We were *made* to hear His voice. His voice is what makes us come alive on the inside. His voice is what makes our hearts *burn* within us! We are His sheep, and He is our Shepherd. We know His voice and follow Him. *This* is the magnificent new nature we wear as His much-loved children (see John 10:26, 2 Corinthians 5:17).

An Unwise Exchange

While this time was so wonderfully sweet, I'm sad to say I started listening to other voices again. I remember thinking, *I can't go too deep in my relationship God because then I won't feel right about going back to Manny if he and I get back together*. I want you to notice that *I* withheld. *I'm* the one who drew back. *I* leveled off and made an exchange of the worst kind. *I* did this—*not* God. I exchanged eternal, perfect love for something that didn't even *come close* to love. It couldn't because Manny didn't know what love was, and I decided to settle for something less than love. Even now, my heart breaks at the thought.

Every day, I would pray for God to bring Manny and me back together. And every day, God gave me really good reasons as to why that wasn't wise. "Hope, he doesn't know how to love; he's never been taught, nor does he ask Me to teach him. He's mixed up with someone else, and it will only add to your heartache. You will be settling for less than My best for you."

And every day, I'd come up with objections to my Father's infinite, invaluable, wise words. "But God, I'll love us enough for the *both* of us. I don't care if he's mixed up with another girl, I'll win him back. Then he'll remember that *I'm* the one he wants. I'm not settling because I know *this* is what I really want. I think *I* know what I want more than *you* do." (*Yikes.*)

Those were some *incredibly* unwise words, but I didn't know it at the time. I sincerely thought I knew what the secret desires of my heart were better than the One who put them there in the first place. Here's the truth, God doesn't withhold romantic love from us—He simply wants us to wait for the one *He* deems worthy of receiving our love. The truth is, I didn't trust that what He had for me would be better than what *I* thought I wanted. So, I fought for what I actually didn't need, and eventually, I found it was also what I really didn't want.

When we finally did get back together, it didn't take too long for us to fall right back into old patterns. Big surprise there. That's what happens when you don't address under-lying issues. At first, he was surprised and grateful for how forgiving I'd been of his indiscretions, but it wasn't long until his gratitude wore off into indifference.

Looking back now, I realize I'd made a great big blunder in the process, several actually. While love always forgives, love also sets healthy boundaries. But at that time, I didn't even know what boundaries were. (We'll talk more about boundaries later, what they are and why they're absolutely essential.)

When he finally came clean about how he'd been unfaithful, but still wanted our relationship to work, I should've taken the time to think about my response before jumping right back into his arms. The issue itself warranted a wise response. Unfortunately, I didn't have one. As soon as he said he wanted to come back, I immediately embraced him like nothing ever happened. I'm sure you can imagine how this set off a super unhealthy series of events.

Settling the "Settle for Less" Lies

What do you want out of love, my friend? I think it's safe to say that we all want a love that is faithful. A love that is loyal, honest, and true. A love that rejoices in what is good rather than what isn't. We want a patient love that bears with us as we grow. A love that isn't self-centered or prideful, doesn't point out our flaws, and endures to the end. A love that overcomes every obstacle and wins every war.

I believe this is the love we all want because it's the love for which we've all been made. But when our love tank is empty or running on fumes, we tend to make irrational decisions and compromise an awful lot to gain very little. The exchange is severely uneven and does not weigh in our favor. But when we're desperate, we make ourselves susceptible to anything that remotely resembles what we *assume* love looks like. Because we won't know what *real* love looks like until we've *experienced* it for ourselves. So then, how can we know what love looks like to recognize it, or where we go to find it?

Earlier, we said God is love. And we talked about how His love looks like everything we'd ever want out of love. But sometimes, we settle for less because we think we don't deserve this loyal of a love. Sometimes we settle for less because we don't believe God's good love actually exists, or we've simply never experienced it for ourselves, so how do we know it's real. And sometimes we settle because it doesn't seem worth the risk when we feel like we're always being let down by love.

I'm sure by now you know I empathize with how hard it can be to trust in love when we've been hurt by it before. But here's the thing, the difference between God's love and self-consumed love is as stark as day and night. The two are totally incomparable.

If we want to experience God's love and all the goodness He has for us, we must first make ourselves *vulnerable* to it. Otherwise, we'll stay in abstract, detached linear thinking regarding the One who is supremely passionate about us encountering Him. Vulnerability beautifully bridges the gap between our *heads* and our *hearts*. Helping to frame the foundation for our experience with the Designer of the highest form of pleasure—encountering His love for us.

John 1:4–5 tells us the Light of the world came into the world and gave us life and a light that always overcomes the darkness. When He walked the earth, Jesus referred to Himself as this Light—the Light of the world (see John 8:12). He is the self-expression of the Father—what the Father looks like and how the Father speaks is all reflected in the life of Jesus. What I'm getting at is God is love (see 1 John 4:7–8), and Jesus is what God's love looks like lived out. So we know God's love is full of light because Jesus said He is the light of the world.

God's love overcomes *every* darkness, including doubt, deception, and every sort of destruction. Often, when we feel like we've lost our belief in love, it's because we've been believing a lie that was born out of a dark place or period in our lives. When we've been hurt by something or someone, we tend to put that pain onto Perfect Love whose plans for us are only filled with purpose and hope.

I get that it sometimes seems easier to cut love out of our lives by saying it no longer exists, but just because I say the sun doesn't exist, doesn't make it go away. I will have to live in denial of its light, warmth, and brilliance every day. When instead, I could actually be enjoying its many benefits. The same is true of God's love, denying Him, doesn't make Him go away.

And saying He doesn't exist doesn't make Him nonexistent. We live with His love wrapped up in creative expression all around us every day. But whether we choose to be aware of it or not is up to us. When we refuse to believe in God, the only thing this does is withhold us from receiving the *full* expression of His many benefits.

I say *full* expression, because Jesus said the Father causes the sun to shine on the evil and the good, the rains to fall on the just and the unjust (see Matthew 5:45). We live, we breathe, we have good things because God is a good Father who's always reaching out to us. All of us. Even those who haven't reached out to Him yet. Still, there's a fuller and greater discovery of God's goodness that only comes from a heart of surrender to this Perfect Love.

But then there are times when people, who are *supposed* to look like love, live in a way that looks nothing like it. For that, friend, I'm sincerely sorry. If you have experienced the heartache that comes from unloving people, particularly, those who are supposed to be known by their love for God and others, I'm here to apologize and ask for repentance on their behalf. I've experienced this kind of pain myself. So I can empathize. I've found the best thing I can do in this circumstance is forgive, as forgiveness releases me from false responsibility and empowers me to move on. (We'll talk more at length about forgiveness later.)

It's sad that some people choose to live like this. But the reality is, we're each responsible for our *own* choices. I shouldn't allow what *you* do to determine what *I* do or don't do. What *I* believe or don't believe. And vice versa. The power we have to make up our own minds is extremely profound. It's a great gift and it's a great responsibility.

Jesus commissioned us as His followers in Matthew 5:14–16 to reflect the Father's Love when He said, your lives are the light of the world, your lives are a city set on a hill, shine your light for others to see. We must live our lives like God's love is real—because it is!

I don't mean we put pressure upon ourselves to save everyone we encounter. It's not our job to save people—it's our job to point them to the Savior. But it is our responsibility to reflect what Jesus' love looks like, the same way He reflected the Father's love when *He* walked the earth. So when others see us, they no longer see *us*; they see God's irresistible, irrefutable love shining *through* us.

Jesus told us to love others *as* we love ourselves (see Mark 12:28-31). If we don't love *ourselves*, we're not only going to have a hard time giving and receiving love; we won't be able to sustain love. We'll have a propensity to sabotage every relationship we cultivate with neediness and fear of rejection. When we feel unworthy of love and/or live in fear of losing love, we're more likely to smother people or reject them before they can reject us.

When we tell ourselves that we're not worthy of real love, we'll actually work our relationships around this unhealthy, poor perspective. So the relationships we *do* choose will not only *not* be worthwhile; they'll only work to reinforce the lies we're carrying around about our identity.

Not knowing or believing we were created to receive God's love does nothing for us but make us susceptible to lies. Lies that say we must earn His love to feel like we deserve it. Lies that tell us we're unlovable. Lies that tell us we're unworthy. The truth is there's only *One* worthy. And *He* makes *us* worthy. Romans 5:8 says God proved His love for us in this—that while we were still stuck in our sins, Christ died for us. Even when we couldn't pay Him back, earn it, or reciprocate it, Christ loved us.

Believing God loves us helps us to believe we're someone worthy of love. Believing we're someone worth loving positively affects our relationship in every way. And it all starts with making ourselves *available* to encountering His perfect love.

Vulnerable to Love

I used to think vulnerability only applied to my relationships with other people; I never thought of it relative to my relationship with God. And if I'm being completely honest, I kept my heart guarded for a long time.

> *I used to think vulnerability only applied to my relationships with other people; I never thought of it relative to my relationship with God.*

I remember feeling like I couldn't completely trust *anyone* with my whole heart. I felt I had to guard my heart against friends and family because I never knew when the conversation would turn to why I went back with Manny. At the same time, I had to guard my heart against him since there was so much uncertainty surrounding our relationship and interactions.

If you ask me why I stayed, all I can say to try and explain is that twisted sort of sickly relationship somehow becomes addictive after a while. If you've ever been in one, you know what I'm talking about. Or maybe you're in one right now, and this gives you the language to what you've been wondering. If you're fortunate enough to have not experienced this kind of relationship, all I can say is praise God, and please don't ever settle.

I remember guarding my heart against the words, "Hope, I have to tell you something." I *dreaded* those words; somehow, they always seemed to end in earth-shaking news and a shattered heart.

I found myself constantly defending Manny, and in turn, defending myself for staying with someone so many people said I shouldn't be seeing. Sometimes, I would actually *hear* what I was saying, as if I was standing outside of myself. I remember thinking, *What are you doing? Do you hear how delusional you sound? Why in the world are you fighting for someone who isn't even here for you and who's hardly ever here with you?* After a while, I learned how to look like I was okay on the outside, but inside I was screaming, swallowing my sobs.

I wish I could say this was the wakeup call I was waiting for. Unfortunately, it took a whole lot more to wake me up out of my stupor.

What I wanted was to feel more secure, but what I did was run deeper into my delusion. I convinced myself that a firm future with Manny would certainly be a solid source for stability. What I was about to experience was even less stability or security than I already had. Codependency really is an addiction. And while it sometimes involves substance abuse, it always involves our interactions with others. We'll talk more about codependency a bit later. For now, let's get back to how we find the wise balance between guarding our hearts and being vulnerable.

I need to be clear, friend, my message isn't, don't ever guard your heart. That's just silly. Guarding our hearts can be a good thing when it's done the right way and for the right reasons. Proverbs 4:23 tells us to guard our hearts with all vigilance for from it flows every issue of life. So, what's the difference in how we guard our hearts? The difference is, what are we guarding our hearts *against*?

I wish I would've done a better job of guarding my heart against unhealthy relationships because I actually had a lot more say in what happened within them than I originally realized. I wish I would've known how to guard my heart against what others had to say about me, because now I know, my life isn't the sum of what others say. My identity is firmly founded in who my *Father* says I am. I wish I would've understood how to guard my heart against letting my emotions run wild because I feel so much—but now I know I get to *filter* what I feel.

This kind of guarding is good. We guard our heart wisely and tenderly according to the wisdom of our Father, not the wisdom of this world because every issue of life really does flow from our hearts.

So, while we want to guard our hearts against making ourselves vulnerable to unwise relationships and routines, we don't shut ourselves off from holding out our hearts to the One who holds His heart out to us. Jesus totally made Himself vulnerable to us by coming and living among us. He didn't do it simply to see what it would be like. He did it so we can make ourselves vulnerable to Him and walk as He walked—in victory!

Here's the thing about vulnerability: I can't guard my heart against God's love and make myself vulnerable to it too. I mean, God is gracious and will fill us to whatever capacity we allow. But why would we want a *thimbleful* when He has *oceans* of love available for us? This is why we ask Him to *expand* our capacity to receive because it's our Father's delight to give us the Kingdom (see Luke 12:32).

I think sometimes we're afraid to make ourselves vulnerable to God because we're scared we're the one He's going to forget or overlook. This lie is straight from an orphan spirit who wants us to believe our perfectly good Father plays favorites. The reality is those who experience God's love in powerful and profound ways are doing so simply because they've asked and made themselves fully available and vulnerable to it.

Many heroes of the faith have been and are willing to give up house and home, life and limb for God's love. It doesn't mean they have, but their hearts are postured in such a way that they refuse to position anything else above His love. Because once we've truly encountered His burning love, there's simply no risk we're unwilling to take.

We've all heard that without risk, there can be no love. That's true ... and it isn't. It's true that we run the risk of leaving personal empires and selfish notions behind when we really go after God's heart. But it's also true that whatever we lose will be *nothing* compared to what we gain.

When I left what I thought would make me feel secure, I found true security. When I lost what I thought were my dreams, I learned how to truly start dreaming. When I stopped telling God the way I wanted things, I found the way to really live. When I finally quit feeling sorry for myself, I found all the compassion I will ever need in my King. When I stopped acting like everything was hopeless, I found everlasting hope. When I ceased obsessing over what would make me happy, I found unstoppable joy. When I surrendered my poverty mindset to my Provider, I found true prosperity. When I stopped thinking like a victim, I became a victor.

Whatever we refuse to keep close-fisted becomes kindling for love's fire, a beautiful flame. I'm saying, whatever we do in the time between the need realized and the need met, isn't merely a painful, pointless process. It's vulnerability. That time does a lot more than we may realize at the moment because it forces us to draw out into deeper waters, as the shallows no longer satisfy us. When we're hungry to encounter real love, we'll be willing to take risks because playing it safe simply isn't able to feed love's ferocious fires.

Making ourselves vulnerable to God's love doesn't make us victims; it makes us victors. Victors who avail themselves to all His love has to offer. Take that leap today, my friend. Make yourself available to the most amazing love you'll ever experience. Ask Him to encounter you, my dear, and you'll finally find the Love you've been looking for all your life.

1. Taken from 1 Corinthians 13:1, note e, page 469 in The Passion Translation, The New Testament with Psalms, Proverbs and Song of Songs, Second Edition

2. Taken from 1 Corinthians 13:1, note e, page 469 in The Passion Translation, The New Testament with Psalms, Proverbs and Song of Songs, Second Edition, (emphasis added)

CHAPTER FOUR

How Do You *See* Me?
(Our Need for Attention Redefined)

True humility is not thinking less of yourself;
it is thinking of yourself less.
—C.S. Lewis

Have you ever lived with the fear of being found out? Found out that you aren't as put together as you project? Or that you don't feel as confident as you come off? Have you ever lived with the fear that if they knew who you *really* were, they wouldn't really like you? I have. On all points and more.

I was so afraid that students from other schools would find out how badly I was bullied. My fear was, if they knew, then they would begin to bully me too. Or at least think less of me. I was constantly covering up any kind of trail that could connect me to my classmates or others at school.

Of course, these were the days before social media, so finding information on me wouldn't have been easy. I simply avoided the places students from school would populate. This cut back on a lot of my social activity, so I found myself spending a lot of time alone. But this is what we do when we react out of fear, right? We isolate.

The thing is, the fear of being found out was all in my head. I don't really know how my friends (from other schools) would have reacted, but I know now if they were *real* friends, it wouldn't have mattered. Even though that fear felt very valid at the time, I didn't realize that by *living* in it, I was inviting it into the rest of my life. (That's *so* not okay.) Living in fear was all a set up. A set up to keep me settling in life. And settling for less led to some seriously foolish decisions. But isn't this also what we do when we react out of fear? We settle.

The shame and fear I felt about myself didn't stop after I graduated high school. It followed me into every single college class I ever attempted. After ten years of hearing how stupid I was, I'd become convinced that I was incompetent. Rather than making up my own mind about myself, I allowed their words to determine who I was. It's something I still wish I would have done differently.

But God's grace restores more than our *lives*. It restores our *time*. Not that we get to go back and do it all over again, nor would I want to. Restoration comes as we yield to the One who has written redemption into our every story with His very own blood. When we put our hope in Him, our hearts are positioned in a place where we can receive the *much more* He has for us.

Even in seasons when we feel like sorrow is the only emotion we know, we can hold fast to His promise that those who sow in tears will reap in joyful shouting. We hold onto His promises to restore what's been broken even as we're in seasons of brokenness. Yes, especially then. For He's the One who works wonders for us. The One who crowns us with joy and draws with us with an everlasting love.

He's the One who is our Redeemer, and as our Redeemer, He promises not only to restore what's been lost but also to redeem the time; even the time we feel like we've wasted. Because God wastes *nothing*. Every broken piece of our lives will rise up and declare Him worthy because He brings beauty even from ashes.

I'm grateful to know this now, but I didn't know this back then. I just kept dragging what others said or did into my everyday experiences, piling one on top of the other. Like layers of clothing, I wore their words. I had no idea I was making agreements with the enemy, effectively giving my yes to the one who wanted to destroy my life, by believing their words.

When we run with a thought, we are making mental agreements with the source of it. When we make mental agreements with things like fear or compulsion, they're not content to stay compartmentalized to one little corner of our lives. Their goal is to get us to take on whatever *their* identity is. They do that by giving us their thoughts (but we don't have to take them).

So let's say the spirit of fear starts whispering to us, his goal is to get us to feel like that fear is ours—but it's not—it's *his*. The enemy doesn't want us to know that he's already a defeated foe, for Christ Jesus overcame him at the cross. Neither does he want us to know that the only power he has, is the power *we* give him. The devil is a fear monger; he'd much rather us walk around feeling terrified and defeated all the time so he can sponge off our power by getting us to agree with him.

The agreements I'd made with fear left me feeling forgotten, like I was always overlooked. I wish I would've gone to God to meet my need to be noticed. Instead, I listened to the lie that said His love would reject me, just like everyone else. I wasn't really certain if that was true, but I was too afraid to find out because if it was, I simply couldn't stand up under that sort of rejection. So, I avoided the One I needed the most and looked to others to appease my appetite for attention, which only worsened my pattern of people-pleasing.

People-Pleasing

Simply put, people-pleasing is just that, it's pleasing people. Which seems innocent enough, right? Well, yes *and* no. When we serve others from a place of pointing people to the Father, though we consider the people we want to help, our heart is really running after our Savior. We want to reflect His wonderful love in every way, including the way we assist others. When this is the purpose behind our aiding and uplifting one another, we not only please *people*, we please our *Poppa*. But when people-pleasing becomes the source of our identity, we run into some pretty big problems.

When people-pleasing becomes the source of our identity, we run into some pretty big problems. My problem was I wanted others to think more of me than I was willing to think of myself. I didn't like me, yet I wanted everyone else to.

My problem was I wanted *others* to think more of me than I was willing to think of *myself*. I didn't like me, yet I wanted everyone else to.

I mean, how do you like someone you don't even know? But that's right where I was. Stuck in a place where I no longer knew myself. It got so bad that I started having internal anxiety attacks when others would ask me simple questions such as, "What's your favorite color?" When I realized that I honestly had no idea, it scared me.

But rather than pushing me into some seriously needed self-discovery, I decided to ignore the issue altogether by asking others' their opinions, then turning them into my own. In other words, I became completely *un*original. Rather than choosing to positively impact whatever environment I was in, I allowed myself to become internally affected by the external environments around me. Not only is this a really unwise way to live, it's how we become quickly dissatisfied with life.

I wanted everyone to be happy with me, so I found myself catering to others all the time. But this only caused more problems when my worlds ran into each other. When you act *one* way around one person and *another* way around another, what do you do when they come together? Particularly when their lifestyles and opinions are complete opposite of each other. Which version of *you*, will you be?

When we're stuck in a cycle of people-pleasing, this causes a real-life crisis. That's the problem with being *un*original. Well, that and the world misses its chance to receive what only we can bring when we're not bold enough to be our real selves.

When we rely on the opinions of others instead of thinking for ourselves, we'll experience even more anxiety because not everyone's going to agree about what you should do. At least that's the way it was for me. I'd toss and turn all night with their words whirling around in my mind as I mentally weighed out which one would work best. Especially when it was about Manny, everyone had some pretty strong opinions about him, and of course *theirs* was always the right one.

Here's another problem with relying on other people's opinions: Sometimes, they actually get offended when we don't take their advice. Which opens up yet *another* problem as we work through who will be *least* offended when we don't listen or follow through with what *they* think we should do. But *they're* not the ones who have to live with the outcome. See how it works against us when we depend upon the opinions of others?

I'm not saying we don't ever seek out wise counsel; that's just silly. But the keyword I want you to catch here is *wise* counsel. Proverbs 15:22 (NIV) puts it this way, "Plans fail for lack of counsel, but with many advisers they succeed." The point is, we need to be keenly aware of where and with whom we seek out advice.

Please don't do what I did and ask everyone else their opinion about your situation—let me spare you the stress. But there is a lot to be said about having a select, core group of people we talk to about our issues. They're the ones we're willing to make ourselves vulnerable to, the ones we allow the room to tell us when our attitude or emotions aren't what they ought to be. Friend, I'm certain you can see how this isn't at all the same as asking everyone their opinion.

Why is it important for us to surround ourselves with wise counsel? Think of it this way: People have a huge impact on culture, and the kind of company we keep determines the kind of culture we create. If you don't like the kind of culture you're in, you may want to reconsider the kind of people you're around. Because we really do become like the people we surround ourselves with the most.

Not thinking for ourselves creates a culture of unrest within us as we're constantly wondering what everyone else is thinking. And not knowing that our true identity flows from who God says we are can actually cause us to think our identity comes from what others think about us.

Not having these pillars of thought in place is how we get roped into people-pleasing in the first place.

The thing is, we were *wired* to want attention and *created* with the need to be noticed. I realize this is contrary to what religion tells us. Religious teaching tells us that humility is thinking less of ourselves. But humility isn't thinking less of myself, because at the end of the day, my focus is still on *myself*. Humility is redirecting our focus off *ourselves* and onto *Jesus*.

To believe it's okay for me to entertain thoughts about myself, so long as they are poor, is preposterous! Not to mention in total opposition to the way Jesus lived. He was *fully* confident in Himself, still there has never been anyone humbler than Him.

Knowing we were wired for attention and created with the need to be noticed can actually be catalytic to us catching, keeping, and advancing the fires of our Father's love. But if we want to encounter and advance His fervent flames, we must first learn how to filter through these wants and needs wisely.

Attention Hoarder

I was ready. Every hair was in place, my makeup fully accented every feature, and my dress was, well, *barely* a dress. With my four-inch stilettos and snakeskin clutch in tow, I was sure to get some second glances throughout the room. All so *my man* would know how lucky he was to be with me.

Looking back now, my heart hurts at how often that young woman sacrificed something as precious as her dignity only to draw attention to herself for a few short moments.

Listen my dear, if someone pressures us to prematurely reveal parts of ourselves that are meant to remain hidden to defend our dignity and ensure our integrity, they're *not* asking out of love. They're asking selfishly because it's what *they* want. And sometimes, they're asking as a result of the momentum of the moment. Proverbs 12:19 (NIV) puts it this way, "Truthful lips endure forever, but a lying tongue lasts only a *moment*. (emphasis added)"

We've all experienced the heartache that comes from compromising when we've listened to lying lips. But when we step back and get some perspective, we all know it's not worth compromising what is sacred for lies—not even sugar-coated ones. Because lies never satisfy.

It doesn't matter how dark or dim it is, when we strike a match, it lights up everything around us. Right? Because light *always* overcomes darkness. In the exact same way, even the simplest truth overtakes every single lie. And when we get ahold of the truth that we are actually the sons and daughters of God; it changes the way we interact with our need for attention in the most wonderful way!

For the sake of this subject, I must skip ahead several years in my story. About a month after I *finally* left Manny, I encountered Jesus in a more extraordinary way than ever before. He gave me a vision. (If you're not sure what a vision is, it's simply when God uses our imagination to speak to us through mental and/or visual images and is often accompanied with words, feelings, promptings, and impressions.)

In this vision, I was a little girl in a grand ballroom wearing a beautiful pastel pink ballgown. Suddenly Jesus appeared, dressed in His kingly attire, and asked me if I'd like to dance. Bashfully, I replied that I didn't know how. He looked down at His feet, and I followed His gaze. With shining love in His eyes, He chuckled, "That's okay, simply step on, and I'll lead you!" As I climbed on, I was met with the most wonderful flush of warm emotion I'd ever felt, as Love Himself held me. The One whose hands swept away the sins of the world were now sweeping me off my feet. How could I do anything but sink deep into His affectionate embrace?

Time passed as we danced, and I went from resting in His arms to wanting to peek around the room. There were so many people and pillars swirling all around us and I suddenly realized I could run into someone or something and get hurt. Reading my thoughts, Jesus leaned down, looked lovingly into my eyes and warmly whispered, "Just hide your head in my chest and rest here. There's no need to look up and around. I promise to get you from one end of the ballroom to the other safely." After He spoke, I remember leaning *all* my weight against the only One worthy of all my trust—the only One who would twirl me into eternity.

As I lingered in His love, He laid on my heart that the ballroom was representative of my life. And I saw myself through His eyes, as a little girl because He was restoring my innocence and renewing my mind. These two were intertwined. He was in the process of restoring my innocence, as I was partnering with Him in the process of renewing my mind. By really getting to know *His* heart, I was really getting to know my *own*.

From this place of clarity, I could finally see how *He* was the answer to my need for attention, all along. Only His Love was enough to silence my innermost screams to be noticed. I no longer needed to look around and wonder at what could go wrong or be absorbed in another's identity and mirror it as my own. All I had to do was rest in the arms of the One who promised to twirl and swirl me through every season of my life.

I walked away from that encounter truly changed. Feeling far more prepared for whatever was ahead. My identity wouldn't be found in what Manny (or anyone else) thought I should be. I'd been set free from the life-sucking lie that *his* life had to be my *whole* life. For the very first time, I was finally seeing that my identity could only come from loving and accepting who *God* created me to be.

True Humility Leads to Love

There's really only one of two ways to live. Full of love or full of fear. When we're not plugged into love, we walk out our identity from a place full of fear, subconsciously leeching our identity off others. But here's the thing, it's really hard to believe in yourself when you're letting everyone else do the thinking for you.

We're often taught in Western civilizations that not thinking much of ourselves is what humility looks like. If you don't believe me, watch the way others react next time you pay them a compliment. Actually, you might not need to look any further than your own reaction to encouragement. When I say something complimentary to others, I've found that three out of five people will reply with appropriate social responses, followed by fifteen reasons why what I just said is wrong. Like, they'll never be as good as so-and-so. Or they rolled out of bed late and look like a hot mess. Or they haven't slept well for six months and are amazed they can even remember their own name, let alone the lyrics to the song they sang a moment ago. You get the point.

And the point is, humility isn't thinking *less* of ourselves; it's thinking of ourselves less. It's the joyful freedom from self-absorption.

We don't have to do mental self-rejection exercises to maintain a healthy level of humility. I mean, why do the enemy's job for him, right? Psalm 139:17 (TPT) says, "How precious and wonderful to consider that you cherish me constantly in your every thought." That's so beautiful! God cherishes us in His *every* thought!

I feel like I may not be fully getting my point across in the way I want to. *So, let me grab you by the face, look you in the eye and say it this way:*

We all know God's been around for an untold and uncountable amount of years, right? Hang with me here for a second. So before God, from out of His mouth ever said in Genesis 1:3, "Let there be light," God, from within His heart said, let there be *you*. Before the earth was ever formed; before the evening and morning were the first day, second day, third day and so on, and before He ever rested on the seventh, God carried *you* around in His heart.

That's how long He's been thinking about you. And in *all* that time and *all* those thoughts, He's been *constantly* cherishing you! I mean, *wow*. Let that really soak in before you rush on ahead, cherished one.

False Humility Comes from Religion

When we've been taught that God's thoughts toward us fluctuate depending upon what we do, those who've taught us these untruths were likely regurgitating religious lies. Lies, they learned from someone who was *also* regurgitating religious lies that *they* learned from someone else. Do you follow me? What I'm saying is, religion, like codependency, is cyclical. And like codependency, it's rooted in *control*.

Except, where we employ codependency to help us feel noticed (or numb the pain when we're not), religion teaches us our need to feel noticed is not only unnecessary, it's a need with which God is not pleased. When really, *He's* the One who gave it to us in the first place!

So, when someone does something really wonderful, for which others appropriately want to applaud, if they're stuck in the ways of religion, they've been programed to respond with some ridiculous and even painful replies. "Oh, it really wasn't that great; I wish it would have been better." Or "It wasn't me; it was just Jesus." Or "Oh, thank you but I was almost embarrassed to go after sister-so-and-so; she's so much better than me."

I mean, the religious culture leaves *absolutely no room* for feeling good about yourself. In fact, feeling good about yourself is often viewed as arrogance. When really, feeling good about what God made gives Him *glory!* Now obviously, we can take this too far and get into pride. But when we know we're unable to do what we do on our own, apart from Christ, and we know everyone else knows it too, our only appropriate response is one of *absolute* gratitude from a heart overflowing with celebration. *This* is the response that gives God glory because in it, we're magnifying *Him* as the Master Creator who makes everything beautiful in its time (see Ecclesiastes 3:11).

Friend, it's time we get real. We've got to stop quoting Scriptures without letting them make an impact on our hearts. If He makes *everything* beautiful in its time, that means *we're* beautiful in *our* time. So let's live like we're beautiful—because He says we are! We just read it. He calls us His greatest creation, His masterpiece. The Star-Breather says you take His breath away. The One who filled the oceans wants to dance with you on the deep.

He's not satisfied with only half our hearts, but that's what religion does. It puts walls around our hearts. Because it's hard to make ourselves vulnerable to Love when we're being taught that He's only pleased with us when *we* think less of ourselves. When this is what we're taught, naturally the takeaway is, it must be because *He* thinks less of us too. Friend, *nothing* could be farther from the truth.

Shalom

We really can't afford to have a thought in our head about ourselves that God doesn't have. And He doesn't have one negative thought about us. Not a single one. Jeremiah 29:11 (NKJV) says, "For I know the thoughts that I think toward you, says the Lord, thoughts of peace and not of evil, to give you a future and a hope."

That word peace here in Hebrew is *shalom*, which means safety, welfare, health, prosperity, contentment, friendship, and covenant relationship. That's priceless! The thoughts God thinks about you are thoughts full of hope for your future but they're also full of peace, prosperity, safety, welfare, health, and contentment. But He doesn't just stop there. Friendship and covenant relationship are the words He uses when you're running through His mind.

God loves you with an everlasting love, my friend. What's more, He *likes* you. He enjoys you, and He *sees* you.

Our Need to Be Seen

As we said earlier, we've all been created with the need to be seen. God knit this need into the fabric of our existence when He weaved us together in the secret places of the earth. For our need to be seen exposes us to our need for His encouragement.

Something happens to the self-esteem of a child whose parents praise them. Regardless of their age—two or sixty-two—the effects are the same. You want to increase your kids' confidence? Compliment them. (This actually isn't exclusive to your kids; it'll work on anyone.) And I mean do it *sincerely*, none of this half-hearted junk. Call out the *gold* in your kids because it's in there. If you don't see it, it might just be because you haven't called it forth. (And remember, this isn't exclusive to your kids; it applies to everyone ...)

Please don't misinterpret this as me accusing you of being a bad parent. I'm not. I'm simply saying your kids never tire of hearing how proud you are of them. Whether we're running around in diapers or running around as adults, we delight in knowing we make the hearts of those who raised us happy. You know why? We were designed for the absolute delight of feeling the heart of our proud Poppa.

Our identity comes from *knowing* we're His kids. The same way I know I'm Harold and Candy's daughter, I know I'm the daughter of the God of the universe. *I'm His daughter!* That's supposed to absolutely amaze me! And let me tell you, it absolutely does!

But the spirit of religion wants to swoop in and say the Father's heart carries anger and disappointment toward us because it wants us distracted and stuck in a web of lies. We're not a threat to the enemy's territory when we're doing his job for him. This is why self-pity and false humility can carry such an appeal. The devil wants to draw us in through our preoccupation with ourselves, rather than being consumed with our Bridegroom King. Because when we know who we are, the sons and daughters of God, the Bride of Christ, the threats we cause to the enemy's kingdom are not only *immense*, they are *eternal*.

The thing is, the spirit of religion doesn't have a voice unless we give him our ear, so let's stop listening to his lies. Even if the enemy's accusations reflect the words and actions of those who raised us, God renews our perspective as we partner with Him in the renewing of our minds. The One who makes all things new, cancels out the lies of the enemy with His love.

When we know His love, *by experience*, we're not afraid of interacting with the Father's heart. His love helps us tear down the strongholds of thought where the enemy hides his lies. We no longer expect to find anger or disappointment or forgetfulness in His heart. Those lies don't have a voice when we refuse to listen to anything other than the song of love our Father is singing over us.

Secure in Our Attention

When I'm refusing to entertain thoughts God doesn't think about *me*, I'm far less likely to entertain thoughts He doesn't think about *you*. Why? Secure people are not given to building cases against others. They're less inclined to go into a room and pick everyone apart by appearances or abilities, just to make themselves feel better. They're confident enough to celebrate everyone's strengths while maintaining their own identity.

When we realize our Father's heart is big enough to give all His children attention, we step *out* of need and *into* faith. I don't become apprehensive in my Father's love when I hear the testimony of how He touched you. I know His love for me isn't any less because of His love for you. In fact, the more I experience the Father's love, I'll find it only grows stronger and greater as it spreads—much like a wildfire.

This is what security looks like lived out, and true security only comes from making ourselves available to the Father's love. Friend, our need for attention isn't offensive to God. He designed it to drive us to Him. When we know

He's the only One who can satisfy our need to be seen, we'll stop criticizing ourselves (and others) for needing to be noticed. Instead, we'll run into the arms of our Father who always responds to the cries of our heart. We captivate His attention, and by His affection we are satisfied and set free. When we live in His fullness, we invite others to come and see—simply by being our beautiful selves!

CHAPTER FIVE

How Do You *Hold* Me?
(Our Need for Security Redefined)

Justice is not something God has.
Justice is something that God is.
—A.W. Tozer

L et's take a few minutes now to talk about our search for
security. Go ahead and grab a mug of your favorite hot
beverage, wrap your hands around it, and get all warm and
cozy. That's what I just did. I'm all curled up on my couch,
sipping on some mint-matcha from the first mug my hunky
hubby ever bought me. It's orange with brown writing that
says "HOPE" on it. (Thanks, babe. I still love it even after
all these years, just like you. Except I love *you* much more!)

Okay, are you all comfy? Yes? Then, now we're ready for
a good old-fashioned heart-to-heart chat. I've promised to
always be real with you, my friend. So I pray you'll always
be real with me, and more importantly, real with yourself.

Let me start by asking, have you ever put your trust in someone, and they let you down? I'm assuming you're shaking your head yes right now because we're all going to let each other down at some point or another (intentional or not).

But how about this, have you ever trusted in someone whose choices pushed you beyond the reaches of disappointment and into the realms of despair? It may have been a parent or guardian, a family member or a close friend; maybe it was your pastor or a well-known, well-respected individual. It may have even been your spouse.

Here's the thing, risks are possible with any relationship. That's what safe boundaries are for, we'll talk more about boundaries in a bit. But the outcome will always be disastrous when we put our *complete* and *total* trust in people. People are not God. Therefore, people are not perfect, and we set ourselves up for some serious heartache when we expect them to be.

Wedding Bells and Broken Hearts

The day I thought I'd never see was almost here! After years of convincing and coaxing, Manny finally fumbled through what I accepted as a proposal. In the months following, I kept telling myself, *this is exactly what you've been wanting ... so why don't you feel happier? This is going to fix everything!*

Fast forward eleven months later and there I was on the eve of my wedding, dreaming about the future, hoping this was what would finally settle my wondering heart. Everything was ready. My gorgeous wedding gown was fitted, pressed, and now hanging on my closet door. Its satin and lace lines draping down like so many symbols of hope dancing in the dreams of all our tomorrows. The church was booked, and the responses returned. The caterer and reception center had both been slated, prepped, and paid, and now every decoration was in place. The rehearsal was rehearsed, dinner was done and as far as I knew, everyone had turned in for the night.

Everything was ready.

Then, at two o'clock in the morning on the day of our wedding, my world turned up-side-down. Manny called to tell me he didn't think he could go through with it. He wanted to cancel the wedding. We'd already had a pretty rocky engagement as it was, and to be honest, I don't know why I hadn't called it off months earlier. I mean, what bride-to-be wants to walk down the aisle toward a man who's kicking and screaming for her *not* to come? "Do you take this woman...?" A groom shouting, *"Please, don't make me!"* while violently shaking his head isn't exactly the stuff of every girl's dream!

I guess the reason we stay or don't stay in a relationship points back to where we put our security. I was undoubtedly putting all my hopes and dreams—not to mention pressure—upon a person who, quite frankly, wasn't ready for any adult responsibility apart from caring for himself. But *I* wasn't ready for the responsibility of facing life without him. See how twisted this gets?

So there I was on the other end of the line and I remember thinking, *I can't believe this is my life.* Yet somehow, I wasn't surprised. Stunned? Sure. Surprised? Not exactly. I guess you could say, I was getting used to getting let down. I know what you're thinking because I'm think it too, now that I'm on *this* side of the situation. If all he did was let me down, why in the world would I have ever even *considered* marrying him?

I see now that I wasn't asking myself this question because I didn't actually want to know the answer. Because real questions, lead us to real answers. And real answers lead us to real accountability for those answers which, if we allow, will lead us into real change. Apparently, I wasn't ready for *real* change. That's why I wasn't asking *real* questions.

As I lay there listening to him drone on about everything he *couldn't* do, I remember how surreal it was having this conversation with my wedding dress staring right at me. What once stood as a symbol of hope for our future, now hung there mocking my dreams. Its delicate lace lines, turned deadly cords, were choking me, cackling at all my misery. It was *too* much! It was *all* too much!

After all the uncertainty of our relationship ... After all the tireless efforts I'd put into planning our wedding ... After investing all my funds into our future and now hearing *this* ... It was all *way* too much!

At this point in the conversation, I started shouting something like, "You've got to be kidding me. This is *crazy!*" That's when my parents met me in the hallway where I'd been pacing. I must have woken them up with all my shouting—*go figure*. The last thing I remember was going down. *Lights out*. My mom must have grabbed the phone from me after I fell to the floor because when I came back to, she told me she'd told Manny that he needed to call our pastor.

After all the terrible transactions of that morning, a switch flipped on the inside of me, and I felt like I could *finally* see what everyone had been saying all along. But hours later, after he called saying he was willing to go through with the wedding, so long as I promised to do *everything* I could in my power to make him happy (a statement that still makes my stomach sick), that switch flipped back.

There was *so* much wrong with his unbelievably one-sided statement. And *even more* with the fact that I didn't recognize just how wrong it was.

So, after my mental switch flipped and I had my moment of clarity, why do you suppose I flipped back? I mean, if I could finally see *why* everyone was saying, *what* they'd been saying all along, why would I ever agree to go back to someone who was obviously only in it for himself? That's a great question, and its answer is, again, rooted in security.

The little bit of self-esteem I had before I met Manny was now all wrapped up in him. As we discussed earlier, when a person (or group of people) become our means of security, we'll do anything to hold onto them. Never mind that this sense of security is all an illusion, one which could shatter at any moment. We're so caught up in the emotional entanglement of it all that we lose sight of what is real. This is what happens when we go to a *resource* rather than *The Source* for our security.

When these are the steps we take to feel secure, the outcome will never be what we were expecting. Because what we are expecting, won't ever stand up against what is real. We have all these ideas of what things will look like, but our ideas aren't actually what *is*; neither are they what *will be*. Therefore, we're only setting ourselves up for things like deep disappointment and heartache. We might realize this once we're on the *outside* looking in, but when we're right there in the thick of it, we simply can't see it.

It's like standing in a super dark room and not being able to see your hand, even though you're holding it five inches from your face. Same concept. Deception works really hard to keep us in the dark, so we don't see Christ reaching out His hand, right there in front of us.

I put my security in what I *chose* to believe and what I *chose* to see and blinded myself to all else. Here's the thing,

I really did only want to believe the best in Manny. I mean, as "good Christian people," this is what we're taught to do, right? But blithely believing the best in others, without the Holy Spirit's wisdom, can lead us to disastrous undoing. Our desire for their best will run us right into our inclination to enable if we're not walking in wisdom. They may be a great person, full of potential, but the extent to which they run in their potential is really up to them. Even God, while He's obligated Himself to fulfill all His *promises*, He leaves our *potential* up to us.

Before he called the second time, all I kept thinking was what in the world am I going to tell everyone? Everybody was right. I feel so ashamed and look like *such* a fool. Did I really want to call all those people and tell them the wedding was canceled because the guy ended up being exactly who they said he was? Did I really want to run the risk of hearing over a hundred people telling me all the reasons why they knew it wouldn't have worked? Did I really want everyone feeling sorry for poor, little, helpless Hope? Absolutely not! So when he did call, it was really easy to slip right back into old ways of thinking, without even realizing it. Now I didn't have to worry about saving face. And maybe, just maybe, everything really would work out for our happily-ever-after.

The Choice

There are some of you here with me today, who have experienced unspeakable, unbearable heartbreak and pain. And you want—no—you *demand* to know where God was. How could He have let those horrible things happen to you? But that's just it—*He* didn't. *His* plans for us are *always* good. *He's* not the thieve. *He* doesn't steal, kill, or destroy. *He* came to give us abundant life (see John 10:10).

In Luke 9:56 (NASB), Jesus said, "the Son of Man (speaking of Himself) did not come to destroy men's lives, but to save them." When we weep, He weeps with us. When we hurt, He hurts. He holds us through the hardest times, even when we don't realize it or feel His arms around us. He's still there. And He's never gonna leave.

Why, then, do we experience hurt? Why do horrific things happen, even to good people? How do we find our security in God when pain is so often a part of our process?

My beloved, it all boils down to *choice*. The choice Adam and Eve made back in the garden opened us up to a world of hurt that was never in God's heart for us. Yet God gave and continues to give us the freedom to choose. Because love cannot exist without choice.

Love cannot exist without choice.

What each of us does with our own choices is up to us. Yet even in our ability to choose, God has not left us without guidance. He's given us His very own Spirit to help us in our decision making if we'll only listen. That's the key. Proverbs 4:20–22 tells us when we listen to and honor what God says, His words become life and health to us.

Choice is God's gift to us because He wants relationship, not robots. By His very nature, He is a Rewarder (see Hebrews 11:6) and He sets us up to be rewarded by making choice available to us. We can choose Him and His ways or our own. When we choose Him and His ways, not only are we walking in wisdom, we're exposing ourselves to His reward. We're His children, and what good dad doesn't want to reward His kids for doing the right things? If *we're* wired to reward our kids, how much more is *He?* The stirrings we sense to reward and recognize comes from Him because we've been made in His image and His likeness (Genesis 1:27).

When we ignore God's voice and stubbornly fight for our own way, we not only make ourselves and others around us miserable, we actually step outside of His protection. We remove ourselves from the safe place of His shelter. I want to be clear—*He* doesn't remove us. *We* remove ourselves.

By no means am I suggesting that when we are walking in step with God, we won't ever experience difficulty or adversity. But focusing on our Father keeps us in perfect peace on the *inside*, regardless of the pressure on the *outside*. Our internal world isn't in disarray because of the disasters around us since our security isn't in what's happening, it's in knowing who God is and who God is for *us*.

I'm also not suggesting that God is out to get anyone. As if He's waiting for someone to miss a step so He can scold them. The truth is, His mercy *triumphs* over judgment. I'm simply saying, when we choose our *own* way over His, we make ourselves far more susceptible to the attacks and accusations of the enemy.

Along with our ability to choose comes a whole gambit of decisions to be made. Some we hit right on the mark, while others we miss by a mile. Here's the thing about choice—we never make decisions in a vacuum. What I do affects my loved ones and those around me, and the same goes for you. So we need to be careful with our choices because they really do make an impact, not only in our lives but in the lives of others. Something we should all be asking ourselves as we progress in our decision-making process is, are my decisions rooted in *love* and founded on faith, or are they coming from a place of *fear?*

The Voice

I felt sick as I stood before him shaking, heart pounding, palms sweating, barely able to breathe. I may have been breathless—but not in a good way. I wasn't breathless for all the anticipation I felt for our future. I was breathless because I was terrified, I was making the wrong decision.

Let me back up a bit.

It seemed the overall consensus was to put the morning's phone call behind us and move ahead. I don't really remember talking it over with anyone or discussing how I felt about it; I just remember sort of pushing it to the side and going on autopilot from there. On one hand, I think this was partly due to the fact that I was an adult, and everyone assumed I knew my own mind (boy did I have *them* fooled). On the other hand, I think since I'd been going in this direction for so long, everyone was finally willing to let me follow it through. I'm certain they were as emotionally exhausted as I was from the last several years.

So there I was on my wedding day, finally standing before Manny, and it took *everything* in me not to bolt back up the aisle, storm out the door, and take off running until every memory of us vanished like a cloud of smoke mingling with the sunset sky. Tears were rolling now, uncontrollably down my face, but they didn't feel like tears of joy. They felt out of place and time, much like me.

That's when Manny held out his hands for me to see how steady they were (unlike my own) leaned in, and said, "Sorry about earlier. I'm ready now." I gave him a weak smile and remember thinking, *Good for him, but now I don't think I am.*

As I looked into his eyes, my heart sunk; I knew I couldn't hurt his heart by leaving him to stand there all alone. And as I gazed out across the sea of faces, it felt like everyone was collectively holding their breath, along with their hope, for our future. Coupled with my sheer stubbornness, these were enough to keep me standing right by Manny's side.

No sooner had I resolved to stay when a soft whisper, like a punch in the gut, screamed inside me, "*He's not the one.*" It was the same whisper I'd heard when we'd first started dating years before. It wasn't that I didn't recognize the voice, but I didn't want to believe it then, and I sure didn't want to believe it now.

As I turned to face him, all I could think was, I don't want to believe I've wasted the last six years of my life. I could hear my own voice repeating my vows to him, "I take thee, Manny, to be my lawfully wedded husband, to have and to hold..." But *inwardly*, I was wrestling with myself. Not wanting to believe I'd allowed myself to fight for the wrong one. "...From this day forward, for better or for worse..." *I don't want to believe everything I've done has been for nothing.* "...For richer, for poorer, in sickness and in health..." *I don't want to believe that I've forced myself to feel something for someone I might not even have any real feelings for, all for the sake of familiarity and a twisted sense of security.* "...To love and to cherish, till death do us part..." *I don't want to believe that what I feel for him isn't so much love as it is pity, coming more from a mother's heart than a lover's heart. I couldn't get those two confused, could I? No! I don't want to believe it! I won't believe it! So, I refused to say anything other than,* "I do."

The problem wasn't that I didn't recognize God's voice. The problem was that by this point, I was so full of confusion that I didn't know where His voice fit. Does that make sense? I see now, it needed to fit *first*. It came *first*. Before every other decision. Before every other promise, vow, or choice I made that day. Before I cared about how *he* felt about us, I should have cared about how *He* felt about us. Before I cared about what *they* thought, I needed to care about what *He* thought.

But honestly, I wasn't confident in God's care for me at this time. I mean I didn't know *with my whole heart* that God considered me valuable. I wasn't confident that He had something better for me than what I could contrive on my own. I thought it was more about do's and don'ts than it was me giving Him the freedom to fully express His Father's heart toward me. I didn't really know what that looked like. I hadn't really had anyone sit me down, grab me by the face, look me in the eye and say, "You are worth *so much more* than the way he is treating you," in a way that *stuck* with me.

I think after a while, everyone just got so tired of fighting with me about our relationship that they eventually rolled over and gave in. And while I certainly was strong-willed and fighting for a relationship I shouldn't have been fighting for, the truth is, the entire time, I was secretly waiting for someone to validate me and tell me I was worth *so* much more than what I was receiving. Rather than making excuses for his behavior or mine, rather than psychoanalyzing every last inch of our interactions, what I *really* wanted was someone to make me aware of my worth. To make me feel *secure*. It's only now, on *this* side of things, I see, *Someone* was. I simply wasn't listening.

Friend, can you see how essential it is to know the Source of our security if we want to make wise decisions? When we don't, we end up ignoring the whispers of the One who wants more for us than we want for ourselves. Then we make bad decisions from broken perspectives and blame God for the pain we've unintentionally brought upon ourselves.

He wants us to hear Him and know His voice that's always loving and full of life. Even when it holds correction,

His voice is so full of love. He's never about shaming us; it's simply not in His nature. Love doesn't shame. Love lifts us up and helps us out of the pit. Yes, even the ones we've dug ourselves. Beloved, He wants you to listen close. Because He's leaning in, holding your face in His tender hands, looking you in the eyes, and whispering to your heart, *"You're worth so much more than you can imagine,"* in a way that will *stick* with you for the *rest* of your life.

> *Jesus is leaning in, holding your face in His tender hands, looking you in the eyes, and whispering to your heart, "You're worth so much more than you can imagine."*

How do I know? Because the One Who loves us best told me so.

As Manny and I turned to face our guests and take our first walk down the aisle as man and wife, I immediately knew I'd made a big mistake. My spirit was so grieved that I was sick to my stomach. Still, I tried to ignore the sinking feelings swarming on the inside of me. Like maybe if I acted as though those feelings weren't there, I could save myself from drowning in the worst decision I had ever made.

Yet the days and weeks ahead would only confirm my convictions.

Head over Heart?

This was *my* story of misplaced security arising out of the broken places and bad decisions of my life. But *you*, my friend, may have faced terrible difficulties not because of what you did, but because of what you've encountered. Maybe it was someone imposing their will upon you or a natural disaster or life-changing diagnosis. What then? And what do we do with the statements people make such as, "God allowed this to happen to you," or "Well, you know, God moves in mysterious ways," or "God's in control, so He did this for a reason."

The thing is, that's easy for *them* to say, when they're not the one hurting. When they're not the one wrestling all night with the memories of what happened or living out the loss, grief, and aftermath of the experience. If you're anything like me, the more you hear these cliché, trite responses, the easier it is to become frustrated with people and distrustful of God; this is especially true when we don't know His nature for ourselves. How can we be expected to find security in Someone we feel like we can't even trust or we don't even know?

So, for my sake and yours, let's shine some light on this subject. It's true, God *is* good. All the time. It's also true that He's in charge. But there's a *world* of difference between being in *charge* and being *in control*.

Let me give you a brief, easy example to portray this difference. Let's say I own a company. I'm in charge of this company and have employees under me, I'm also in charge of them. Part of my responsibility as a business owner, is cultivating an atmosphere where my employees will receive every effort to succeed and follow through with the purposes within their positions. While I am in *charge* of these employees and give them the tools, resources, and opportunities they need to be successful, I cannot *control* the outcome of their success. The ultimate outcome of their success is up to them because they have the *right* and *gift* of free will, and only they can decide how, and to what end, they will use it.

I cannot control whether they use their free will to advance and increase in opportunity in my company or embezzle money; that choice is theirs alone. If they choose to embezzle money, will others accuse me of being involved? Perhaps. But only because I'm in charge. I'm the owner and for good or bad, my employees reflect me, my heart, and my company.

It's the same with God. He's in control of what *we* surrender to Him. When we give God our "yes," we yield our will to Him—we *give* Him control of our lives—which is the *wisest* thing we can ever do. I used to think surrender came by a huge effort, a one-time heavy heave-haul of my burdens at the altar. The problem with *this* version of surrender was, it revolved around *me* and *my* efforts. So, when I'd find myself under the weight of all those burdens again, I'd also find myself under the weight of unnecessary guilt coming from the hiss of the accuser; blaming me for not trusting God, suggesting I wasn't really His daughter since I wasn't in surrender.

Saying surrender is a one-time big, showy deal *sounds* really spiritual, but in reality, surrender is simply what happens in the intimate moments of our everyday lives. It's in the intentional minute by minute, sometimes second by second choices we make. I surrender my control and will to God—and I *keep* surrendering my control and will to God. This is what true surrender looks like. We let it go and we *choose* to not take it back, by *choosing instead* to remind ourselves of all the reasons we have to trust Him.

Can this be easier said than done sometimes? Sure. But only when I'm believing lies about who He is. More specifically, when I'm believing lies about who He is for *me*, or when I fight against the purposes, people, and perspectives with whom He's asked me to align. But God is *so* gracious, and we're all in-process, and He's here to help us through the process and into success. *He* wants us to succeed even more than *we* do!

If we look around, we'll see He's provided us with all the tools, resources, and opportunities to truly know His heart and be successful in our time. He's given us His Word, His Son, and His Spirit. He's given us His power and authority through His Son's blood and name. He's given us all the wonderful gifts and dimensions of His Spirit, and He's given us His glorious nature to know, explore, and enjoy. His nature is evident in His Word and it's wonderfully displayed in all of creation and our everyday lives. If it doesn't look like love, it didn't come from Him for by His very nature, He *is* Love.

Rape. Murder. Molestation. Disaster. Violence. Racism. Abortion. Hatred. Abuse. Addiction. Betrayal. Divorce. Miscarriage. Cancer. Deception. Stillbirth. Disease. Pain. Anxiety. Aids. Disorder. Starvation. Fear. Genocide. *None* of these originated with God. Let me say it again. *None* of these came out of God's heart. For He is *only* love; "God is light and in Him is *no darkness at all"* (1 John 1:5, emphasis added).

At the same time, I realize there are lots of people running around doing and saying things "in the name of God" that *definitely* aren't in line with His nature. This isn't *God's* doing, but if we have the perspective that God is a controlling God who manipulates or controls people's choices, we can find ourselves thinking it *is*. Throw in natural disasters, wars, and rumors of wars, and if we think God's up there pulling the strings, it can feel like we're all just a bunch of pawns on His Chessboard.

Back in the garden, God gave Adam and Eve dominion over the earth and told them to *subdue* the earth and fill it. According to Merriam-Webster's Dictionary, subdue means to conquer and bring into subjection, bring under control, especially by an exertion of the will. The Hebrew word for subdue here is *kabash,* and it means to subject, force, keep under, to bring into bondage, make subservient (it's where we get the saying, "put the kibosh on it or them"). This is eye-opening, right? God gave the first people on the earth the *command* to conquer, subject, and keep control of the earth and fill it. You might not agree with what I'm saying, but it's right there in your Bible in Genesis 1:28, like it is mine.

God gave us all free will as a gift because like we said before, love cannot exist without choice. And He created us for the purpose of *love*, not *control*. But back in the garden, Adam and Eve, using their gift of choice, traded in their dominion and authority over the earth when they *chose* to believe the enemy's lie that God was withholding from them. When they *chose* to believe the enemy's lie, they didn't only *choose* to not believe *God*, they *chose* to believe the devil. Effectively trading masters.

From that moment on, actually, *before* that moment, God had a plan to redeem humankind from sin, restore us to right relationship with Himself, and reinstate our authority over the earth. If you'll remember, we talked earlier about how God, through the spilled blood of Jesus at the cross, cut a new covenant with us—one of *love*, not of *law*. (The covenant of law is what resulted from the fall in the garden, the covenant of love—which trumps the covenant of law—is what came from the cross and blood of Christ). Father God signed and *forever sealed* this new covenant with us through Jesus' blood. It can *never* be annulled!

I want you to see how in Matthew 28:18–20, Jesus reinstated—*He gave us back*—our authority and dominion over the earth. Because of the cross, we have been forever redeemed, and our rightful dominion and authority is restored to us the *second* we receive Christ as our Savior.

The issue is, sin still has a lease on our planet, we see this evidenced in creation as the earth groans with labor pains, as Paul put it in Romans 8:22. The enemy no longer has authority because Jesus stripped it from him at the cross (see Colossians 2:15). *That's* why He could say, "*All* authority in heaven and on earth has been given to me" in Matthew 28:18 (NIV, emphasis added). If Jesus has *all* authority that means the enemy has *none*. While the enemy has *no* authority, he does have power, but he only gets his power by getting us to give him ours. satan operates through those who are not walking in full surrender to Jesus. This is why it's *so* vital and such a joy to lay down our lives in surrender to Christ because it's our only way to real freedom.

We need to take seriously our position and responsibility as believers. For this is *our* time to shine. It's *our* shift to shake the heavens, to take a stand as intercessors and say, *enough and no further. This is our watch now.* Jesus has taken back the authority and dominion over the earth and given it to *us*.

We're back to living under God's original command to *subdue* the earth and *fill* it for His Word *never* returns to Him void. That command is *still* rolling through the ages and is as momentous now as ever. Now is not the time to sleep on our shift! It's time to subdue the earth—to bring it under the subjection of Heaven—and fill it! For we've been given authority and dominion to proclaim God's heart to be done on earth as it is in Heaven. This isn't only His *heart*; this is His *will*.

So, when I see someone with cancer or hear about an impending hurricane, I take it personal. I remind myself that God has given me authority over these things, *and they will bow!* Regardless of whether I see it revealed today or tomorrow or when I'm in Heaven, the things that rise up against God and His goodness *will bow*. They *have* to. This is how it was when Jesus walked the earth, and we've already established that He's our Savior, but He's also our *model*. We are to imitate Him. It's *our* time.

Heart over Head

When we've lived through something awful or traumatic, most people want someone—*anyone* to blame, so most blame the "Big Guy." They blame *something* they cannot understand on *Someone* they do not understand. But when we know God's nature by *experience* from encountering His kindness and tasting His goodness, our heart finds its home in His love. When our heart is at home in His love, our head—the way we think of Him—catches up and we'll find it's not in *His* heart to hurt us.

At the time of this writing, we recently had an F4 tornado rip right through the center of our city, doing all kinds of damage to the downtown area. Homes and businesses all over the place were demolished, trees were snapped in half, debris was everywhere.

Sadly, the worst of the wreckage happened in areas that were already impoverished. It's tragic to see people pitching tents and boarding up homes with wooden planks and blue tarps as they wait for the relief of more permanent repairs. It's heartbreaking to see that lost look in their eyes, like a little child who has lost track of his mama. All you want to do is hold their hand and help them find their way back home; and we can, when we know the Way Maker.

We have the most important thing they need—we have living hope on the inside of us. Unfortunately, it can be really hard to help them receive His hope when it's impressed upon them by society, the news, or even those who confess to follow Christ that something like this is God's judgment. Ouch. BIG misconception. HUGE. I mean, how does that help someone in *this* sort of situation?

I can't stand there and tell you God is good and also tell you He's the One who sent a storm to tear down your house to teach you some sort of a lesson or get your attention.

How can we expect Him to be our security if we can't even trust that He is good?

Yet most of us have been taught, or at least it's been implied that God will be out to get us if we're not living up to a certain standard ... but it'll all be for our own good, of course. What a lie! There's a vast difference between being all-*powerful* and all-*controlling*.

God's not only good all the time, He's always in a good mood. He's not the cranky, crotchety old man He's been depicted to be throughout the years. Nehemiah 8:10 tells us the *joy* of the *Lord* is your strength. God gives us His very own joy to strengthen us, which means He has more than enough to share! This isn't exactly the picture of someone who walks around, furrowing His brow in displeasure, looking for someone to punish.

No matter what *life* throws our way, God is good. No matter what *others* may do or say, He's still good. Even when people around me or those I love aren't good to me, *He is*. He is *always* good. Even when churches unintentionally end up hurting more people than they help by regurgitating the lies of religion, God is still good. I can't blame Him for a broken system He didn't set in place. *He's* not the One who takes a handful of verses and says, this box shall be our belief system and we shall oppose anything and everyone outside of its walls. *He's* not the One with the issue of control—*we are*.

When we're finally ready to stop trying to understand with our *heads* what is meant to first be explored with our *hearts*, understanding will follow. Why does it work this way? Because diving into the depths of God's love requires far more than an ascent into mental consciousness. Diving into the endless depths of God's love is more about knowing *Who* is waiting to catch us and less about *what* we're diving into. When we know the One waiting is faithful and true and His arms are sturdy and sure, it's easy to kick up our heels and just jump in.

What gives us security isn't having every last question answered. That actually only leads us to more questions. What gives us true security is encountering the Father's heart for ourselves and from that place of experience, discovering that He really is who He says He is. *He really is good.*

If you haven't yet discovered His goodness for yourself, my friend, I encourage you to talk with Him about it today. Ask Him to show you in undeniable and irrefutable ways that He's not only good—*He's good to you.*

When we know God is good, we have a greater peace and a greater propensity to place our life in His very capable, faithful hands. As we live life in surrender, we'll find it's a life full of adventure! One we get to joyfully discover with Jesus every day. He's the One who made you, and He knows better than anyone what makes your heart soar. He loves to see you smile and He puts things in your path just so you do. He's so beautiful!

My friend, knowing we were made for God's pleasure and living from this place of passion with Jesus is not only the inlet of our *identity*, it's the source of our *security*.

CHAPTER SIX

The Battle Between Our Ears
(How to Win the War for Your Life)

*What comes into our minds when we think about
God is the most important thing about us.*

—A.W. Tozer, The Knowledge of the Holy

I *hated* what I saw as I stood before the mirror. Huge thighs and a disproportionate body stared back at me, mocking all my weight loss efforts. It seemed like no matter how much I worked out and cut calories, my chunky arms and chubby thighs would *not* go away.

If only I could lose a couple inches here or my body was shaped differently there ... I meticulously studied my body from all angles and concluded only one thing was to be done—*More weight had to go.*

My mind rapidly turned to what I needed to do next, *I can't eat much of anything and I'll have to make sure I quickly dispose of what I do eat if I get weak and give into the enemy—food.* The wheels in my brain started revolving around this idea, *I'll lose the weight twice as fast if I work out, but I'll have to be careful not to eat as many calories as I burn, otherwise it won't work as well—or as fast. Yes, I know it's exhausting, but you know it's totally worth it, so get it together girl! Now's not the time to be weak; you're almost there! Besides, you can quit whenever you want. You don't have to do this forever, only until you finally like what you see staring back at you in the mirror.*

I struggled with eating disorders for well over ten years. But no matter how hard I worked, I never liked what I saw. I never felt satisfied and secure no matter how thin I got or how many "goal pants" I slipped right into.

I'm pretty sure everyone's had a pair of goal pants or two in their time, right? You know, the ones you stopped wearing six years ago but swear you'll wear again someday and therefore refuse to give away. Chances are, they're still stuffed in the back of your closet to this day. You know, *goal pants*. Well, I had a slew of them and kept buying smaller sizes just to make sure I was continuing to lose weight. Eventually, I was able to slip all of them on without unbuttoning them. That should've gotten my attention right there.

Red flags and blaring sirens should have been blasting in my brain. Instead, the extreme weight loss only fueled my self-destructive fire. Each time I purged, a chemical reaction triggered in my brain, giving me an intense high feeling, like I was weightless. As if I could fly higher or run farther and faster because there was *nothing* weighing me down.

But an hour or two later, the crash came. Then simply putting one foot in front of the other was a real chore. Every time the high receded, I felt hopeless and *so* discouraged; absolutely *sick* of the struggle within me but so afraid that if I stopped, I would also stop *losing* weight and start *gaining* it.

I was sure having the "picture perfect body," would solve *all* my problems. If I had a perfectly shaped body, I'd finally be happy with myself and satisfied and successful in every area of my life. I was neck deep in this delusion, so I couldn't see that what I was chasing, was about as real as a unicorn or pot of gold at the end of the rainbow.

I can see now, these were outright lies sent to destroy my life. I also see that those lies were allowed in my life because *I* allowed them. I agreed with the lies and therefore I empowered the liar. But now I also know that if I've empowered the liar, I can also *disempower* him, by breaking the agreements I made with him and taking my thoughts captive to Jesus. We'll talk more about this in just a bit.

I'm relieved to say that I now also know there is *no* such thing as a perfect body. Not on this side of Heaven anyway. But back then, I was sure if I worked at it hard enough, it would happen. But the more I worked at it, the worse I felt—in every way. My body was sick, my emotions were a mess, and my mind was foggy all the time. Everything in life, including my relationships, became really overwhelming because I was *always* exhausted. I may have been closer to a certain size, but it did *not* change *one* thing about my self-perception. I was as insecure about myself as ever, *if not more*.

It took more than ten years to put the eating disorder behind me, and I'd be lying if I said it's never been a temptation since. But thanks be to God for the support, people, and programs He's placed around me to help me recover. By His grace *alone* am I able to walk in victory from this very addictive, self-sabotaging cycle.

Actually, if I'm being completely transparent with you, sometimes I still get thoughts about it. But *now* I know, entertaining those thoughts and keeping them to myself is how I get into trouble. I've set healthy parameters in place to ward off those destructive tendencies: Trusted friends and loved ones I turn to for accountability, prayer, and encouragement, scriptures I'll speak over myself until my heart and head have caught up with what I've read.

To this day, I must surrender my body and beauty to the Lord. I must practice a well-balanced lifestyle that reaches far beyond fitness and nutrition and stretches to the pools of praise for being uniquely created just as I am. Just as God wanted. Anything less and I find myself critically scrutinizing every square inch of my body.

You see, any beauty I possess is *His* beauty. As David wrote in Psalm 16:2 (NIV), "I say to the Lord, 'You are my Lord, apart from you, I have no good thing.'" I *now* know, God *alone* is my good.

He is my beauty.

It is hidden in *Him*.

Just as *I* am hidden in Him.

The only beauty I now want others to see in me is the glorious reflection of my beautiful Jesus. Because He alone is my good. And I get to share His goodness with them when they see His goodness in me. And honestly, friend, the stress and strain to find beauty any other way is just vain. It's vain. It's empty. And truthfully, it's plain old exhausting.

I don't want to be exhausted by beauty any longer. I want to be *exhilarated* by it.

You'll Eat Your Words

When I focus my thoughts on things that are upsetting, it won't be long until I feel upset. If I keep with this train of thought, not only will I *feel* upset, I'll start to *talk* about upsetting issues. The more I talk about upsetting issues, the more I'll see them manifest in my life. All because of what

I'm entertaining on the inside. What I entertain on the *inside* absolutely influences what happens on the *outside*. This is true for everyone from all walks of life.

Our thoughts become our words, and our words become our reality. Proverbs 18:21 (NLT) puts it this way, "The tongue can bring death or life;

> *Our thoughts become our words, and our words become our reality.*

those who love to talk will reap the consequences." You could say we'll literally *eat* our words. It sounds like controlling our tongue is a really big deal. I mean, if by our very words we rise or fall, I think this is a subject that's very worthy of our attention, don't you agree?

If we want to tame our tongues, we must first learn how to control our thoughts. The Apostle Paul said it this way in Colossians 3:2 (NASB), "Set your mind on the things above, not on the things that are on earth." Basically, if it's trashy, tormenting, or tears down, it's not something we should be entertaining.

One definition for the word entertain means, *to admit into the mind*. That's a big deal. This means we're influenced not only by what we see and hear, like we talked about in chapter two, but also by what we're entertaining between our ears. So, if we *suddenly* realize our lives are full of frustration and drama, you can bet those things didn't just come on *suddenly*. We've likely been allowing them admittance into our minds, so whether we realize it or not, we've also been giving them influence over our lives.

This is why the Apostle Paul also told us what we *should* admit into our minds. In Philippians 4:8, he tells us to *dwell* on things that are honorable, just, pure, lovely, and of a good report. The word *dwell* in this verse is the Greek word, *logizomai* and it means to meditate on, to take into to account, to purpose.

When we meditate on something, we turn it over and over in our minds until that thing becomes ingrained in our thinking. Biblical mediation is meant to fill our minds with God's Word by expressing Scripture over ourselves until we can feel our hearts reflect what's been written on the page. It's not the same as memorizing and reciting Scriptures, though it involves that. We literally allow the Scripture to expand in our minds by meditating on its meaning and validity, especially as it pertains to our life and circumstances.

God gave us His Word to speak into our lives in real, active, and personal ways. When we meditate upon His Word, we are filling up with Truth that is *superior* to what we see, inviting the atmosphere of Heaven to come and invade every impossibility. That's why we need to take Scriptures that relate to our circumstances and *personalize* them.

For example, Psalm 125:1 (NLT) reads, "Those who trust in the Lord…will not be defeated." You'd personalize Psalm 125:1 as "*I* trust in the Lord…and will not be defeated." What a difference this makes! Suddenly these promises aren't just for a far-off people from long ago; they're for us. They're *personal*.

This is how we get God's Word rooted deep down within us. We take firm hold of His promises and turn them over and over in our head until they become the echo of our heart.

The Law of Attraction

When I was little, I was afraid of practically *everything*. Planes, trains (no, not automobiles, for all you movie buffs out there) but yes, car crashes, storms, thunder, and lighting, tornados, and torrential down pours. I mean, I had irrational fears of things I'd never even seen or experienced before like sharks, open water, outer space, deep-sea diving, and giant pink cats (okay, not really the cats). If it was out of the ordinary and unexpected, unexplained, or unknown, it scared me.

I often prayed from this place of fear and my imagination would run wild with scary scenarios. I didn't know what I was doing, and I didn't realize I could partner with Jesus to overcome it. I only knew my brother and sister were annoyed that we couldn't watch Scooby-Doo since it gave me nightmares.

When I was older, my mom and I discussed this issue and she told me that when she was pregnant with me, my dad often got a rise out of her by pretending to race oncoming trains to their railroad crossings. He'd shout something like, "We're gonna *beat* that train across the tracks before it *beats us!*" Of course, he never really did, but it upset and scared her all the same. Apparently, her response was always, "Harold, if you don't stop doing that, you're gonna strike fear into our baby!"

My parents were young when they started our family, young in their faith as well. They didn't know about the realities of spiritual warfare, such as being mindful of what we entertain and agree with since we give those things access to our lives through our thoughts, words, and emotions.

Later, as she grew deeper in her faith and relationship with Jesus, my mom came to believe fear was transferred to me while I was in her womb due to those crazy train track experiences. This would have been a large part of why I was so fearful throughout my growing-up years. I agree.

You see, the kind of environment we cultivate matters. In fact, it's a *really* big deal. And the environment we cultivate—both internal and external—comes from what we entertain. Like I said before I'm not simply talking about what we listen to or watch, while we should certainly be wise with those too, I'm talking about what we admit into our minds and emotions. Remember we said earlier that what we think about influences our emotions and drives what we say? These things matter because we make agreements with invisible forces—whether Heavenly or demonic—through our thoughts.

Let me say it this way; *we attract* what we think and feel. In quantum physics, it's actually called the Law of Attraction, where we *attract* what and who we're in agreement with. Since I struggled with so much fear, I experienced a lot of anxiety, dread, and terror. These were attracted to me because I was, unknowingly, making mental and emotional agreements with them. I mean, I didn't know what I was doing. I was only a little girl.

My parents would pray and read Scripture to me and taught me how to pray against fear, but it wasn't until I was much older that I found fear had *already* been conquered. Before then, I simply hadn't known that I could pray and fight *from* the victory of Jesus, opposed to exhausting myself in efforts of fighting *for* the victory. *What a revelation!*

I no longer had to stand in defensive mode against fear. Instead, I could just ask Jesus to help me see fear the way He does—as a defeated foe. This gave me the upper hand. It helped me break agreements with any demonic entities I'd allowed in my life through what I'd entertained. And I was able to do so without fear when I realized those entities have no rights to me, because I've surrendered all my rights to Jesus!

He rescued me *out* of the darkness and brought me *into* His marvelous light! From His Kingdom I now operate. This puts me on the *offensive* team where I can pray, declare, and decree over any situation like it's already won because in His perspective it is!

Amazing Grace

Grace is what saves. Grace is also what transforms. God's grace empowers us to change, grow, and work at whatever we do with all our heart, as unto the Lord (Colossians 3:23). In 1 Corinthians 15:10 (TPT) the Apostle Paul wrote, "... God's amazing grace has made me who I am...for His empowering grace is poured out upon me."

Grace that is taught unto salvation *without* transformation is a message of immaturity that says you can get saved and still live for yourself, as if no life-change has happened. But true grace—*God's grace*—always leads us into a place of identity as sons and daughters of our Heavenly Father. Grace isn't what allows us to live like sinners; grace is what *redeems* us from sinners to saints (1 Corinthians 1:2).

God's grace flows through us as power, enabling us for every good work He has prepared. Second Corinthians 9:8 (NKJV) puts it this way, "God is able to make all grace abound toward you, that you, always having all sufficiency in all things, may have an abundance for every good work." The Greek word for grace here is *charis*. It's the holy influence and power of God's Spirit resting upon us to turn us to Jesus and strengthen and kindle us to walk in the character of Christ and the calling He has for our lives.

I want to be crystal clear; we don't work to *earn* our salvation. Ephesians 2:8 tells us that by *grace* we have been saved, not by works so no one can boast. Grace is the power God gives us to press into what He holds in His heart and will for us. And as Jesus taught in Matthew 6:9-10, God's will is for Heaven to invade earth—for the Father's Kingdom to come and will to be done on earth as it is in Heaven. This is God's will for everyone and all of creation. The grace He gives empowers us to use the gifts He's bestowed for the sake of seeing His will fulfilled (see

Romans 12:6, 1 Peter 4:10). Ephesians 4:7 (KJV) puts it this way, "unto every one of us is given grace according to the measure of the gift of Christ."

The Greek word for grace, *charis*, also means that which gives pleasure, joy, and delight. We're not only given power to enable us for the gifts and dreams God calls us to, but the things He calls us to will give us pleasure, joy, and delight! The apostles were filled with great power and grace was upon them all, not only to do what they needed to for the spreading of the gospel of Jesus Christ, but also so they would find joy, delight, and pleasure in doing it (see Acts 4:33, 5:41).

God's grace is far too kind to leave us to ourselves, unchanged. He knows that the deep yearnings of *our* heart for Him, cries out to the deep yearnings of *His* heart for us. It's only in the center of His heart that we'll ever truly find satisfaction. But to plunge the depths of His heart, we must first shed the fear that keeps us floating around in the shallows. His grace is what gives us the courage to ditch the life preserver and dive into the deep.

Would God's grace have been okay with me slowly starving myself to death? Absolutely not! His grace was what sparred my life. His grace is what said, these eating disorders are not okay and there *has* to be a change if you want to live.

I think sometimes, we get confused on the meaning of grace because someone, somewhere along the line, thought it was a good idea to take *compromise* and *complacency* and call it *grace*. To say, it's okay that you have this addiction or that destructive habit; God loves you anyway. It's true, God *does* love them. No matter what state they're in, His love for them will never change. But because God *does* love them, in His grace, He calls them to turn from what is ruining their life.

Let's go back to that Greek word *charis* for a minute. Like we said, *charis* means grace, but it also means favor. Jesus had to grow in favor with God and man (Luke 2:52). Though He was like God in everything, He did not consider being equal with God as something to be used for his own benefit. Instead, He emptied Himself of His outward glory, humbled Himself and became vulnerable. He chose to do everything He did as a man in obedience to His Father. He was a perfect example, even in His death and crucifixion (see Philippians 2:6–8). Jesus is our model that means if *He* had to grow in God's favor, we do too.

Favor isn't the same thing as love.

There's *nothing* we can do that can ever make God love us any more or any less. But we *grow* in God's favor by wisely *stewarding* it. We steward favor by putting to good use the gifts and talents He's given us, the power and influence He's put in and upon us. The more we exercise these, the more we grow in favor. In its most elementary form, stewardship is essentially utilizing and enjoying what God has already given and saying, "Thank you Poppa, I'd like more please." God, in His goodness and grace designed it this way.

Let me show you.

When I was struggling with eating disorders, I wasn't growing in favor because I was walking in disobedience. I was disregarding God's command to take care of my body and treat it well because it's His dwelling place. I was straight up lying to my parents and friends who were rightly concerned about my weight loss. Playing it off as if I simply had some stomach issues (which I did, but they were related *to* the eating disorder, as well as stress). And I was more consumed with the vision of a perfectly thin body, than I was the vision He'd placed in my heart of helping others grow in their God-given gifts and callings.

Looking back, it's easy to see how I could barely care for myself, let alone anyone else. But while I was in it, I thought I was fine. At least, that's what I told myself.

During that season, I tried starting several women's groups where, funnily enough, we were to discuss our security in Christ and how we could grow deeper in Him. I wanted to create a safe place where we could share our thoughts and hardships, victories and testimonies. Not one of them flourished—*not one*. In fact, all of them ended quite abruptly.

What felt like rejection and failure, was God protecting me from overextending myself and hurting others by spreading the lies I'd been believing. I actually had nothing to pour out because I wasn't filling up. I would spend time in prayer and reading God's Word and other biblically inspired books, but it was from a place of obligation and fear, rather than a real desire to experience intimate relationship with the Father.

I wasn't seeking His presence, I was checking the boxes, fulfilling the lists. I was approaching my relationship with God the same way I was approaching my body, and it all came down to one word—*control*. I wanted to feel like I was in control. I'll tell you right now, friend, that's a *sure* way to put a wet blanket on any kind of fire you have for Jesus.

It took me over ten years to learn how to relinquish control and surrender. But when I finally stepped into that place of wonderful, beautiful surrender, I started seeing myself with a redemptive perspective. *God's* perspective. When I finally came to terms with the fact that I had a real problem and needed help, the Lord led me through a deep cleansing, healing process inspired by the Holy Spirit. He gave me the grace-power and tools I needed to transform my thoughts by renewing my mind with His Word. He helped me make wiser decisions, as well as relationships.

The process He took me through brought restoration to my whole being—spirit, soul, and body—and deepened my relationship with the One who sets my heart on fire.

Throughout the remainder of this book, we'll be exploring and using these Holy Spirit-inspired tools to help us change the way we think about ourselves and others, as well as to help us grow in intimacy with the *only* One who can set our souls on fire. And it all starts with transformative grace.

Familiar Struggle, Familiar spirits

I not only thought the perfect body would fix all my problems, I thought it would make me irresistible to Manny; surely he'd be convinced to come around more often if I appeared a certain way. I was a woman obsessed. I truly thought I could control my circumstances by controlling the way I looked.

Now, I realize this was only an illusion. A *delusion*. Merriam-Webster's Dictionary defines delusion as a fixed false belief that is resistant to reason or confrontation with actual fact; the act of tricking or deceiving someone. This describes my experience to a tee.

The enemy works hard to delude us. To deceive us. You see, not every thought we think is our own, and if he can keep us deceived, he can keep us distracted. Distracted from discovering the truth of our identity and destiny in Christ. Distracted from soaking in the Source of our true security and distracted from releasing the message of His hope everywhere we go.

When we're under the enemy's influence—his *delusion*—the threat we pose to his kingdom is thwarted, or at least lessened. You see, when we boldly walk in our identity as God's sons and daughters, we'll find we're destined to change the world in the most wonderful ways! This strikes great fear into the enemy, and it's why he works so hard to keep us deceived, deluded.

Several years into *my* delusion, I realized my plan wasn't working. My life was still a mess, and Manny was as evasive as ever. But by then I was so addicted to the endorphin rush and rapid weight loss that I didn't *want* to stop. Even if Manny didn't react the way I wanted, at least I seemed to attract more attention than ever—which made *him* jealous and gave *me* a false sense of security. My thinking was, why *should* I stop? He's finally seeing that I'm desirable, maybe *now* he'll step it up. Of course, I had no *real* confidence, it was all an illusion. A *delusion*.

As I said earlier, I finally got free from eating disorders many years later. This came several months after I left Manny, who, I'm sorry to say, only supported my habit.

But even years after breaking free, food phobia was still a familiar struggle for me. You see, the enemy sends familiar spirits to plant thoughts in our minds that we think are normal. We might *think* these thoughts are normal, or that they organically come from us, but really, they are snares set by satan. See, a familiar spirit is something that so stealthily attaches itself to our personality that we're inclined to think the thoughts they feed us are ours. But as we said earlier—not every thought we think is our own.

The enemy of our soul is an illusionist. Sometimes he disguises himself as an angel of light, and sometimes he disguises himself as *you*—he comes as *your own* voice. But the thoughts he brings will only ever argue with or twist what God says. satan's words are full of contradiction and confusion, accusations and arguments; he'll argue against your identity and authority in Christ, how God sees you, and what God says about you.

When we think thoughts of self-hatred, suicide, and destruction, we can know with certainty that these thoughts are not our own. God didn't create us to hate ourselves, and He certainly didn't create us to destroy ourselves—that's actually unnatural. Look at any caged wild animal and tell me otherwise. God created us to *live* and not die; He created us *for love* and to *be loved* (see Psalm 118:17; 1 John 4:7–11). This means these thoughts come from *another* source; not from ourselves and definitely not from our Father God.

> *When we think thoughts of self-hatred, suicide, and destruction, we can know with certainty that these thoughts are not our own. God didn't create us to hate ourselves, and He certainly didn't create us to destroy ourselves— that's actually unnatural.*

Familiar spirits are assigned to set a stronghold (a wall or fortress used for a place of hiding) around the struggles that are or have been familiar to us. For instance, let's say you often find yourself expecting something bad to happen. Well, if you've been thinking this way most of your life, you're not going to know this thought pattern *isn't* normal to everyone, because it's familiar to *you*. Often, there's a twisted, fleshly feeling of false comfort to these demonically planted thoughts, such as self-pity or offense, so it can almost feel like a violation of our will to refuse them.

Honestly, sometimes I still get thoughts about how to quickly dispose of calories or ways to curb my hunger, so I'll eat less. But now I know these thoughts aren't from me. They're lies from a familiar spirit sent to torment me and trick me back into bondage. But I don't have to take the bait. The times I did made me feel dirty, discouraged, and disconnected from the ones I love. This is exactly what familiar spirits want—to tempt us with what's familiar, then accuse us when we give in. Then, they want to guard that process, so we do it over and over and over again—often without even realizing it. This is their only purpose; all to torment and torture us and keep us disconnected from each other and distracted from our God-given destinies.

I'm so grateful Jesus set me free from this stronghold, but it's up to me to *stay* free. I must guard what thoughts I entertain, because whatever I entertain in my *mind* influences my *life*. The same goes for you, friend. Remember, *not every thought we think is our own.*

The Battle Between Our Ears

The enemy works hard to keep us preoccupied with problems, so we won't see God-given solutions. His strategy is to make himself look bigger than, or at least in opposition to God. But he's not; he's a *created being*. He's not God's rival—*God has no rival*—satan has *never* been, nor will *ever* be, more powerful than God. He's a defeated foe!

He works to wage war in our minds, by presenting thoughts that are in opposition to the knowledge of God. Like it or not, we have been born into a war. A war between Heavenly and demonic forces and a war between the spirit and the flesh. Like it or not, the enemy will never take a day off, which is why God has given us mighty weapons. Weapons not empowered by the by the natural (physical) realm, but divinely empowered with *His* power.

"For although we live in the natural realm, we don't wage a military campaign employing human weapons, using manipulation to achieve our aims. Instead, our spiritual weapons are energized with divine power to effectively dismantle the defenses [strongholds] behind which people hide. We can demolish every deceptive fantasy that opposes God and break through every arrogant attitude that is raised up in defiance of the true knowledge of God. We capture, like prisoners of war, every thought and *insist* that it bow in obedience to the Anointed One" (1 Corinthians 10:3–5, TPT, emphasis added)

This is our battle strategy: To cast down, pull down, and throw down every thought that isn't in line with God's truth and tell it that it must surrender and obey Jesus, or it must go. *We* tell our mind what to think. *We* give our mind scriptures to think on or listen to. *We* make our mind come into alignment with the truth of God's Word and *we* give it *no* other option because no other option leads to life, peace, and victory.

We don't pity or entertain the thoughts satan throws at us; we filter them out and cast them down. We don't simply *suggest* he leave—we *demand* it. In fact, Jeremiah 1:10 (NKJV) says we are called "to root out and to pull down, destroy and to throw down." This strong, rapid succession of action words exemplifies how confronting and capturing wayward thoughts isn't a complacent thing. No. We capture and confront arguments that rise up against the knowledge of God when we *feel* like it—and when we don't—I'd wager to say it's even *more* important to do so when we *don't*.

One thing we *must* remember throughout this process, is that we do *all* this from a place of victory, knowing the enemies of darkness have been rendered powerless! "Jesus made a public spectacle of all the powers and principalities of darkness, stripping away from them every weapon and all their spiritual authority and power to accuse us. And by the power of the cross, Jesus led them around as prisoners in a procession of triumph. *He* was not their prisoner; they were *his*" (Colossians 2:15, TPT, emphasis added)!

In chapter two, we talked about how the only power the enemy has is the power *we* give him. The only access he has to power is through the agreements *we* make with him. When we agree with him, we empower him by giving him our own power; the power Christ gave us through His finished work of the cross. This is why satan wars against our minds, so we'll agree with him through thoughts of worry, strive, lust, fear, offense, insecurity, pride, gossip, depression, addiction, anxiety, hurriedness, negativity, and every work of darkness. And this is why it's so important to guard our thoughts and refuse to allow our minds to run wild. We tell the enemy *access denied* when he works to plant thoughts in our minds.

The good news about all this is demons don't have staying power. They don't have the tenacity you and I are privileged to, when we're tucked into the heart of the Father. When we're tucked into His heart, we rest in Him and allow Him to tell and show us all He is and all He wants to be for us; which is absolutely *revitalizing* for us and totally *terrifying* to the enemy.

Intimacy: Our Greatest Weapon

When we talk about intimacy in Christ, we're talking about living and abiding in a place of soul-deep rest in Him. It's a rest that flows from *our spirits* connected to *His Spirit* and governs our soul (our mind, will, emotions, affections, and attentions).

So whether I'm boldly decreeing and declaring God's promises or resting in quiet faith, through it all, I'm keeping *my* eyes on *His* fiery eyes of love (see Revelation 1:14). In fact, the more I abide in quiet rest with Him, the bolder I become in my declarations. Because *trust* comes out of quiet rest, and *boldness* is the byproduct of trust.

When I'm keeping my eyes on His, I don't have time to entertain the lies of the enemy, what's more, I recognize them from a mile away. I recognize them because they don't look or sound anything like God's love.

This posture of resting in Christ and keeping our eyes on His is how we experience intimacy with Jesus. It involves a vulnerability, where we allow Him to see into us, and He calls us to see into Him and explore the depths of His heart.

When we look into His eyes, we'll see His heart for us. And when we look into His heart, we'll find He's made Himself completely vulnerable and available. He's withheld *nothing* from us.

Our Father's heart is so rich with love, so purely good that He gave us His very best so we can have much more than a token relationship with Him. God didn't send His Son to the cross just to give us a place to go on Sunday, then live six days out of the week like He doesn't matter.

Jesus overcame at the cross so we can experience intimacy with Him, the Father, and Holy Spirit. Intimacy with God is the most exhilarating and awesome privilege we'll ever experience in life. It brings us joy and peace like *nothing* and *no one* else can. It will wreck and ruin everything else in life for us—in the most wonderful way. Leaving us only wanting more. Because intimacy with God is an *eternal* need and temporary solutions to an eternal need will never satisfy us. God created us to *long* for Him, friend, so looking for this eternal need in anything less than Him will only leave us frustrated and unfulfilled.

Everyone's relationship with God is personal. That's why it's called a *personal relationship*. Some may express their love louder or quieter than others, but He calls *all* to experience intimacy and closeness with Him (John 17:21–23). When we harden our hearts and resist Him, God calls it rebellion. As it is written in Hebrews 3:15 (NLT), "'Today when you hear his voice, don't harden your hearts as Israel did when they rebelled.'"

Intimacy with Jesus looks like finding what we were born for: to worship God and give Him glory. Everything comes out of that place; from the river of life running within us. We step into its flow by going into the depths of worship for the One who is worthy of it all. All our worship. All our devotion. Our adoration, praise, and thanksgiving. Worthy of our entire life. Intimacy looks like turning away from the things that compete with our love and devotion for Him—those lesser loves—and laying them down as a sacrifice, an offering of love because He matters more.

Intimacy looks like praising Him, even when it's hard and I don't understand because I don't have to understand to trust Him. When discouragement knocks on my door and I have plenty of questions but don't have any answers, I remind myself of what He's done, and rest in the One who *is* the Answer. Intimacy is not allowing my heart to harden when I experience adversity and refusing to attribute it to the One who's only good. It's trusting the revelation of His nature, even in the tension of the mystery.

We pursue intimacy with God purely to be with Him. To encounter Him, His presence, His face, and go deeper into His heart than we have before. We pursue intimacy because we're hungry for more of God and to know Him better. Intimacy means learning how to host His Spirit by finding out what He likes and what doesn't and why—we're allowed to ask Him—in fact, He welcomes it. He likes it when we come to Him with no self-appointed, preset agendas, but simply because we want to know and love Him more.

Sometimes, we approach intimacy with God because we want to *get* something in return. But here's the thing, pursing intimacy with God to get anything out of it other than His love and presence, is like pursuing *professional* intimacy. When we worship God for effect, it crosses the line from worship to prostitution—where we *give* something to *get* something. Worshiping with ulterior motives is like trying to use and manipulate God, but Jesus said the Father is seeking *true* worshippers who will worship Him in *spirit* and in *truth* (John 4:23).

In poverty or abundance, during unexplainable chaos or times of prevailing peace, in loss or in gain, when we feel like it and when we don't, may our worship be the same: Coming from a place of reverence and love for our King Jesus. For He *alone* is worthy.

Worship is where we empty ourselves so we can be filled. It's where *we* are the sacrifice, awaiting His fire of love. As the Psalmist so beautifully said in Psalm 5:3 (TPT), "Every morning I lay out the pieces of my life on the altar and wait for your fire to fall upon my heart." This is the worship that is pure, true, and honest. It's the worship our Father seeks. It's the more excellent way Paul described in 1 Corinthians 13 where *love* is our motivation for everything (see 1 Corinthians 12:31—1 Corinthians 13:3). This is the worship that changes lives, heals bodies, repairs broken relationships, redeems, and sets free because it's the worship that ushers in the very Presence of the Spirit of the Living God. And when the presence of God is present, *nothing* is impossible.

Living out of this place of intimacy with Christ is so threatening to satan's kingdom because we aren't moved by anything other than our King. Just as David was not moved by the size or intimidation of Goliath. In this way, intimacy becomes our greatest weapon and by it, *we* become the one who intimidates as we carry within us a righteous indignation against anything that tries to come between our love and Him; anything that tries to rise up against His Name and Truth. As we spend time with Him in intimate worship and rest, we find everything must bow to His name. From this place, *we* take territory from the enemy, he doesn't take it from us!

True intimacy with God leads us into a healthier relationship with ourselves. And having a healthier relationship with ourselves leads us into having healthier relationships with others. So, if healthier, happier relationships is what we seek, we would be wise to start with our intimacy with Jesus.

CHAPTER SEVEN

Because I *Felt* Like It
(Addressing the Issues of Emotional Self-Sabotage)

*Your attitude tells the world what you expect from life
and you will receive exactly that, no more no less.*
—Kathryn Kuhlman

I looked out the window of the plane as we descended through the clouds; I could feel my heart and hopes descending right along with it. Our honeymoon had brought out a whole new side of us. We laughed, we played, we explored. The fresh island air brought out the best in us both. But the moment we boarded the plane to head home, I knew something had shifted.

Manny had grown indifferent and edgy again. While he reverted back to his old self, I had no idea how to help him stay the fun-loving, easy going, affectionate, guy he'd been on vacation. And quite frankly, I no longer had the motivation to try. So I sat silently in my seat, hands folded across my lap as I whispered prayers for wisdom and renewal all the way home. The moment we got back to Ohio, he didn't even wait for the plane to come to a complete stop before he reached over and whispered to me, "We never should have done this. I'm not attracted to you the way a man should be attracted to his wife. I'm still not ready; you need to give me more time." And so began the long, drawn out period of separation as if our marriage failed before it even got off the ground.

As we waited our turn to unload our luggage and disembark the plane, my mind drifted back to those crazy exchanges the morning of our wedding. Now more than ever, I deeply regretted going forward with the ceremony. Even though Manny said he was ready after his momentary wave of doubt, deep down in my heart, I knew he really *wasn't*. I had hoped I was wrong. Still, I knew I should have walked away before saying "I do," no matter how embarrassing and awkward it may have been in the moment. Saving my sanity should have been more important to me than saving face. My focus should have been on reverencing God rather than fearing people.

I have to be honest; my memory is a little fuzzy about what came next. I was so broken and upset that I moved through the next several weeks like a zombie. I was hurt not only by *his* decisions, but by my *own*. I do remember immediately moving back home with my folks; I just can't recall how all my stuff got there, or maybe it never left. It all just sort of runs together.

To make matters worse, when Manny and I flew home from our honeymoon we had a layover in Atlanta, so I decided to use some of this time to go through my voicemails; well, I came across one that said I shouldn't come into work when I got back into town because the company I was working for went out of business. No joking.

So there I was, husband-less, jobless, and wondering *what in the world* was going on with my life. I remember being consumed by grief for quite some time. And a while after that, shame really started to sink in. I was terrified of running into the wedding guests who hadn't known what happened, as they would naturally ask me how married life was going.

I felt so foolish and fragile in those moments, so ashamed of myself. I half expected my friends and family, who knew my situation, to laugh in my face and tell me I had it coming, or they could see it a mile away, something sarcastic like that. I was relieved when they never did. Still, I lived with the plaguing thought that I was the topic of conversation behind every closed door. That every whispered comment, every sideways glance, or hushed tone was about me. If you let him, the liar can make you really paranoid, and I was letting him. Believing the lies and empowering the liar.

You can drive yourself crazy this way, you know? Imagining what everyone is saying or thinking. Imagining what your life would be like "if only I would have ..." or "if only he would have ..." I'd spend hour after hour in my room weeping, crying out to God to comfort me. At the same time, hating myself for missing and still wanting to be with Manny. Knowing if he called and said he was ready for me to come home, I'd go running into his arms.

Through the grief arose a deep longing for more to life than what I was experiencing. I knew there must be *something* more to life than mourning my loss and looking for new jobs—there *had* to be. When life takes unexpected twists and turns such as these, we can either become depressed and bitter or remember we have an anchor of hope for our soul, steady and secure in Christ Jesus. I was tired of living in the former and ready to explore the latter. I could feel Jesus pursuing me, reminding me of what it was like to be enveloped by His love. Reminding me how sweet the seasons were when I'd given myself to Him.

My parents, being the loving parents they are, suggested I move into the room above their garage so I could feel more independent and freer. They even recommended I give it a fresh new look and make it my own. The idea was really pleasing to me and gave me a sense of purpose, a project through which I could sort out my thoughts and feelings. I remember using this time to reconnect with God. Worshiping Him in the midst of my mess. As I started repainting the walls of my living space, the Lord started repainting the walls of my heart.

My mom and I would take weekly, if not daily walks. The whole time, she would lovingly listen, allowing me to pour my heart out to her as we rambled throughout the wooded trails and riverways. Walking among the beauty of God's creation, listening to my mommy's soothing voice of wisdom brought little pieces of my heart back together.

As often as he worked and even amidst all his other responsibilities, my daddy still made time to show me that I was one of his top priorities. He'd hold me in his loving, protective, fatherly embrace as we sat on the couch. He'd put his arm around me as I rested my head on his shoulder, and every time he'd tell me how much he loved me and how proud he was of me. *Talk about tears.* They'd stream right down my face, softening the soil of my heart a little more with each embrace. Later, he told me how God had charged it to his heart to be a *tangible* example of how my Heavenly Father was holding me, loving me, and cherishing me.

I'm so very thankful to have had my parents and their Spirit-filled wisdom and love throughout this tremendously difficult season. I sincerely don't know how I would have got through it without them. God is so gracious. From the bottom of my heart, mommy and daddy, *thank you.* I'm incredibly blessed by you both and hope you know how loved and appreciated each of you are.

Cornerstones

I didn't know it then but looking back now, I can see God was rebuilding the cornerstones of my life through this difficult time. He was speaking to me and showing me how His love never fails. Without even trying, joy and hope began to surface in my heart. They came solely by looking at Jesus and allowing Him to capture me with His love.

I'm not saying I never had sad moments; naturally, I did. Manny and I spent, what would have been our first Christmas as a married couple together, apart. I remember that being a terribly difficult and depressing holiday season for me. We should've been celebrating with our families, deciding whose house to go to next. Instead, there was only radio silence. Talk about feeling invalidated and insignificant to someone to whom you're really supposed to matter.

Throughout this time, he would periodically call to try and sort out where we were heading. He fluctuated from the extremes of saying maybe we should walk through these issues together and just see where we land, to saying he was preparing the papers to dissolve our marriage. And while I was reconnecting with God, I still allowed Manny to toy with my emotions. I felt like a rag doll being pulled apart at the seams. I hadn't yet discovered how to set boundaries with him and stand up for myself—that part of me was still very much in process.

At that point, I really wanted my marriage to work. Though I knew I shouldn't have hitched my cart to his horse, so to speak, I still wanted to honor God with my marriage in whatever way I could. Looking back, maybe I should've just moved myself right in with him and said, you're simply going to have to learn how to deal because we *both* said "I do" to this thing. Yet I see now how this wouldn't only have been unhealthy—it would have been unsafe.

The truth is, I needed to separate my emotions from my situation so I could get some clarity and connect with God's voice. The problem was, I didn't know how to do that. My emotions were so wrapped around Manny that I couldn't see my way of escape from emotional self-sabotage as I allowed his words and actions to interfere with and hinder any sort of healing or progress I'd make. But the truth was—and *still* is—God *always* provides a way of escape. First Corinthians 10:13 (TPT) says, "We all experience times of testing, which is normal for every human being. But God will be faithful to you. He will screen and filter the severity, nature, and timing of every test or trial you face so that you can bear it. And each test is an opportunity to trust him more, for along with every trial God has provided for you a way of escape that will bring you out of it victoriously."

The one thing I knew with all my heart was I wanted *more*. I wanted more than this back and forth with Manny. There *had* to be more—more joy, more love, more happiness, but I honestly didn't know how to find it. I thought it would come from him, now I know it comes from *Him*.

Maybe you've been there. You thought everything you ever wanted would come from that one person, only to be let down time and time again. Friend, let me gently say this in the best way I know how, while they might be responsible for some of your disappointment and pain, the real heart of the issue likely lies within you. What I mean is, you have more say in the way you live your life and what goes on in it than you may have realized. We'll dive deeper into this in the following chapters.

Listen, I know what it's like to *sit around* and wait for that certain someone to finally *come around* and make everything seem alright again. Maybe you do too. If you do, then you know it feels like the only time you can really breathe is when they're with you. Here's the thing about that though we could be holding our breath for a *lo-ong* time until we see them again. (And we gotta breathe, right!)

I'm saying, sometimes, we really just need to (sigh) *exhale*. We need to let them go, take a deep, cleansing breath and just *breathe*. Breathe, even if it's only for the sake of breathing. Breathe, because *you're* worth breathing for and your life is worth living.

By "breathe," I'm assuming you know I mean more than just the act of inhaling air into and out of your lungs. I'm saying, it's a metaphor for the invitation we've been given to stop putting our lives on hold and live them to the fullest—with *joyful abundance* in our hearts! I'm saying, we are *not* victims of our relationships—*unless we chose to be*. I know there are always those special circumstances. Trust me; I definitely get it. But even then, no one can rob us of our right to choose. We have to *give* that right away.

> We are not victims of our relationships—unless we chose to be. I know there are always those special circumstances. Trust me; I definitely get it. But even then, no one can rob us of our right to choose. We have to give that right away.

That's exactly what I was doing: giving away my right to choose and speak up. I was so used to him either invalidating my emotions or using my own words against me later that I became a silent spectator in my own life. Yet, I was so tired of living between the extremes of, let's work this out, to it's really over. On his good days, I remember Manny saying, "It's gonna be like you've always dreamed. I'm going to

137

give you the happy ending you've always wanted; just like in the movies you love. I'll be the one who finally comes around, swoops in and saves the day."

I hate to admit it, but you know, I actually believed him. I was young and so very impressionable at the time, and I remember how much I really wanted my life to turn out as I had dreamed. So, this all sounded quite appealing to me. Now, I can see how manipulative it was for him to prey on my extremely raw emotions. What I didn't take into consideration, as I was dreaming of this grandiose ending, was I wouldn't even need *swooping* and *saving* if he'd simply stop *hurting* me. How contradictory and totally twisted to personify yourself as the one who comes in and saves the day, when you're also the one who's creating the context out of which I needed saving. I mean it's absolutely absurd!

The problem with putting my hopes in what Manny would say was he'd eventually change his tune to the other extreme. So naturally, the more I put my hope in him, the more miserable I became. On the other hand, as I spent more time with *Jesus*, enjoying His presence, delighting in Him, and delighting in how He delights in me, I found He became the source of my hope. He became the source of my joy.

False Responsibility

Finally, after about six months of separation, I found myself all moved in with Manny. The month before, he'd called to say how sorry he was for all the ways he'd hurt me and for being so back and forth about us. But all that was behind him now. He was fully onboard and ready for married life together.

After a few weeks of feeling him out, I believed he was sincere, and to an extent and for a time, I believe he was.

I believe *he* believed what he was saying, and *I* certainly wanted to believe him. I wanted to believe his words were the answer to my prayers. Later I realized, I needed more than his *words*; I needed his *actions* to back up his words.

Here's the thing, the only way true transformation *sticks*, is if we do it for ourselves (not somebody else) and we do it *with* God—because we can't do it alone. So when someone has experienced true transformation, their character will show it and show it *consistently*. I'm not saying they'll be perfect. I'm saying they'll be committed to the process of change—because it's what *they* want. So even if or when they have momentary lapses, they'll recognize it, repent, and pick right back up where they left off.

This is what I was expecting to find from Manny, and for a few weeks I did. Then suddenly, he started to get extremely agitated, irritable, and became difficult to be around. He'd vacillate between violently blowing up to completely ignoring me for days and weeks on end if I said or did anything to offend him. And since I didn't always know what that was, I found myself walking around on eggshells most of the time.

I remember waking up every morning with a sense of dread, unsure of which version of Manny I'd encounter and doing everything in my power to make him happy. While trying to make him happy helped sometimes, more often than not, it only seemed to make him more irritable.

That's when he started finding reasons to be gone *a lot*. He had to work late, or he was going to the gym after work, he was meeting up with the guys, or was going to play basketball. Whatever the excuse, week after week I found myself spending more and more time alone.

It quickly turned into a very dark, depressing time for me. I remember bearing my soul to my journal because I was ashamed to talk to anyone about what was happening.

Wishing with everything in me that I could make Manny happy, so he'd want to come home and become the man he said he wanted to be for me. The man that would worship and pray with me, explore the goodness of God with me, attend church with me, and lead us in our walk with Jesus together. I was literally living in the exact opposite of that as he started to become more fascinated with the kingdom of darkness than the Kingdom of Light.

Looking back now, I realize that while I was responsible for contributing to a healthy environment where we could both experience happiness and every blessing of joy, I was *not* responsible *for* his happiness. *He* was. And the more I tried to *make* it my responsibility, the less respect he had for me. Because we teach others how to respect us by the way we respect ourselves—and I wasn't. I was reducing my worth in my *own* eyes by taking responsibility for his unhappiness, thus reducing my worth in *his* eyes. All the while teaching him it was okay. When really, it *wasn't*.

When we fill our minds with thoughts that we don't matter and our lives aren't worth respecting, we inadvertently give others the permission to view us the same way. Even if we want them to, we can't expect *others* to respect us if *we're* not willing to respect ourselves. If we stay stuck in these patterns of thought, our interactions with them are liable to become more destructive and even dangerous. This is exactly where I found myself when I tried to stand up to Manny—in a very destructive and dangerous environment. He immediately went into a rage—punching walls and throwing furniture at me as I ran down the hall to lock myself in another room.

I had gotten in the habit of keeping a packed bag in case I needed to quickly leave; but as it turned out, I didn't need to sneak out because he kicked me out of the house.

Telling me he wouldn't be disrespected in his own home and making it obvious that I wouldn't be safe if I stayed.

Less than a week later, I was right back at my parents' home. Staring at the same four walls and left to wonder *again* what in the world I was doing with my life.

Where Happiness Is Found

Any of us can look around and see that the world is hungry for love. The thing is, it's looking and pointing to all the wrong places to find it. Society screams at us that happiness is found when we *finally* find that one person who can complete us. And while our happiness hinging on one person is a bewitching idea, it's also totally bogus. But back then, I didn't know that and maybe you don't either.

> *While our happiness hinging on one person is a bewitching idea, it's also totally bogus.*

The idea that our world is set right, so long as that *one* person is in it, is not only deceptive, it's downright dangerous. I mean think about it. We disengage from our own ability—and *responsibility*—to find happiness within ourselves when we engage with this lie. Giving others the authority to control and even manipulate our emotions. We make ourselves susceptible to their ulterior motives and hidden agendas this way. Not to mention that a sure-fire way to ruin *any* relationship, is to expect the other person to meet *all* our needs.

No person, let alone relationship, can withstand that sort of pressure for an extended amount of time. It's exhausting, and inevitably they're going to do something—if not several things—that make us unhappy, intentional or not.

What are we going to do then? Throw a tantrum? I mean, who wants to stick around while we act like a three-year-old throwing a fit when we don't get our own way?

That being said, I also don't think anyone (okay, very few people) *consciously* go into relationships thinking, I'm really gonna suck this person dry. I'll get everything I can out of this one, then move onto the next.

I'd say most people probably aren't even aware that they're trapped in this sort of a cycle. So when you try to approach them about it, they become defensive and irrational because it's actually an unhealthy stronghold in their lives. A snare set by satan to trap them, distract them, and keep them disconnected from their God-given identity and destiny. If you'll remember, we talked more at length about this in the previous chapter.

Here's the thing, if I don't know that God gives me every opportunity to experience happiness and joy *in* Him, I'm going to go looking for it *outside* of Him. I'll go to every Tom, Dick, and Harry to satisfy my needs. But when the demands I place upon them to make me happy become too great, they're going to turn and run the other way. Leaving me, yet again, to wonder why I can't find happiness and love. Not knowing both, are not only within my power to attain, but also part of my inheritance as God's child.

The truth is, I need to look no further than my relationship with my Heavenly Father to find all that fulfills me, including happiness and joy. Speaking of the Lord, the Psalmist wrote, in the latter half of Psalm 34:8 (CSB), "How happy is the person who takes refuge in him!" Happiness isn't found in money or the sweetest ride or from having the hottest clothes. And while relationships *add* to our happiness, they are not the source of it—the same goes for the stuff we have.

Happiness is the result of putting our trust in God. That means, even when I'm all alone or my circumstances, according to the world's standards, aren't conducive for happiness; happiness is *equally* as available to me as when I'm surrounded by the ones I love, my bank account is overflowing, and all is right in my corner of the world.

Let me back up to Psalm 34:8 for a minute. The beginning of this verse tells us to "taste and see that the Lord is good." Combine that with the rest of the verse, and we realize *that's* how we come to trust Him, and in turn find happiness. We *taste* and *see* that the Lord is good.

Now, when we're sitting down before a delicious spread of food, what's the first thing we do? We *look* at it, right? We can smell it, see it, and sometimes we can even hear it. But when we first come to the table, what do we usually say? "My goodness, that sure looks good!" Right? We see *before* we taste. But here, God's Word tells us to *taste*, and then we can clearly *see* that He is good.

The Kingdom of Heaven is up-side-down to ours. God doesn't think like we do. His thoughts and ways are *so* much higher, still He chooses to reveal His heart and will with us by His Spirit (1 Corinthians 2:10). He's so wonderful! He knows we can't *see* that He is good until we *taste* of His nature and know what He's like.

God wants us to actually *know* Him: To encounter and experience real relationship with Him because it's in the context of relationship that we discover what He's like. And when we discover what He's really like, we get a taste of His nature. And when we *taste* of His nature, we start to *see* He really is good. When we taste and see His goodness, we stop living like He's out to get us and start living like He's on our side. When we know the God of the universe is with us and for us and has given us the spirit of adoption, by which we call Him Daddy, our perspective on

143

life's issues dramatically change. This is when things start to get really exciting.

We *stop* seeing ourselves as victims of fate, waiting on that certain someone to finally come around and make us happy, and we *start* seeing ourselves as victors who walk around full of joy! Because we have Someone who's faithful, loving, trustworthy, and worth more than a million other "someones".

From this place of confident victory and intimate relationship with Jesus, hope starts to come alive on the inside and joy begins to bubble up and overflow. We look at hardships and circumstances completely different because now we know we have our Father behind us, which means *nothing* is impossible. That doesn't mean we'll never experience adversity, but it does mean we walk *through* adversity with hope in our hearts, peace in our minds, and a joyful song on our lips.

Happiness versus Joy

God is *always* good, so are His plans for us. No matter what. Period. No take backs. But if I don't taste and see that He's good, I'm missing out on experiencing His goodness for *myself*.

I can hear others talk about it. I can see the fruit of it in their lives. They might even let me sample that fruit, but until *I* decide to step into His goodness, I won't taste or see all the goodness He has for me. Don't get me wrong, it's by God's goodness we live and move and have our being; His goodness is what gives us *access* to all He has for us (Acts 17:28, Romans 5:1-2). And since every good thing comes from Him, if I want to know more about His *goodness*, I simply need to know more about *Him*.

If you want to get to know a friend, you spend time with that friend, right? Well, the same goes for God. He's our *Best* Friend! The more we spend time with Him and bring Him into all we do, the more we'll get to know Him, and in turn, get to know what He's like. His nature. His unrelenting kindness and love. His laughter and smile.

As we invite Him into the time we spend reading and decreeing His Word, His Word comes alive and impregnates us with His promises, and we become an expectant people. As we breathe Him in, stilling ourselves in His presence, His voice effortlessly flows from His heart to ours, lighting up our minds with thoughts that are higher, better, and farther reaching than our own. And all we have to do is simply come and be with Him. He's already proven by His own blood, how much He wants to be with us.

We are vessels who will fill up with *something*, so He invites us to be filled up and flowing over with His Spirit. He wants us to encounter His Presence so we can experience His fullness. The fullness of His Spirit, joy, and peace all come out of encountering His sweet Presence. He really wants us to *experience* Him—to taste and see. This has been His heart since the very beginning. But *how* do we experience His fullness? How do we *access* it?

It's simple really, all we have to do is *ask*. Jesus has already done the rest. He *is* our access to the faith and grace we need to step into the Kingdom of God and receive every good thing He has in store for us. We simply ask for the fullness of His Spirit and choose to receive, with gratitude, His fullness by faith. Knowing that the fullness of His Spirit, His goodness, joy, and peace aren't anything that can be *earned*, they can only be *received*. This is why Jesus says childlike faith is so important. All we need to do is receive be grateful. And a *grateful* heart is a *joyful* heart.

Choosing to trust and receive all the fullness He has for us, is choosing for His goodness to be revealed in greater measure in our lives. Because God cannot be separated from His goodness, no more than He can be separated from His holiness or His glory. *Good* is who He is. And when we choose to taste and see that God is good, *for ourselves*, His joy overwhelms us in the most wonderful way.

People often confuse joy and happiness or joy and pleasure. They think as long as they've got everything going for them, they'll finally find joy. But joy is actually found in the person of Jesus. He *is* joy. In Fact, we can think of it like this: J.O.Y. Jesus. Overwhelms. You.

Where I can get worn out by chasing happiness, joy will give me strength because it comes with a promise from God *for* strength. Nehemiah 8:10 (NKJV) promises, "The *joy* of the Lord is your *strength*" (emphasis added).

Joy was the reward Jesus received for the cross. Hebrews 12:2 tells us, for the *joy* set before Him, Jesus endured the cross and scorned its shame. Joy brings with it, supernatural strength to endure even in the toughest times. Joy is remarkable. Even when we walk through seasons of difficulty, we won't just find strength, we'll find gladness, delight, and laughter—all attributes of joy. How? By fixing our eyes on Jesus. The author and perfecter of our faith, as Hebrews 12:2 tells us; "looking unto Jesus, the author and finisher of our faith, who for the *joy* that was set before Him endured the cross, despising the shame, and has sat down at the right hand of the throne of God." (NKJV, emphasis added).

I truly believe Jesus' joy came from fixing His eyes on His Father. Psalm 16:8 (NIV) says, "I keep my eyes always on the Lord. With him at my right hand, I will not be shaken." I believe David wasn't only speaking of himself in this Psalm, he was prophetically describing to us what happens when we keep our eyes on the Lord.

Jesus knew this Scripture; He knew it even in the midst of horrendous pain and agony. And keeping His eyes on His Father and what was in His Father's heart for us is what strengthened Him. Even in unfathomable circumstances, Jesus modeled to us how to live a joy-filled life—with eyes ever focused on the Father.

That's the difference between happiness and joy. Happiness comes from my happenstances while joy comes from experiencing God. One fluctuates based on what's happening around me. The other is constant like God's nature. He's constant. He was. He is. He will always be. So it is with His joy. His joy was. His joy is. And His joy will always be.

Now, *that's* something to smile about!

Transitions

I know it might sound strange, but while Manny and I were apart this time, I felt like I was starting to feel alive again. Like, I was finally starting to learn the dance of the joyful. I even started thinking for myself, rather than through the filter of what he would've wanted.

Right around this time, I got really into *The Lord of the Rings* movies. As I sat there watching these heroic characters coming together to fight off the enemy and destroy this tiny little ring, which had the potential to destroy them all, it spoke volumes to me.

You know, no one would've thought one little ring could destroy a whole land, but it wasn't simply the ring itself. It's what the ring represented—evil, destruction, darkness. I guess it made me ponder my own life and how I'd allowed one person to control my thoughts and emotions, and if I kept going down that path, I, too, was headed for destruction.

I was relieved by the thought of my life not being controlled by Manny any longer, though I still had to learn how to *apply* this thought and live free from his influence. After all, I was still living in the tension of not knowing whether my marriage was even going to make it.

To be honest, I didn't take any recovery classes or get counseling during this time but definitely should've been doing both. I do remember asking God to be real to me and heal my heart. I asked Him to draw me deeper into His love and bind up my wounds. To reach down and pull me up out of the pit and set my feet upon His solid rock. I asked Him to raise me out of the ashes of yesterday and help me laugh and live lighthearted today.

As I learned to live from God's heart, I remembered what it was like to be held by His love and I knew *that's* what I wanted for the rest of my life. I know now this was Holy Spirit reminding me of His perfect love, which was with me throughout my entire life, drawing me close, even when I didn't feel like I deserved it. Meditating upon God's love helped me make myself vulnerable to Him again. *I* may not have known how to stop letting Manny control me, but I knew *He* did.

I started feeling more confident about myself, more competent too. It's absolutely amazing what hanging around with Jesus does for your self-esteem. An employment opportunity opened for me at another corporation. They told me the position was mine if I wanted it because they saw me as being a great fit for their company. I love how God opens doorways for us as we simply fix our eyes and attention on Him. We just enjoy Him, and He does all the rest! Amazing.

Finally, after a few months of being separated the *second* time, on a humid July afternoon with the sun beaming in the sky and the sweet smell of lilies in the air, Manny came knocking on our door. With tears in his eyes and repentance in his voice, he went on to explain how he'd been having an affair, which was why he'd been treating me so awful before. He'd actually got caught up in a relationship with this woman before we ever even said "I do," but never told me about it because he told *himself* that once we got married, he'd end it right away.

The problem is it's never that simple, is it?

When we hide and conceal things like lies, they start to take over our lives, steal our joy, and create a life of their own. Pretty soon, we start answering to *them*, rather than having them answering to *us*. The truth is, exposing anything that wants to stay hidden in our lives is not only essential, but it's also our way to freedom. Keeping it all inside leads to our misery. From misery, we run right into depression. And depression, if left unchecked, can run us right into sickness and disease. All because we kept a lid on the truth.

Now don't misunderstand me, I'm not suggesting you go stand on your front porch and shout it out for all your neighbors to hear. I mean, if that's what you're into, I can't stop you, though you might think better of it later. I'm talking about going to your spouse, a trusted friend, a counselor, or your pastor, and get those things out in the open air. Let it vent so healing, mercy, and joy can arise and restoration can begin (James 5:16; Proverbs 28:13; Psalm 32:1–5).

To the tune of the squeaky front porch swing with lawn-mowers humming in the background and ice tinkling in our lemonade, we sat and talked for hours. Well, mostly he talked, and I listened. I listened as he told me he was broken up about what he did to me and so very, very sorry. I listened as he said it was officially over between him and the other woman and that she wasn't what he wanted because she wasn't me. I listened as he said how much he regretted hurting me and how he never meant for it all to happen.

I listened ... and I listened ... and I listened some more. As I sat there quietly trying to process all he was saying, I studied a bee who'd landed on the outside of my glass searching for sweet escape from the heat. I knew how he felt. I continued to listen as he said he'd never do it again and if I gave him one more chance, he'd make it up to me by cherishing me all the days of his life. I listened until purples, pinks, and oranges swept across the horizon. And as the sun set on our conversation, I was reminded that even when one season ends, the promise of a new season begins.

As I listened, I remember thinking it all sounded good, and I had never seen him follow up his words with such contrite and sincere actions before. He had me convinced that this was finally it. The man I'd been waiting for, the marriage I'd been praying and dreaming of was finally sitting before me. And while I knew it would be hard, I decided I'd rather give our marriage another try, than never try to make it work again.

As we headed inside, I was full of mixed emotions. I didn't know what the future held for us, but whatever it was, I was hoping *this* time, we would face it together.

The truth is, I was completely unprepared for what happened next.

CHAPTER EIGHT

Digging Deep
(Unearthing the Layers of Your Life and Processing Past Pain)

God never hurries. There are no deadlines against which he must work. Only to know this is to quiet our spirits and relax our nerves.

—A.W. Tozer, Knowledge of the Holy

A couple of weeks later, we were all moved into our home—*again*. And for the first few months, it seemed like we were really going to make it. We were laughing, happy, and what I thought was in love. That's when I decided to take a few night classes to help advance my career, which meant for several months, I would be gone most evenings. I honestly didn't even give it a second thought; I mean we were doing so good. Nothing to worry about, right?

But a couple of months into my classes, I remember we just felt *off.* You know that feeling you get when you know something isn't right, but you can't actually prove it or put your finger on it? Well, I simply couldn't *shake* that feeling. So one crisp autumn afternoon, with the golden fall sunlight flooding through our kitchen window and the smell of dinner simmering on the stove, I sat across from Manny and shared what I was feeling with him. I asked him if something was going on that I needed to know about, and if so, it would be better if he told me *now*, rather than later.

He swore up and down that there was nothing and I was simply being overly sensitive and emotional. So, I decided to shrug it off and go about my day, I mean I didn't want to argue or think the worst of him. The problem was, days turned into weeks, and weeks turn into months, and I *still* couldn't shake that nagging feeling. After I approached him about it a few more times and got the same responses, I finally chalked it up to nerves. He was rebuilding my trust and I needed to let him. That couldn't happen if I was being paranoid. Little did I know how *off* everything really was; I certainly couldn't have imagined what was coming.

Out in the Open

I should've trusted my instincts, but when someone is *really* good at making you feel like you're crazy or always at fault, that's pretty hard to do. I figured the problem must have been me, and he was all too happy to let me think so and often steered our conversations in that direction. Things were starting to get rocky with his moods again. So I was afraid to stir the pot too much concerning what I was feeling, for fear he'd kick me out or leave, which is something he'd often threaten me with if he felt I was putting too much pressure upon him.

Finally, in the spring of 2006, Manny sat me down and soberly said he had something to tell me. I could tell by the way he was acting it wasn't good news and I was about find out why my instincts had been working overtime. He took a deep breath and asked, "Remember when I told you I had an affair?" I nodded my head, slowly saying, "Yeeess." He continued, "And remember when I told you it was over, and I'd never see her again?" I gave him the same response. Then, he took another long, deep breath and said, "Well, she came to see me at work a couple of months after you moved back in and told me she's pregnant. She's due in three days."

I was speechless—absolutely *shocked*, to say the least. *That* certainly wasn't what I was expecting to hear. He went on to tell me she wasn't even supposed to be able to conceive, so they never bothered to use protection. He never told me about it earlier because he was afraid I'd leave.

I was *so* upset. Here, there really *had* been something going on but every time I approached him, he made me feel like I was crazy or imagining things. I started pacing the room, shouting something like, "I gave you *every* opportunity to tell me! And I told you if you were honest *now*, it would be better than coming clean *later*!"

He just sat there with his head in his hands as I went on ranting, "How could you keep something like *this* a secret? I deserved to know, and I deserved to know *months* ago! Now I have *no* time to process all this, since the baby is due in *three short days!* Did you *really* expect me to just magically roll with all this? What were you thinking, Manny? I mean, are you kidding me right now?"

I took a deep breath to collect myself, and as I did a logical thought arose within me, "How do you even know the baby is *yours?*" His exact words were, "I just know. She's not been with anyone else but me." The truth is, there were absolutely no words he could use to make me feel *any* better.

All I could do was sit there, as the gravity of the situation started to sink in, becoming heavier with each passing minute. Pictures started flying through my mind of them being at doctor's appointments, picking out baby clothes, having baby showers, choosing baby names. I thought I was going to be sick. "Did you start up a relationship with her again through all of this, it would be hard not to get close? Were you guys *together?* Does your family know? Does *she* know about me?" He gave me the responses in rapid succession, "No. No. Yes. Yes." But how could I *truly* trust them? Nothing he could say could make me feel any better because none of his words meant anything anymore. With *one* word, in *one* single second, my *whole* life blew up in my face. How do you prepare for that? You can't ... you just *can't*.

That night, he received the phone call that she was in labor. He told me he wanted to be there for the birth of his baby. It was all so wrong. So backwards, up-side-down, and inside-out. So surreal. The next several days went by like a bad dream. I totally disconnected from reality, staying in my pajamas, binge-watching movies, and barely getting off the couch. I didn't call anyone or tell anyone about what was happening because I was so embarrassed. And I mean, what do you say? How do you talk about something you can barely believe yourself?

How did I keep getting stuck in these disgusting cycles with him? I had never felt so ashamed and alone before. I knew God was there with me. He's literally what was keeping me alive, but I allowed the lies of shame to block my closeness with Him. The lies whispered, ridiculing me with their accusations that God was sick of me, I'd gone back and forth too many times. He didn't want to hear it anymore. *This* is exactly what shame wants us to believe—*lies*.

The following weeks went by like a blur. I told myself I had to pull it together, put on a happy face, and get back to work. Then, I told Manny if we had any chance of making it, I needed to be involved, so I wanted to meet the baby and the mother. She needed to accept my involvement, even if she didn't like it. He responded by saying that he'd set up a meeting for us all to sit down together, a few weeks after they got settled in at home. I could understand how the mother needed time to get her baby into a routine, so I agreed. I patiently waited a couple of weeks and then a couple of weeks more. Finally, I told him if he didn't set something up for us all to meet, I couldn't stay in our marriage any longer. It simply wasn't going to work.

The next evening, he picked up his phone and called her in front of me, she didn't answer so he left her a voicemail telling her all three of us needed to meet—or at least I *thought* he did. Over the next month, he left her several supposed voicemails, all in front of me. Eventually, he started blaming her, saying she wasn't getting back to him because she didn't want to meet. Instead, she wanted to ignore the situation altogether. Weeks later, I learned he never even made the calls; it had all been for show. Talk about feeling foolish—I'd been taken for a ride once again.

I didn't even know where I belonged in our marriage anymore. I couldn't see how I would fit into the picture if we didn't all get on the same page. Crazy as it sounds, I still wanted to make my marriage work, so I suggested counseling. And while he agreed, I let him put stipulations on what we could and could *not* talk about during our sessions. Of course, him having an affair and a baby with another woman were both off-limits, as were his emotional, mental, and physical abuse toward me. If I stepped outside of those parameters, I knew I'd pay the price for it later. Still, I pursued, praying the counselors would sense there were deeper issues not being exposed during our sessions and pull them out of him.

Since we didn't talk about what was really going on, they had us do very basic assessments, surveys, and strategies opposed to the deep, intense counseling we *actually* needed. And just like he manipulated me, he manipulated our sessions. Making himself out to look like the victim of a wife who had unrealistic expectations upon her husband.

I want to be clear; this wasn't the counselors' fault. I allowed him to control the flow of the sessions. Each time we went, I allowed him to decide what we would and wouldn't talk about before we even stepped out of the car. *I* allowed him. *I* let him take my voice and actually use it against me. And every time we came out of our appointments, it looked like *I* was the problem: A possessive wife who only wanted to control her husband's every move.

I can see now how I was *part* of the problem. *I* allowed him to control what I said, did, and even thought. *I* chose to live in denial. *I* chose to not respect myself. But I did not make his choices. His decisions and the outcome of those decisions were of his own making. It took me a long time to see that. Please, my friend, never let someone steal your voice—especially when you are in search of the truth that sets free.

> *Never let someone steal your voice—especially when you are in search of the truth that sets free.*

After a couple of months of chaos and confusion, the day came when all hell seemed to break loose when the mother of the baby pulled up to our house. *Immediately* Manny was beside himself with fear as he exclaimed, "Hurry up!" Guarding himself before the front door, he looked over his shoulder at me, "Run back to the bedroom and lock yourself in!" I stood there blinking, puzzled; I'd never seen him so upset. Seeing my confusion, he hurriedly shouted, "I don't want her knowing you're here, if she does, she may literally go crazy and try to hurt you!"

As I started racing back to our bedroom, I remember feeling even more confused and overwhelmed than I already did. How did she not know I was here? I mean, Manny said she knew about me, but she didn't want to meet me or have my involvement in any way. That's when I heard her crash through the door yelling and screaming at Manny, throwing furniture around, breaking the pictures of us she found, along with anything else she could get her hands on.

Finally, I'd *had* it. I was *not* going to be a prisoner in my own home any longer! I was done being quiet and uninvolved like I was someone to be hidden away. I wanted answers, and by golly, I was gonna get 'em. I came marching up the hallway with all my courage gathered about me, and in my sternest voice, demanded, *"What do you think you're doing destroying our home!"*

The second she saw me, she went *off* and began shouting, *"You said you were divorced!"* She then proceeded to pick up the thing closest to her, which happened to be a wrought iron candlestick and started swinging it at Manny, who went running out the back door with his hands up to protect himself. I watched, stunned, as she followed him, swinging and screaming all the way. Both of them were running and shouting down the street, making a huge scene for the entire neighborhood to see.

And there I was, just watching this spectacle unfold out the front window, knowing full well, my neighbors were likely watching right along with me. I mean, how could they miss it, between all the screaming and shouting and running down the street and through the yards? I felt like I was glued to the flood, stuck standing in front of the window, absolutely dumbfounded and completely overwhelmed, fully expecting the cops to show up any moment. Finally, I started looking around the house at all the mess, our pictures and belongings carelessly flung about, and I began blinking like I was coming out of a thick fog or bad dream.

As looked around in disbelief, I started saying to myself, "How did I *get* here? How did I get *here?* How is *this* my life? *What in the world* am I doing here? I *never* wanted my life to look like *this! How in the world did I get here?*"

Soul Ties

My dear friend, who you do life with *really* matters—because *you* matter, and your life has great value. Relationships play a key role in where we go in life, so if you're not surrounding yourself with wise relationships, chances are you'll end up asking the same questions I did over thirteen years ago. *How did I get here? How is this my life? What in the world am I doing?*

Soul ties are what happen when we wrap our soul (our inner self—our emotions, mind/thoughts, and will) around a relationship, circumstance, or memory. Think of soul ties as the bonds that are formed from physical or emotional connections and exchanges. However, they lie not only in the connections or exchanges we've shared but in what we *believe* about those exchanges after they've taken place.

The phrase "soul tie" often drums up some negative connotations, but the truth is, soul

158

ties aren't inherently evil or bad. It really depends upon who and what our souls are tied to. For instance, my soul is tied around the Lord, and I *want* it to be. I want my soul to be utterly and completely wrapped around Jesus (see Song of Songs 1:7, TPT). I find my soul is wrapped deeper in His love the more I simply say "yes" to Him, for He's already made all His endless love available to me. You see, it actually *takes* God to *love* God.

I also have a soul tie with my hunky husband, Alan, and it's wonderful and beautiful and godly. Sexual intimacy is not only God's gift, it was His *design*. He created pleasure for our benefit! Sexual intimacy wraps our souls around each other, making us vulnerable to the one we're intimate with, which is why God created it to be safely expressed within the healthy boundaries of marriage. Marriage, the way God intended, is built upon covenant—two people, a man and woman—who willingly lay their lives down for each other in the process of becoming one.

Simply put, living in covenant is like living our lives in a way that asks, "What can *I* do for *you?*" Rather than asking, "What can *you* do for *me?*" In this environment, where we consider the needs of our spouse over our own needs, intimacy (both inside and outside of the bedroom) reaches glorious climaxes that self-gratification could never come close to touching. And there is no regret or remorse resulting from the act. It's fulfilling. It's beautiful. It's lovely, pure, and all the good and pleasant things God designed it to be.

Emotional attachments are another way we form soul ties. In the context of *healthy* relationship, this is a good thing, but it stops being healthy or good when we look to a relationship or group of people to meet *all* our emotional needs. In this context, emotional soul ties become perverted and distorted and we're no longer in right relationship with others; we're either consumed with the demands we're placing on them or the demands they're placing on us. Fear and insecurity are often the fruit of this sort of twisted attachment.

Sometimes, we can get emotionally wrapped around more than relationships. Sometimes, our souls get tied to experiences that have happened in our past. Pretty soon, our lives get lost in reliving the memories of *yesterday*, which can keep us from fully enjoying the blessings of *today*. Whether our souls have been tied to partners or emotional experiences, these unhealthy attachments can interrupt the flow of intimacy with those in our lives, including our spouse and even God.

When I used to sit and ruminate on the rejection I'd experienced in my past, to feel sorry for myself or figure out what I should have done differently, I was actually forming an unhealthy emotional soul tie to those memories. This attachment ultimately affected my relationships, as I was tied to experiences in my heart that told me I needed to be on guard for when I encountered rejection. In my mind, it was a matter of *when* not *if*, I encountered rejection. I had allowed my past experiences to paint the way I perceived and even shaped my present and future realities. I started to exhibit defensiveness and rejection toward others as a method of protecting myself from any possibility of them rejecting me, in effect telling them they couldn't reject *me* because I was rejecting *them* first.

Had this pattern been allowed to continue, I would have likely sabotaged every relationship I ever entered. All because I allowed rejection to wrap itself around me by repeatedly revisiting those painful memories and emotions. The thing is, I wasn't even cognizant I was doing this. Instead, it was like a program continuously running in the background, junking up the memory space in my brain. Overly crowding my brain caused me to mentally and emotionally process slower some days than others, as I would subconsciously sort through what happened in the past, trying to come up with ways to fix it.

But the truth is, *I couldn't* fix it. Only *Jesus could*. He's so wonderfully willing and able to set us free from any physical and emotional exchanges we've experienced that have formed unhealthy soul ties within us.

If I hadn't been freed from this unhealthy soul tie to past experiences, not only would I have continued to sabotage my relationships, I would have continued to attract the *same kind* of relationships. And they'd most likely be filled with rejection, as I'd be trying to sort out and make right what happened back in the past, in my relationships today. This process would only continue to repeat itself until the soul tie was cut out of my life.

Which brings us to the question of the hour, *how do we* cut toxic soul ties?

Cutting Toxic Soul Ties: The Process

I feel it's important to start this part of our conversation together by first explaining that anytime we revisit our past, *apart from the blood of Jesus*, we make ourselves susceptible to the spirit of deception. The same way I was totally unaware of the soul tie I'd formed with rejection by revisiting painful memories, we can be walking in deception and not even know it. Such is the nature of deception—we are oblivious to it until it is exposed. This is why we need to give Holy Spirit free reign in our lives by asking Him to expose what needs to be exposed, in His perfect timing and His perfect way. Then, we need to trust Him to show us what we need to see. He's such a kind Father. He's not

161

going to show us what He's not prepared and equipped us for, and He only exposes to set us free, never to shame.

When we ask Him to bring to the surface those things we need to cut or break or work through—past relationships, painful memories, or just the junk we're tied to in our soul—He's faithful to do so in ways which will *empower*, not cripple us. The beauty of our past is, *we* don't own it. *Jesus* does. Isn't that wonderful? We no longer have to live with what we tell ourselves about our past; we get to live with what *God* says about it!

When Jesus died on the cross, He didn't just die *for* us, He died *as* us, and when He resurrected to new life, we were raised to new life and a new nature *with* Him. Old things—past things have passed away. The Greek word for away is *parerchomai* and means to perish, to omit, and indicates persons moving forward. When we receive Christ as our Lord and Savior, we are what the Bible calls, born again; we're invited to consider ourselves *dead* to sin and *alive* to Christ (John 3:3-5, Romans 6:11). That means our old, sinful nature is dead because it died with Jesus at the cross. We are fully permitted and encouraged to look at our past as having *perished* because God *omits* it from our record in Heaven and we are now fully able to *move forward!* I love that!

Not only does God omit past sins and soul ties from our record when we repent, He actually rewrites our history. Our history then becomes *His-story*. In His very own blood, Jesus puts His pen over our past and gives us a new story fully of redemption and hope. It's of utmost importance to revisit the events and experiences, relationships, and exchanges in our past through His perspective. Otherwise, we're looking through the wrong lens.

Many of the heroic stories in the Bible are sprinkled with sin, yet sin isn't recounted against these heroes of faith in the historic and heroic chapter of Hebrews 11. Likewise, God does not count our sin, doubt, and immorality against *us* when we repent, as they did. Repentance means to turn. It's a *conscious* process of turning *away* from that which brings bondage (sin, lies, and lesser loves), *to* that which brings freedom and healing (God, His truth, and His love for us).

Repentance brings justification and immediately restores us to the pinnacle—the highest place of right relationship with God—as if we've never sinned. So when Holy Spirit makes us aware of issues we've already repented from, it's not because those issues still exist in His eyes. It's because our soul is still unhealthily tied around them, giving us a wrong perspective of our past, and He wants to restore us to *His* perspective.

So you see, friend, those connections and encounters, those memories and experiences, none of them exist any longer according to *our own* recollections, for they've been rewritten. So let's ask God to help us see them as *He* sees them—from *His* redemptive perspective. *This* is how we begin to break ties with the junk we've got tangled up in our soul.

I realize it can often be tempting to want to dig around in our past, apart from Holy Spirit's promptings, this isn't something I recommend. We can end up getting into all kinds of self-shame, confusion, and resentment this way because we're honoring the issues of our past (the problem) rather than the One who is the *solution* to the problem.

Sometimes, the *effects* of soul ties are more obvious to us than the soul tie itself. For instance, if I can't function without having a giant piece of chocolate cake every night, it shouldn't take too long for me to I realize that I have an addiction to sugar. But *what* is the sugar substituting? What's driving my cravings, my choices, thoughts, and behavior?

This is where I need to ask Holy Spirit to take the lead and guide me into what's going on in my heart. For if I want to adjust my *behavior*, I first need to address my *heart*.

Honestly, when Holy Spirit revealed the rejection I was tied to in my soul due to the issues in my past, I hadn't gone looking for it. Like I said before, when we're deceived, we don't recognize the issue until it's revealed. To be totally transparent and quite vulnerable with you, what brought this soul tie to the surface was a couple of nasty arguments my (present-day) husband, Alan, and I had, had. The effects I was experiencing from my soul tie to rejection were adversely affecting my marriage, and we simply couldn't seem to shake this emotionally frustrated funk we were feeling toward each other.

It's not that we were fighting all the time, it's more like there was this internal ickiness churning between us. So I think we both felt as though we had to tread carefully around the other to avoid unleashing the ugly that was happening on the inside of us. Finally, one day I completely exploded, spewing awful words everywhere. Oh my goodness, it was so nasty, and I felt absolutely terrible afterward. This was more than just a warning sign that something wasn't right. It was full-blown, in your face, undeniable evidence that my attitude toward my marriage, like unattended fruit, was starting to rot. I needed prayer, deep repentance, deliverance, *something* ... because my fruit was *stinkin'!*

Soon after, I called a dear friend of mine and confided to her about our situation and my behavior. I told her I needed and *wanted* to truly change, but I knew I needed to start with my heart. For behavior, as we said a moment ago, begins in the heart.

Rather than going right into a counseling session and walking me through my past, my friend and I simply turned our eyes upon Jesus. We started talking about His beautiful nature, which organically moved us into worshiping Him for being the Healer and Mender of broken hearts and broken homes. With a heart of true worship and repentance, we praised Him for His faithfulness, for His love, and for restoring us to the pinnacle the *very second* we repent. We praised Him for how He helps us turn from what ruins to what renews. And how even when we don't understand what's going on in our lives, we can still trust Him because He's only ever good.

As we worshiped, not to manipulate Him for answers or as a means of warfare against our enemies but out of a spirit of true, honest worship, He began to work on my heart. He started softening my heart toward my husband while simultaneously showing me certain things in my past I had been unconsciously holding onto.

One of the memories He brought to my attention was an unpleasant, recurring memory I would often have of a field trip I attended in my early elementary school years. The trip ended with my entire class gathered in a circle laughing and pointing at me as I stood in their midst, the object of their bullying. This memory had especially troubled me, yet I didn't understand why, as bullying wasn't an unusual occurrence in my past. I only knew it was very vivid and made me feel sad when it flashed across the screen in my mind.

Rather than dismissing this uncomfortable memory and pushing it out of my mind, as I would have before, Holy Spirit asked me if I wanted to see it through *His* perspective. I was amazed and absolutely overcome by what He showed me. As I told Him I trusted Him to show me the truth, a vision of Jesus appeared beside me in this memory. He knelt to my eye level and lovingly whispered in my ear, "Don't look at them," making a swooping motion with His hands at my classmates, "Look at *them*." And in the vision, He opened a doorway to Heaven and showed me the great cloud of witnesses cheering me on. They were jumping up and down, shouting "Go, Hope! Don't give up! Keep going! You're doing great! Yea, Hope!" (Cue tears.)

He closed the door, looked me in the eyes, and affirmed with a smile, "They've been doing this your *whole* life, and whenever you've experienced rejection, they've cheered you on *even more.* So anytime you feel rejected or sad, *rejoice!* For the Kingdom of Heaven is greatly rejoicing over you!" (Cue *more* tears!)

In this time of deep prayer, Jesus revealed to me this memory had especially troubled me because that was the moment I made an agreement with the spirit of rejection by letting it attach itself to my soul. At that moment in time, I had internally agreed with rejection and allowed it to take up space in my soul, directly affecting my decisions, affections, emotions, and attention—my life.

God showed me *this* was what was churning between me and Alan. This spirit of rejection was working overtime to try and divide what He had unified. Suddenly, I could see the ruin rejection had spread throughout my past relationships, ambitions, confidence, you name it. But God didn't show all this to me to leave me in it! (Thank goodness!)

In these moments, when God so kindly puts His finger on the things working to interfere with His love, we have a choice. We can choose to continue to give it a place of influence and access. We can live in denial of it (which will *still* give it a place of influence and access). We can try to control the issue(s) ourselves (which will *also* continue to give it a place of influence and access). Or we can praise Him for exposing it to us, so we can turn from it unto Jesus, and walk in the truth of the One who *sets* us free and *keeps* us free. Remember, He never exposes to shame us but to *empower* us.

When He asked me if I wanted to see that painful memory from His perspective, I could have said no, but I knew if I did, I'd miss out on the blessing of surrendering to God's goodness. I could have protected that memory and protested, "No, don't touch it. I know I'm a victim of my past and I always will be," and continued to live out the rest of my days from that self-fulfilled prophecy. I could have said no, I'm afraid of what I'll see because it was really hard, and I don't want to go back there. To be honest, this was *almost* my response were it not for God's grace infusing me with courage and strength.

Fear is driven out by God's perfect love. And the moment I said yes to God's love, His love came rushing into my memory with its piercing, white light, washing away all shame and sorrow, all remorse and regret. His love reminded me, I'm not that person anymore. That was the old me who was crucified with Christ, and I've been given the beautiful permission to move on into the newness of who I am in Him. What wonderful news!

Now I get to stand in *His* victory. And in everything I do, I get to *start* where He *finished!* I get to stand in the truth that I'm fully accepted and loved by Christ. I'm free from rejection's lies and he can't conquer me because God's love already has! The answer to every issue we'll ever face, be it soul ties or addiction, self-sabotage or insecurity is and forever will be surrendering to the love of the One who paid it all to redeem us all.

Cutting Toxic Soul Ties: Don't Get Stuck in Denial

What do you think takes greater faith: to ignore an issue like nothing is wrong or recognize there's a problem but refuse to give it a place of influence in the way we think, feel, speak, and live? It doesn't require faith to ignore a problem. That's an exercise in *denial*—not faith. It takes faith to look at the issue and restrain ourselves to say only what *God* is saying about it. It takes faith to walk in His promises as we're walking through the challenges of life. To celebrate His goodness when the report isn't what we were hoping, or when there's too much month and not enough money, or when they let us down *again*. It takes great faith to keep our eyes on God's promises in these times rather than the problems.

Here's the thing, it can be quite easy to convince ourselves that denial is in the same family as faith; when really, it's *anti*-faith. Denial is the fruit of *fear*, not faith. You see, when we live in denial, we enslave ourselves to our past, to fear, and to bondage. Often, when we fear facing our past it's because we feel powerless against it. But for those of us who are being saved, the truth is we have the power of God actively working within us through the message of the cross (see 1 Corinthians 1:18)!

When we live in fear of facing the past, it's really easy to stay in a state of denial or create alternate realities and egos to deal with the pain. Don't get me wrong, I'm certainly not pointing my finger at anyone; I definitely don't have the right to do so. All those years I made compromises for Manny came out of denial. I was living with my eyes wide *shut*. Now that I'm living with my eyes *open*, there's no way I'd be making those same choices today. But before, when I was with him, seeing things with open eyes wasn't easy—I wouldn't let it be. Let me say it this way: There were moments in my relationship with Manny when I knew—I mean, I *knew* he wasn't the one I was supposed to be with, yet I felt so overwhelmed in those moments that I quickly shut them down.

As we said earlier, the nature of deception is to deceive, we simply can't see the destruction it has on our lives while we're *in* it. So when we finally come *out* of it, and we're free to clearly see, sometimes *what* we see is really overwhelming. Especially when everywhere we look, all we see is the destruction that denial and deception have left in our lives and in the lives of those we love.

This is when the temptation to dip right back into denial can rush in like a river. Hear me clearly my dear, denial is *not* your friend. No more than it is mine. It may *feel* like the solution in the moment but it's not—it's the *problem*.

Just as our eyes adjust from darkness to light, so our hearts adjust when we walk away from denial and into truth. Trust me, my friend, that's an adjustment you want in your life. For if we never walk away from denial, we'll continue to be held captive by it.

It's funny how we use denial as a self-protection mechanism when really it does far more harm than good. If I remain in denial and refuse to work through the painful issues in my past, those issues will only lead me into present-day struggles and patterns I really don't want in my life. Ignoring uncomfortable issues from my past won't make my present-day struggles any less present. The negative effects of being bullied or abused won't go away just because I try to act like they never existed. In fact, it'll likely exacerbate them by keeping the past *inside* my present.

If I refuse to work through and ultimately move on from a painful experience I had when I was sixteen (let's hypothetically say it was date-rape), I will operate from an emotional skillset in certain situations and environments as a sixteen-year-old. I'm susceptible to slipping into a teenage-like emotional role in tense or unsettling circumstances without even realizing it. This can be manifested in such ways as rebellion, resentment, fear, depression, negative attitudes, anxiety, and even violence, and addiction.

My thought life will also unconsciously orbit around these painful, uncomfortable memories if I refuse to rewire the way I think. Throughout our time together, we've often talked about the issue of renewing our minds by changing the way we think. When we discover what God has to say about us, others, and the world around us and chose to willingly align our thoughts to His, our minds are transformed. Cutting unhealthy soul ties is part of this transformation process.

We cannot hold onto past hurts and expect to live from a transformed mind because the transformed mind comes through surrender to what God has to say about our past, present, and future. If we want to live in the freedom of a transformed *life*, we must first find our freedom in a transformed *mind*. This means we must make ourselves available to Holy Spirit's direction in everything, particularly when it comes to the hidden hurts and issues of our heart.

Cutting Toxic Soul Ties: Don't Get Stuck in the Past

Remember when we said God never reveals anything to us to shame us? Well, He also won't expose what we need to see only to leave us in it. (Thank goodness!)

I think sometimes this is where we can get stuck when it comes to inner healing. There's often a tendency to rehash, relive, and reprocess the painful issues of our past on such a regular basis that we keep the past in the present. Whatever we focus on grows larger and more prominent in our minds, as well as our hearts. What we said earlier applies well here—we don't want to honor the *problem*; we want to honor the One who is the *solution* to every problem.

When someone tells me they've been going to counseling for twelve years for the same issue, I'm inclined to think it's not working. Or maybe they just need a new counselor. They need *The* Counselor.

It's important we find the balance between being honest and open and vulnerable with God, while stubbornly refusing to stay stuck in the past—even as we work through it. Remember, we don't own our past, *Jesus* does. So, it's extremely important we never revisit our past apart from His blood, for we'll always be looking through the wrong lens—the wrong perspective—when we do.

Cutting Toxic Soul Ties: The Power of Testimony

So then, how *do* we effectively navigate the process of inner healing? How *do* we find freedom from the pain in our past without getting stuck *in* it? Especially when we hear someone else's testimony of breakthrough and are inclined to think, *That's the answer, I've got to do it that way!*

Testimony is powerful. Testimony stokes our fervor and strengthens our faith, knowing God *can* and *will* do it again. In fact, the word testimony in the Greek is *marturia,* and it means, witness, historical attestation, evidence, judicial or general certification. As in, an inner *witness* of the Holy Spirit *attesting* to us of His power and ability to do what we've heard, *again!* I know people who've experienced healing simply by listening to the testimony of others! I love the strength-giving component to testimony; I could listen to them for hours and walk away filled with refined focus, energy, and encouragement.

We steward what God has done when we give Him the glory through the sharing of our testimonies. To steward means to take care of, attend to, administer, apply, or use what God has provided. We honor and worship God when we steward what He's given us, from money to healing, to talents and giftings, and everything in between. When I have a supernatural encounter with Jesus, I journal it so I can remember the details of the experience and steward that testimony, encouraging myself and others even years after it happened.

Stewarding testimony sets a precedent—a legal Kingdom precedent—for miracles, signs, and wonders to happen again. It makes impossibilities *possible* as they bow to the name of Jesus. Others can actually *break through* to their breakthroughs simply because we have shared what Jesus has done for us! Amazing.

In fact, Revelation 19:10 tells us the testimony of Jesus—the proclamation of who He is and what He has done—is the spirit of prophecy. Meaning, what He has done He will do again, and who He is for *one* He will be for *everyone!*

But we must remember that testimony reveals *outcome*—not *process*. When we put the emphasis on the testimony rather than the One who made the testimony possible, we can quickly grow frustrated because we're not being organic with God. We're trying to emulate someone else's process.

While we would be wise to listen, honor, and remember the testimonies and breakthroughs of those who've gone before us and received what we're seeking; we'd be equally wise to posture our hearts to receive what God has to give us through their testimony in the way *He* wants to give it. You see dear one, God wants to be God for *you*. His interaction with you is as unique and specific to your relationship with Him, as it is mine. It's beautiful the way He relates with us all individually. It means we can fully be ourselves and freely pursue Him first, knowing *everything else* will follow.

We partner with Him in our healing by pursuing Him in total surrender. That's our answer right there. We surrender control, allowing Holy Spirit to have His way in us—whatever that looks like for you and whatever that looks like for me. God rarely does things the exact same way. Otherwise, we'll become fascinated by the *process* and not the *One* who leads us through the process. Regardless of what it looks like, He'll prove His faithfulness to me as much as He'll prove it to you and the journey to our breakthroughs will be as uniquely beautiful as we are.

Cutting Toxic Soul Ties: Where Freedom Is Found

Until I was around fourteen, my family went to a whooping and hollering kind of church. Don't get me wrong, that doesn't bother me a bit. I absolutely love to sing and shout and dance for my King Jesus. But looking back, I can see now that what *wasn't* right was a lot of that whooping and hollering was directed *toward* the enemy rather than *for* Jesus. I observed at a young age that we were supposed to *shout* at satan, and that our authority came in the form of *hollering*. Naturally, I followed down the same path, and I'll tell you what, friend, I felt like I didn't accomplish much with all my screaming and shouting except to wear myself out.

You know, the more we seek Jesus and spend time with Him, He's faithful to show us why things in our past didn't work as we expected—or were taught—they would. As I'm growing deeper in the revelation of God's love, He's revealing to me that I have more authority over the enemy in a *whisper* than I do a shout when I know His love for me and who I am in Him.

It's not that there's not a time for shouting; there definitely is. Look at the nation of Israel and how they won the battle of Jericho by shouting when God said to shout. He's even directed me to roar His roar over certain situations in my own life recently. But if I believe I must always work myself up to win the victory over the enemy that is false teaching, and the enemy knows it. We're not going to walk away victorious when we're living under false teaching. We're going to walk away worn out because the enemy's not going to listen—he's going to laugh.

Our level of authority is directly related to our level of surrender. If we want more authority to break unhealthy soul ties, find freedom, and see breakthroughs, miracles, signs, and wonders, we need to surrender more to God's love and honor who and what He honors. It's that childlike—in the simplest and boldest way. We go low so Jesus can be lifted high. This is the nature of His Kingdom, and it's beautiful because it takes the pressure off of us. All we have to do is simply be willing to surrender control. When we're fully yielded and rooted in God's love, we come with some *serious* power and backing because His love has already won, and we're fighting *from* victory, rather than toward it.

I'll say this, the fight we're fighting isn't fair, but it's totally, one hundred percent in *our* favor! All we need to do is rest in Jesus, and we wear the enemy out with the intimacy we enjoy with our King. Like we said in chapter six, demons don't have staying power. They don't have the tenacity you and I are privileged to when we're tucked into the heart of the Father and allow Him to show and tell us all He is and all He wants to be for us. This is absolutely revitalizing for us and totally terrifying to the enemy.

This means there's nothing—and I mean *nothing*—we have to face in fear. Not our most painful memories or deepest hurts or shocking betrayals because His love for us is *perfect*, and perfect love casts out fear. And there's nothing we'll ever face alone because His love never fails, and it never leaves. He's a Father who will never, ever walk out on us. Through the hard, the ugly, the painful, and the stupid, God will always be right here, reaching us with His love.

This is how we find freedom from toxic soul ties: we turn *away* from what ruins *toward* what restores, effectively replacing sorrow for joy! The process is essentially the same for repentance: it's a lot easier to turn *away* from something if you have something else—or in this case—*Someone* else to turn to, Jesus Christ, our living hope. As we turn our focus to Him, He fills us with energy because His hope brings energy, and His hope brings influence. And we want to influence where we go from here with the energy of His hope.

Cutting Toxic Soul Ties: The Time it Takes

I hear people ask the same question I've often wondered myself, "How long should I expect inner healing to take?"

Honestly, the answer actually boils down to you, friend. The same way *my* healing process boils down to me. The time it takes for our hearts to heal is really tied to how much we're willing to surrender them. So, in a big way, it's up to each of us, isn't it? The question then shouldn't be, how long will it take, the question should really be, how much are we willing to surrender?

The Holy Spirit can absolutely come in and overpower every toxic soul tie and bring inner healing in an instant, and Jesus is absolutely willing. Otherwise, the verse, "I am willing…be healed" (Matthew 8:3, NLT) wouldn't be in the Bible. These moments of revelation when we powerfully encounter the presence and heart of God are astonishing. They're what we cry out for and crave. Still, it's equally as important for us to leave space in our hearts for the *mystery* of God as we do the *revelation* of God.

Please understand, I'm not in the least bit suggesting God mysteriously brings illness or pain or loss in our lives or that He mysteriously withholds His kindness from us. God is mysteriously *good*—not evil. Illness isn't authored by the One who paid the highest price to defeat it. That doesn't even make sense! Illness, pain, and loss are all the work of the devil—*not* God. When I speak of His mystery in this context, I'm referring to the unique, specific, and beautiful way He heals and leads us.

Let's just stop for a second to consider it. Look at Naaman, the leper, in 2 Kings 5:1-19, who searched out the God of Israel for healing and Elisha told him to go take a dip in the Jordan river seven times and he'd be clean. Now, compare that to the blind man at Bethsaida in Mark 8:22-25, who Jesus healed when he spit on his eyes. (Now that's a testimony for ya ... "Jesus spit on me, and now I can see!") And the woman with the twelve-year issue of blood in Luke 8:43–48, who simply touched the border of Jesus' garment and was made whole.

What I'm trying to say, my dear, is we really need to let God do what *He* wants to do in the *way* He wants to do it. We partner with Him in the process when we do.

I have received miraculous healing in my body and soul in an instant. His healing fire has shot through my body, knocking me off my feet as I was caught up in His glory in more beautiful ways than I have words to describe! But I've also experienced the quiet peace and calm of His marvelous presence drawing deep resentment and pain out of me. I wouldn't exchange either encounter for anything; He knew exactly *what* I needed and *how* I needed to receive it in *that* moment. Our healing process is a journey with Him, and *He's* the One who needs to lead it, not us.

If I believe I'll only experience the presence of His healing power in ways He's revealed Himself to me before or in ways I'm comfortable with, I'm seriously limiting the reaches of His power. What a sad thought. I never want to limit my Jesus, I never want to tell Him, "No, it has to look *this* way for me to receive it or for it to be effective." I want Him to reach me in whatever ways *He* knows I need because He knows my heart and what it needs better than I do. Beloved, I believe you want to experience Him in all His manifold and colorful ways, and we will when we let Him have His way in us.

God's ways are *higher* than ours. We must keep that in mind as we're talking about encountering God because sometimes, He encounters us in ways that are offensive to the natural, logical mind. For instance, I've experienced His presence like electricity pulsating right through me. I could not stand for the power of His mighty presence and I shook like a person just who put their finger in an electrical outlet.

The truth is, if we refuse to step out of our comfort zones, our relationship with Jesus runs the risk of growing stagnant quite quickly. Mark 7:13 says we make the Word of God of no effect by our traditions. In others, we deny God His power to effectively work in our lives by worshiping what we know (traditions), rather than the Unfathomable God and the awesome dimensions of Him we have yet to experience.

I've had many people approach me with their concerns saying they don't want to get into any kind of hype. That's good—I don't either! The truth is, when God gets into us, we'll never get into hype because He's *far* better than anything we could ever hype up! Here's the thing about hype, *we* have to maintain it because *we're* attempting to control our time and interactions with God. But it's so freeing when we just let Him be who He wants to be for us, allowing Him the *right*, and the *time*, to interact with us in whatever way He wants. We can trust that He knows best and be exhilarated by our encounters with Him, rather than exhausted by what we're trying to enforce.

While I've experienced His healing in an instant, I've also experienced His healing happen over time. Why does His healing happen progressively sometimes? Honestly, I don't have all the answers, friend. I only know it's essential for us to honor His process and allow space in our hearts for the beautiful, mysterious unraveling of His goodness. Things are being deposited into and drawn out of our hearts through the progressive healing process that doesn't always happen in the instantaneous interactions with His healing power. God cares about healing the whole body: spirit, soul, and body, and often when His healing happens over time, we will not only receive our wholeness, but we will also gain the character, fruit, and disciplines that come with walking through faith-growing trials.

Are there things that can slow or hinder our healing? Yes. Holding onto unforgiveness, resentment, anger, or offense can certainly inhibit healing. Any lies we believe about ourselves, others, or God set up strongholds in our minds against Him and work to withhold our hearts from His, thereby reducing our ability to receive. When we entertain arguments and imaginations that go against God's nature, we give the enemy access into our lives. Choosing to stay angry and refusing to forgive hardens our hearts and gives the devil a place in our lives he doesn't deserve. When we give place to the devil, we also give place to his threefold purpose: to steal, kill, and destroy.

Is God able to override satan and bypass the *yuck* in our hearts and heal us instantly? He absolutely can; He's God! He has no equal or rival. satan is no competition for him. However, because God has given us freewill, He often moves

178

within and upon us to the extent that *we* have given Him permission. His desire is to co-labor—to *partner* with us. So, while there are times He does things *for* us, it's also in His heart to do things *with* us. If He's always doing things for us, our faith-muscles will never grow and strengthen, instead they will be in a continuous state of atrophy from underuse. Then, when we actually need resilient faith for what we're facing, it won't be available since we haven't developed it.

The times when we're waiting for our healing to fully manifest or for our breakthrough to finally *break through*, are the times that produce greater levels of persevering faith. We won't cultivate this kind of faith—a resilient faith that comes with mature character—any other way (see Luke 18:1-8). What we do in these times truly defines and refines our faith.

Will we get into bitterness and discouragement that want to work themselves into our souls when things don't go as we expected or planned? Or will we strengthen ourselves in the Lord as David did in 1 Samuel 30:6–8. When everyone turned against him and his life was on the line, he strengthened himself in the Lord (see verse 6). Before reacting to this life-threatening crisis, David intentionally asked God for wisdom in how to respond. When he was at his lowest point, David didn't need greater strategies, he didn't seek more weapons or look for someone to blame. He needed the strength and wisdom of his God, which led to a great and victorious outcome. When he came up against tremendous difficulty, David sought the Lord and was strengthened and gained godly wisdom for what his next steps should be. We would be wise to take the time to do the same.

When it feels like what we've been praying for is being delayed, it's not time to get wrapped up in fear and defeat. It's time to get wrapped up in God's heart. To sink deeper into the Secret Place—the place of peace He provides us—and seek His face. He's not afraid or disappointed or upset in any way by what we have to ask or say. He already knows! Still, He loves it when we're real with Him because that's when He can really move in our lives. For a tender, open heart is a *receptive* heart (see Mark 4:25, TPT).

As we seek Him with all our heart, He'll show us *His*. Not only concerning our healing and the healing of others; but the issues surrounding and attached to the healing. Issues such as affliction, insecurity, unforgiveness, fear, or any other demonic stronghold. God is faithful to show us what needs to be exposed because He wants for our healing and success more than we do.

As He reveals these issues to us, He'll also lead us in how to overcome them. If you feel like there might be issues or strongholds attached to your healing, I encourage you to prayerfully go back through chapter six and allow the Lord to show you how to walk into your victory because it's already yours. Remember beloved, He never reveals truth to shame us but to empower us and set us free.

Sometimes, God says, "I'll take it from here. Just rest." This is when He's revealing who we are in Him, our identity as precious sons and daughters of a loving Father who is always faithful to provide. Other times, He puts a sword in our hand and with a knowing smile on His face, calls us to our battle arms beside Him. These are the times He's expanding our perspective beyond our identity *in* Him and revealing our authority *through* Him. We are courageous warriors, made capable by His mighty Spirit and power, skilled for warfare and ready for victory. We are both sons and soldiers, two sides of the same coin. We can be confident, whether He's moving on our behalf or calling us to battle, the victory is the Lord's. Therefore, the victory is ours!

CHAPTER NINE

Mixed Messages (Re-Parenting: It Starts with You)

You must come to see how wonderful you are in God and how helpless you are in yourself.
—Smith Wigglesworth

I was racing down the highway, a small overnight bag and purse in the seat beside me. Salty tears streamed down my face and mixed with the cries in my throat as the events of the past few hours replayed in my mind.

I had been preparing breakfast for Manny that morning, walking on eggshells once again and doing my best to keep him from getting upset. Still completely unsure how to navigate the rocky waters of our marriage, especially since it seemed I was the only one putting in any real effort to make it last. His time had been divided between work and spending time with the baby, who I still had yet to meet. I came to understand that as he spent time with the baby, he was also spending time with the baby's mother. I was just expected to trust that nothing was happening. *Yeah, right.* I wasn't the least bit comfortable with this arrangement. How in the world could I be?

I was standing at the counter, putting the finishing touches on his breakfast, as I carefully approached this subject. Trying to gently explain that if our marriage was going to work, we *both* had to be involved. This meant he needed to work on regaining my trust, and I finally needed to meet his baby.

With a violent outburst, he started throwing dishes at me, kicked his chair back, and was suddenly in my face, towering over me spewing threats and profanities in a blind rage. And there I was, cowering before him in total fear for my life and safety. His outbursts were becoming increasingly violent and vicious; I knew it wouldn't be long before I'd be sustaining serious injuries or worse if I continued to stay. And just as quick as a snap of a finger, he grabbed his keys and left for work in an enraged haste.

I stood there shaking in his wake, totally frozen in fear. Finally, something in me snapped and I said out loud, "I'm not in love with *what is*; this *whole* time I've been in love with what *could be*." I don't exactly know how to explain what happened next. It's like I saw every moment and memory of our relationship flash across the screen in my mind in a split second. But this time, instead of seeing them as I always had before, I looked at them with *fresh* eyes and was absolutely *sickened* by what I saw. Building on that momentum, I ran to the back bedroom, grabbed my emergency overnight bag, purse, coat, and keys, and ran out the door.

I blinked, and the events of the morning disappeared, but the pain of its reality hit me like a pang in my chest. I was crying even more now. Crying because I felt like such a fool. Crying for all the years I'd wasted. Crying for finding out the man I'd loved this whole time wasn't at all who I thought he was. Crying for taking so long to do what I was finally doing, leaving—*for good.* Crying because I was *angry.*

I was angry at him for living a life of lies—a whole other life apart from us—I mean how do you do that to someone you *supposedly* love? And I was angry at myself for not knowing (or maybe *not wanting* to know the truth about him)—I mean how could I have been so oblivious?

The tears kept coming, and I let them come. I didn't care about my make-up or what I looked like; I *needed* this release. I finally arrived at my parents, and to be honest, I don't even remember if they were expecting me. I can't remember calling them yet somehow, they weren't surprised at my arrival. I'm sure I looked like a hot mess, with make-up smears and tear stains down my face, still, nothing could hide the resolve I felt flooding my eyes. For the first time, I was certain of my decision moving forward—and it didn't include Manny.

I felt free. *Relieved* even.

This time, I knew I'd left for good. I was *never* going back. This time, I *meant* it. My heart was firmly wrapped around this decision. And even though I had no idea what my future held, I'd never felt so hopeful in eight years.

My mom and dad welcomed me inside, sat me down, looked me square in the eyes, and wisely and firmly laid down the law, "We love you, but this is the last time you can stay here. If you go back to Manny again and things get bad, you'll have to find another place to stay. We're only saying this because we need you to know we can't support you going back into that environment. So, if you do, you'll have to find somewhere else to stay next time."

183

I remember sitting there thinking, *I don't blame them for saying that at all.* In fact, their words only fueled my resolve.

The Power of Words

Like we said before, words really matter. They're far more important than most of us realize. In Job 22:28, God's Word tells us that what we *speak* shall be established. Words are *far* more than breath rolling over our tongue and out of our mouth. They're actual vibrations. When we speak, these vibrations are sent into the atmosphere to attract what we say.

Now before you go thinking I'm some new aged hippie, let me remind you of what Jesus said in Mark 11:23 (NIV), "Truly I tell you, if anyone says to this mountain, 'Go, throw yourself into the sea,' and does not doubt in their heart but believes that what they *say* will happen, it will be done for them" (emphasis added).

I believe Jesus was using this *natural* principle to teach us a *spiritual* law. Here, Jesus is showing us when we speak to our mountains (the issues that loom large in our lives) and believe what we say, they will be *moved*, or they will be *removed*.

We looked at Proverbs 18:21 back in chapter six, but I want to refresh our memory of it here. This pregnant passage of scripture teaches us that life and death are in the power of what we say, and we'll eat—we'll taste the fruit of—what we speak. Are we speaking to our mountains? Or are we speaking to molehills and empowering them to become mountains with our words?

We would be very wise to be far more observant about what we're saying. Are we speaking life or are we speaking death? Are we speaking both and just breaking even, then wondering why we can never get ahead?

When we carefully watch what we say, *what* we say might surprise us. The question is, do we want to be pleasantly or unpleasantly surprised?

Applying our Words

All the other times I tried to leave Manny, I told myself, *I can't do this, I can't do this; he's going to talk me into coming back.* And guess what, I *couldn't* ... and he *did.*

But *this* time, I knew I could walk away and safely stay away because I kept telling myself, *You're going to be okay. God's got you; you're not going back. You don't want to go back.* And I *didn't.* Regardless of how I was feeling in the moment, I wouldn't allow myself to speak contrary to those words. I knew my emotions would pass and eventually even catch up with what I was saying.

This time I set wise parameters for myself. This time, I knew it wasn't enough to simply have resolve; this time I knew I needed to *keep* it. That meant not getting into conversations with Manny, not having conversations about Manny, and not even speaking or hearing his name. I shared these parameters with my mom and dad and asked them to hold me accountable. I then respectfully asked them, along with the rest of my family and friends, to refrain from having any conversation with or around me about him.

I went so far as to give my mom my mobile phone for a month and told her, unless there was a life-or-death emergency, I didn't want to know of any contact from him. I then made arrangements to have my office and friends contact me via my parents' home number. This was how much I didn't trust myself not to talk to him. I knew if I wanted a dramatic change, I had to dramatically change the way I was doing life.

Was it difficult to live without my cell phone for an entire month? You know, I thought it would be, but it was actually a relief. I didn't have to spend my energy thinking about whether I should take Manny's call or respond to his messages. I found my thoughts orbiting less around him and more around God's faithfulness and the hope-filled future He had for me.

It was right around this time that Holy Spirit gave me the vision of dancing with Jesus as I little girl, which I shared with you in greater detail back in chapter four. I was so profoundly encouraged to see myself as He saw me: a dearly loved little girl, cared for, and carefree. That vision carried me through not only this season of my life, but countless others. In fact, the words Jesus whispered to me in this vision to just rest in Him and let Him gracefully dance me to the other side of life were more than encouragement to me, they became my *strength*.

It's like His words lifted me up and over what could have been a traumatic situation, but instead of trauma, I found the sweet song Jesus was singing over me, and I learned to sing it too. Words are powerful, friend. They have the power to literally make or break everything we'll ever encounter.

As we just read in Mark 11:23, Jesus showed us how faith *speaks* and things *respond*. You know what else shows us this? Quantum physics.

Quantum physics, the study of physics at the subatomic level, shows us that *things* obey *words*. That's right—science is *proving* the Bible! What we speak with our lips is what will eventually be established in our lives—this is true of the Word of God and the enemy's lies. Dear one, our lives will actually *respond* to and *obey* what we say.

Now, I didn't know any of this back then. I only knew something *felt* different. I had no idea it was because I was *speaking* and *thinking* differently. I was just overwhelmingly grateful to have a positive and hopeful outlook on my future, even though I knew it was without Manny. Actually, I had a positive and hopeful outlook on my future *because* it didn't include him. I was choosing to not subject myself to his abuse and negativity any longer. Making this choice felt like I was like coming up for precious, sweet air after being held underwater for an elongated amount of time. All the sudden, I could breathe. All the sudden, I could see. All the sudden, I had *options*.

Self-Talk

Everybody talks to themselves. Funnily enough, professionals refer to this as *self-talk*. Reparenting is a term mental health professionals use to describe the process of taking the negative, critical messages we may have encountered from our parents (or teachers, peers, or other persons of influence and authority) in our growing-up years and replacing them with words and messages of love and care. Reparenting is an essential tool to relationship health, especially if we struggle with abandonment issues or we're easily offended or keep getting stuck in the same sort of unhealthy relationship cycles. Reparenting is achieved by speaking biblical truth and healthy, positive messages over ourselves on a regular basis. Quietly and out loud. Whether we want to, feel like it, or think we've earned it is all together beside the point—we do it anyway. When we make

When we make a mess or make it right, we have, in that moment, a choice in what we say to ourselves and the way we say it.

a mess or make it right, we have, in that moment, a choice in *what* we say to ourselves and the *way* we say it.

For example, let's say you wake up tomorrow and pour yourself a cup of coffee, but in the process of grabbing the mug, you knock it over. In this split second, you have a choice to make. You can tear yourself apart for making a mess or you can say, "It's okay, everybody spills things sometimes. There's no sense in getting all worked up about it. Just clean it up, move on, and don't let it ruin your day. God's got goodness stored up for me in this day, and I'm gonna encounter it!"

Here's another example, let's say you exceeded your productivity goal at work. In this instance, you have yet another choice to make. You can have a critical mindset and tell yourself, "You actually should have done better than that. I'm surprised you even did *that* well." Or you can reward yourself by saying, "Way to go! That really took some hard work and dedication! I'm really proud of and grateful for this achievement!" And celebrate your success.

You may feel uncomfortable and even silly speaking to yourself in this way. Especially at first and especially if you're not used to hearing very many positive things about yourself, *from* yourself. You may have to choke out the words, and it might not even feel like they mean anything in the beginning. But as you practice loving and gracious self-talk, I'm confident your emotions will catch up.

It may take some time and you may just have to feel silly and uncomfortable for a while. But keep going! Don't give up! The more you practice healthy self-talk, the easier and better it will become. And pretty soon, it'll be amongst your first responses to the situations you face. Ask the Lord to help you see, treat, and talk to yourself the way He does. He wants us to love ourselves so we can properly love others and be more effective for His Kingdom.

The more you train your thoughts to be edifying and kind, gracious and encouraging, calm and collected, the closer you'll come to parenting yourself in the loving, healthy way you've always wanted. With God's help, you really are strong enough to rewrite those negative messages from your past.

I encourage you to take some time to pinpoint the areas of your life where you're inclined to treat and talk to yourself more harshly. Identify those areas of greater struggle and have new positive messages on standby, ready to replace the old negative ones. These may be messages you've come up with or words from Holy Spirit; they could be quotes that inspire you or verses from the Bible. Please just make sure to have *something*. I promise you; God will bless it because you are blessing and honoring Him and His work when you encourage and strengthen yourself in Him. He is faithful to work *with* us to transform our thinking by the renewing of our minds. Implementing healthy, loving messages and incorporating the truth of God's Word and His love for us into our everyday lives is a great place to start!

Venturing Beyond

Before I left the last time, one of the things that kept me in bondage was the fear of living on my own. I'd never ventured out into those waters, and quite frankly, I was afraid of what I'd find when I did because I was so unhappy with who I'd become. But after taking some time to heal and reconnect with God's heart for me, I was ready to stake my claim, put down some roots, and adventure out beyond anywhere I'd ever been before. For me, that meant living on my own.

I had never felt confident about this decision until now. Because now I knew—like it finally sunk in—that I could never be alone, for my Father promised He'd never leave me. And that's where my confidence came from—*Him*, not me. Boy, did that feel good! It was a *major* victory in my life.

Was I still scared? I'm not gonna lie, I was certainly nervous, but it's like I wasn't paralyzed by fear any longer. The oppressive fear I would feel about living on my own, back when I was with Manny, was gone. Isaiah 54:14 (NKJV) says, "…You shall be far from oppression, for you shall not fear…" It doesn't say we won't fear because oppression will be far from us. No, it says we will be far from oppression because we won't fear. That's exactly how it was. It's like that fear was gone and because the fear was gone, so was the oppression that came with the fear.

Because that fear was gone, I was actually able to *enjoy* life, particularly living on my own. With the help of friends and family, I was able to move all my stuff from his house to my apartment safely. We arranged the move for when he'd be at work, and he was informed ahead of time, so I didn't have to rush around anxiously.

As I walked in the house, the temptation to get sucked back into oppression was there. But this time, I was armed with God's promises and what *He* was saying about my life. I refused to let my mind wander to the memories and words which were shared in that house. Instead, I purposed to say only what God was saying, guarding my heart with all diligence through His words and applying them as a filter to my own.

And for the first time, I felt confident instead of inferior and subservient in that atmosphere. It was another huge breakthrough for me, showing me how far I'd come and how much I really was ready to move on and try new things. I wasn't going to let fear hold me back any longer.

Re-Parenting: Affirmation and Exploration

Re-parenting is process of self-affirmation. But I'm not talking about fluffing ourselves up with empty words and growing big-headed. That's not even *real* confidence—that's just really unattractive—and because it's not real, it won't last. I'm talking about reminding ourselves of where our worth is found, telling ourselves we are people of value because *God* says so. I'm talking about speaking *God's words* over ourselves until they become *our words*.

We may be in the habit of waiting for *others* to encourage and uplift us, to compliment how we look or what we do (even if we only reject their compliments). But the truth of the matter is, we don't have to wait for *others* to encourage or esteem us. We can affirm and uplift ourselves.

> *We don't have to wait for others to encourage or esteem us. We can affirm and uplift ourselves.*

There's a huge difference between building Christ-centered confidence and false confidence—what many people call *swagger*. Being confident in the person God made us to be and valuing the way He crafted us creates beautiful, humble, and happy dependency upon Him. This makes us cognizant that our confidence comes from Christ, not our own attempts to call attention to ourselves (see Jeremiah 17:7).

Arrogance—as pompous and brazen as it is—is actually the outgrowth of insecurity. It's acting on the fear that we're not significant or worthy enough for others to notice without drawing attention to ourselves or our achievements. Self-affirmation is a healthy habit to form. Reminding ourselves of who and Whose we are is even better.

That being said, I want you to grab a pen and paper, whether it's your journal or just the back of an envelope

191

makes no difference, but it needs to be something you'll keep and carry around with you. Got them? Okay. Now I'm asking you, friend, to write down at least ten things you like about yourself. Yes, you heard me right, *at least ten!* These should include your values, your attributes, your personality, and yes, your physical features. If ten is too high a number, then start with five or three. But start *somewhere* and gradually build up to—and hopefully *exceed* ten.

It's not cocky to like and be confident in who God made you to be. It's *false* humility (which is rooted in pride) to believe it's humble to think lowly of yourself. I mean, come on! You're God's creation! He only makes good things! If He says you're good, which He does (see Genesis 1:31), who are you to object? Once you come to know and grow confident in and grateful for who God made you to be, you'll never want to be anyone else.

Remember, as a person thinks in their heart, so are they (Proverbs 23:7). In other words, whatever you think about yourself, that you will be. Please do not skip this very important exercise, even if it makes you feel awkward or uncomfortable. You'll be glad you did it later, trust me. I mean my goodness, you don't even have to show anyone unless you *want* to, this is between you and God.

We all go through difficult and discouraging times. And in such moments, it's good to look back at our lists and remember the good and positive things we've called out and called forth in lives.

Please make certain you do not include things you do for other people or causes. When struggling with codependent tendencies, we often gain our sense of self-worth through the things we do for others. This list needs to be exclusively about you. Things you like (or even *want to* like) about yourself. It should actually be a list we keep adding to because we are ever-changing from grace to grace, so it's good to come back and refresh it. We may want to add some things, change some things, or even make a whole new list all together. Either way, I suggest you don't make this a onetime deal.

As we grow in our Christ-centered confidence, we also grow braver in trying new things. These may be things we've been wanting to do but were too afraid or embarrassed to do before or things we've wanted to try but thought we couldn't. Becoming confident in the person God has created us to be helps us push past our self-inflicted limitations. And suddenly, we find a whole new host of possibilities and adventures await us, and life becomes much more exciting!

Life in Christ is a life rich with opportunities and explorations. While we may be limited in our human ability, the might and power Christ provides is limitless. With God on our side, the only limitations we have are the ones *we* impose.

You've already listed up to ten self-affirmations. Now, I want you to list at least ten things you'd like to try, achieve, and explore in your lifetime. And of course, I encourage you to keep adding to and refreshing this list as you go.

Your list can include ideas you'd like to incorporate immediately such as, every day I'd like to spend an hour or two of uninterrupted quality time with my family. Or I'd like to exercise at least 25 minutes a day, three days a week. Your items can also be long-term, I'd like to save enough money in three years, to travel to Australia. Or I'd like to go back to school to be a nurse.

The items you list should be achievable. For instance, if you can't afford to travel around the world right now, make it your goal to start a travel fund and in the meantime, enjoy exploring nearby cities, towns, and other outdoor excursions. Make sure to include challenging things that will pull you out of your comfort zone. Like taking a cooking class or dancing lessons or attending a Bible study where you can meet new people who will help you grow in your gifts and relationship with God.

Things on your list should be meaningful and fun and include items that make you laugh. For laughter not only increases our endorphins, our confidence, and our intelligence, it also increases our health and faith. Remembering to laugh and play helps us become more childlike and tenderhearted—the very things that *attract* the Kingdom of God and are required to *enter* the Kingdom of God (see Matthew 18:3, Mark 4:25, TPT).

It'd be wise to include items that will help you to achieve the hopes, goals, and dreams God has laid on your heart. Ask Him to help you take steps toward those dreams and goals that are SMART: Specific. Measurable. Attainable. Relevant. Timely. Remember, dream *big*, God-sized dreams, and seek *His* direction for your dreams. Only He knows how to get you from here to there because He is outside of time and sees our past, present, and future in one glimpse. So only He knows what word we need to hear and what direction we need to take to get us there.

In the end, the items on your list should help build a God-given, healthy perspective of yourself, your life, and the world around you. I encourage you, please don't skip these important exercises. They are key to cultivating a happier, more fulfilled, more powerful you.

Our Best Parent

God is the best Father we could ever have; He'll parent us better and more lovingly than anyone else ever could. So, let's make time to encourage ourselves in Him. Let's catch His vision for our lives—He wants to give us His vision, friend, and He's faithful to do so. All we need to do is ask and trust. Let's refuse to entertain thoughts about ourselves (and others) that He doesn't have. Let's restrain ourselves to say only what He's saying and to see what He's seeing, for where there is no vision, the people perish (Proverbs 29:18).

What we carry is *precious*—it's the most important thing about us, for what we carry is the person of God (Father, Son, Holy Spirit). The Best Parent ever. We get to walk into any room and change the options for every person in it because what we carry is not only precious, it's *powerful*. But if we're too busy stuck in the battle between our ears, constantly fighting with insecurity, shame, fear, and defeat, listening to the messages of the *past*, we'll miss out on engaging with the Most Wonderful thing about our lives, here in the *present*.

That's a missed opportunity not only for us, but the world around us. They're hungry and searching for what we carry. Even if they don't know Jesus is who they're looking for—*He's* who they're looking for. He's the answer. He's *always* the answer. So it's really important for us to connect with what He says and stop repeating and reliving the unkind, unpleasant words others spoke over us. We get to replace all that junk with His truth and come out shining—refined and sparking like gold—only more precious and far more valuable.

We get to live above and not beneath. That means we're not buried under all the nasty words of our past. We get to rise above them in victory! For us and those who come after us, for generations to come. The way we talk to and treat ourselves not only teaches others how to treat us, it affects the world around us. Words really matter. It's time we get our hearts and our heads fixed and fastened onto what He's saying and *stubbornly refuse* to change the subject.

CHAPTER TEN

All Bottled Up
(Getting a Healthy Handle on Anger)

*Whether life grinds a man down or polishes him
depends on what he's made of.*
—Kathryn Kuhlman

I was *done* being angry and *so* ready to move on—but that
didn't mean it didn't take my emotions time to catch up.
Sometimes, I could still feel them raging within me, right
below the surface. It was high time for me to learn some
new, healthy ways to channel my anger. To find outlets that
wouldn't adversely affect me or anyone else around me.

What I found wasn't just a release—it was a ground-
breaking revelation for me. Anger, if filtered correctly and
in alignment with God, could actually be *constructive*.
Up until now, I'd only experienced anger in the negative
sense. Explosive, unhealthy anger that went unchecked and
unchanneled. I'd seen and experienced firsthand, the way it

was able to destroy relationships, marriages, and people. I'd seen the resentment unresolved anger could cause because I'd lived with it for more years than I cared to count.

Resentment toward Manny and resentment toward myself. Resentment toward my life and my circumstances. And to be completely honest, I even carried resentment toward others who seemed to have it better than I did. I didn't want to feel that way anymore. For this change to take place within me, I knew I had to do something different with my very real emotions of anger and resentment.

As I sought the One who made my emotions and was able to help me handle and channel them best, He showed me anger isn't sin. It's what we *do* with our anger that matters. How we *act* upon our anger is where sin can come in, by acting upon it in destructive and divisive ways toward ourselves and others.

In the process of working through the emotions of internal heartache and past hurts, you may have noticed some anger stirring up on the inside of *you*, friend. Anger concerning your past and possibly present circumstances. You may not have even realized just *how* angry you are until you started doing this work. I want to assure you; this *isn't* an uncommon reaction.

You might not have ever experienced these kinds of feelings before—especially if you were living in denial for any length of time. You may have also believed yourself to be powerless against your emotions and/or situation. Unable to do anything about them except to wait for someone else to fix them for you, feeling stuck and like a victim of your own reality.

The truth is, you're *not* powerless, my dear. You're not powerless against your emotions or any situation. You know why? Because you're a much-loved child of God Almighty, you've been made in the image of the One Who is *All*-Powerful. He's given us *everything* we need to live victoriously. When we step into that belief it becomes our reality, and when we walk in that reality, we become triumphant over every issue we'll ever encounter.

Heaven's reality trumps our own. It is *superior* and *supernatural* to our natural reality. Ephesians 2:19 tells us we are citizens of Heaven and family members of God; as such, we are empowered with the right to see from His perspective. Armed with this right, we're able to enter into every issue and emotion of life already positioned for victory. As we walk in this triumphant attitude by living *from* Heaven, *to* earth, we become increasingly healthy.

You know what else will happen? Others around us will notice how healthy we're becoming. They will notice the positive change *within* us, which will spread to the environment *around* us. Because the environment inside of us will always affect the environment outside of us. This is why it's imperative we discover ways to healthily work through our emotions and anger. If we want to live in a healthy *environment*, we must first learn how to have healthy *emotions*.

Healthy Boundaries, Healthy Emotions

A couple of chapters ago, we talked at length about unhealthy soul ties, we discussed: what they are; how they are formed; and how to break them so we can walk in freedom. Now I want to take a quick moment to talk about codependency. Codependency is basically the breakdown of healthy relationship exchanges, characterized by an excessive dependence upon or control of anyone or anything. The root cause of codependency stems from the fear of not having our needs met—*particularly* our need for love. When this innate need goes unmet, unhealthy patterns, compulsions, and addictions are often the result as it sends us searching for someone or something to fill our love-void.

Like toxic soul ties, codependency is formed through unhealthy interactions, relationships, and exchanges and the way we view them. These encounters may have happened when we were three or when we were thirteen, but if they aren't addressed, they'll follow us into and well past our thirties. Everything we discussed in chapter eight about breaking free from unhealthy soul ties can be directly applied to codependency since they travel so closely down the same road. If you need to go back through chapter eight with this in mind, please feel free.

With codependency comes a misunderstanding or lack of healthy boundaries, and healthy boundaries are essential to getting a healthy handle on our emotions. If we're someone who struggles with codependency and toxic soul ties, it's common to experience a sense of guilt or denial associated with emotions like anger. As we become increasingly accustomed to putting everyone else's needs above our own, we may feel bad or guilty when we are the ones that have real and valid needs requiring time and attention.

Healthy boundaries don't serve to make us selfish; they serve to make us aware of our God-given value and love so we can become healthily equipped to serve others without trying to be their savior.

This is where healthy boundaries come in. Healthy boundaries don't serve to make us selfish; they serve to make us aware of our God-given value and love so we can become healthily equipped to serve others without trying to be their savior.

200

The Call

The call came from the front desk in the middle of my workday, interrupting my train of thought. "Excuse me, Hope, you have a visitor up front."

"Okay I'll be right there, thank you," I found a good stopping point in my report and walked up the hall that led to the reception area. As I opened the door, what I saw made me sick to my stomach. Manny was hanging over the counter making small talk with the receptionist. I don't know why I hadn't expected him to show up at the office; he'd already tried to track me down everywhere else and in every other way.

Instantly I was shaking on the inside, but I *refused* to let it show. I wouldn't allow him to see how upset I was by his presence. I was a month or more into my codependency recovery and drew heavily upon the boundaries I'd been learning, internally asking Jesus to make them real to me in this moment. A strength, not my own, shot through my soul, as I was reminded of God's great love for me and the worth, *He* says I have. Suddenly, I knew I could face anything because He was with me, working through me. I straightened my back and headed his way, directing him to follow me outside. *I* was taking the lead on the conversation this time—and it wouldn't be before everyone's eyes to see.

I led him to a quiet corner of the parking lot, took a deep breath, and asked him with all the courage I could muster, "*What* are you doing here? You can't just come in and interrupt me at *work!*" My response shocked him; he wasn't used to *this* Hope. Finally, he fumbled around about how he missed me and how life wasn't the same without me ... "Oh, and I came to bring you your mail." (My *junk mail*, mind you, since I'd already transferred my address.) I waited as he muttered around some more until he finally got to his point, "Is there any way you'd be willing to come back home?"

"I have a *new* home now," was my reply, "and I'm *happy* there."

"Is there any way we could work things out? I'll do anything. I'll go to counseling and you can even meet the baby and be more involved. It'll be different this time, I promise, Hope."

My response came so quickly it surprised even me, "What we had feels like a million years ago, Manny. I simply don't feel that way about you anymore." I was overcome, and honestly absolutely relieved, by how naturally those words rolled off my tongue. What would have made me melt like putty in his hands before only served to make me nauseous now. "Listen, thanks for the mail. Just throw it away from now on, and don't come here again. You have no reason to. I won't be changing my mind about us—*ever*. I pray you find God's love and step into peace, but it won't be with me. *He's* the One you're searching for; it's *His* love you need, not *mine*. He's your Savior, not me. I can't be your savior, and I'm done trying."

I turned on my heels and walked away, feeling more victorious than I had in over eight years. A twinge of guilt arose within my emotions and I told it to go away. I didn't have anything to feel bad about. I was finally setting some healthy boundaries, and not feeling bad for Manny was at the top of my list. Because if he could make me feel bad for him, he could make me fall for him again. Neither one of those were healthy options for me, and I refused to go down that path again. I could feel my Father's smile over me as I walked away in victory. I was so grateful for how He used this situation to show me where I was in my healing. I went back inside with such a sense of peace and anticipation for my future. Bring it on. I was ready!

The Secret Place

Sometimes, God calls us *out* of hiding. He calls us to take His hand and run with Him through the open field toward the dawning of a new day—a horizon brimming with new adventures and overflowing with wonderful opportunities. Other times, God calls us *into* hiding. His sweet Presence pulls us into the Secret Place where we learn to explore and grow in our intimacy with God, the place where we find rest for our soul, our mind, and our emotions.

The Secret Place is where we unveil our hearts before our Beloved. It's where we learn how to hear His voice and listen. Listen to what His heart says about us and listen to what He's saying about the world and the lives around us. Here, we learn how to listen and decree what *He* is saying about anything and everything we will ever encounter. The Secret Place is where we go to unburden ourselves from heavy loads and cast our cares and questions onto Jesus. It's where we learn how to seek first His Kingdom and live from Heaven to earth. In the Secret Place, we pull Heaven down as we enter into our inheritance and partner with Jesus, the One who paid the highest price for our partnership.

This is where we learn the greatness and the goodness of our God. In the Secret Place, we learn to trust as we recall His kindness and recount our history with Him. We experience sweet encounters with the Father's heart as we *intentionally* remember what He has done, divinely redirecting our perspective of every circumstance.

In the Secret Place, we learn how to healthily sort through and process our thoughts, feelings, and emotions. Knowing our Father isn't angry at or afraid of our emotions makes all the difference in the world, especially since our discussions so far may have triggered some emotions you didn't even know you had. If we don't know we have a safe place to work through what we feel, we will unwisely try to sort out our own emotions. The problem with that is *we* can't heal our emotions, but *He* can. If we refuse to let Him into the deep places of our heart, we'll miss out on a deeper revelation of who He is and who He wants to be for us.

The Secret Place is where the cup of *suffering* becomes the cup of *joy*. Here we learn the beauty of surrender and how it leads us to life, not loss. As Jesus said in Matthew 16:24–25 (TPT), "...as you continually surrender to My ways...you will continually discover true life."

This is right where I found myself in July of 2007, discovering true life and new ways to live. Manny and I were officially over. The papers were signed, and our court date was freshly behind us. I walked out of the courthouse and released a huge sigh of relief. It felt like I could finally breathe after holding my breath for eight *lo-o-ng* years.

Immediately following our legal appointment, my loving mom planned a road trip for us to visit my beloved great-uncle. He lived deep in the mountains of Kentucky, away from all the clatter and chatter of a fast-paced society. Being one of my favorite spots, it was exactly the therapy I needed, right when I needed it. (Thanks, Mom. You're the best!)

I longed to be tucked away within the shadows of the mountain. Rolling hills covering me on every side. As we drove, I reflected on what a beautiful picture this was of our Father's love. How He tucks us into His heart and how His Presence surrounds us on every side, protectively guarding our lives.

When we got out on the open road, I remember feeling so free. Like someone who'd just served their prison sentence, walking out of the gate for the first time. It was wonderful and yet unnerving all the same. Who was I? What was I going to do now? These questions threatened the corners of my mind. But rather than give them a place to speak, my mom and I used the drive to turn our hearts to the Father. Worshiping and praising Him, the Redeemer and Mender of broken hearts. The One who steadies our feet, so we don't fall.

We finally arrived and settled ourselves into my great-uncle's humble abode. He wasn't a materialistic man of great means. Instead, he held whole-heartedly to the things that mattered most and never seemed to be in want of anything. Lack never even seemed to be something he considered. Laughter was his language, and love was his song and all who came near him couldn't help but sing along.

After we settled in, I started off for a run to release the pent-up anxiety from the events earlier that day. My mom asked if she could join me, so off we went, up and down and around the mountains surrounding my uncle's home. Now, before I go any further into my story, there's something you need to know about me—I *love* horses. I've only ridden a few times in my life, but I find them so beautifully breathtaking and awesome. These gentle giants remind me how power doesn't mean pride, neither should it lead to pain but purpose.

It felt so good to fill our lungs with fresh mountain air as we climbed to the top of the pinnacle. When we finally made it, the mountain leveled out into a lovely, wide open field surrounded by wooden fencing. As we looked around, we saw a huge herd of horses in the distance, and right as we approached the fence, they all turned in our direction and started heading our way. Never before or since have I seen so many horses together in one place. They were beautiful and so friendly, greeting us with nickers and neighs as they allowed us to rub their soft noses and pet their majestic manes. My eyes fill with tears at the memory.

What a tender Father we have to send me this unforgettable gift. As I stood there before these magnificent creatures, I could feel His love surrounding me. I was awestruck by His intentionality. I mean, He knows me better than *anyone*. So, *He* better than anyone, knows how much I love horses. And here, He took what I love and used it to reveal *His* love. It was a tangible, physical reminder of how He tenderly held my heart. I could *certainly* trust Him.

I may not have known what my future held, but I didn't need to know. I knew the One who held, not only my heart, but my future in His hands. He was already equipping me for what lay ahead: winding hills and wide-open fields full of unexpected adventures and treasures. I didn't have to know what was ahead. I simply needed to *follow*.

Reactive Responses to Anger

Do you have a quick temper? Does it come in quickly and exit just as fast? Do you expect others around you to be over it just as easily as you are? Or maybe you suppress your anger—bottle it up and keep a lid on it. But like a shaken can of soda, you eventually *pop,* and what's inside comes spilling out all over you and everyone else around you.

Do you internalize your anger—take your temper out on yourself with destructive decisions and actions? You may be someone who knows how it feels to have others take their anger out on you, and you refuse to pass that sort of pain on to someone else. But anger doesn't just disappear. It's gonna go somewhere. So, you turn it inward. Instead of hurting others, you turn to hurting yourself. Suicidal attempts, self-mutilation, eating disorders, and addiction are not uncommon among those who suppress their anger.

When it comes to anger, maybe you don't really know *what* to do with it. So, you make light of emotionally awkward situations and downplay distressing discussions.

Do you shut down when you're angry?

Give a cold shoulder?

Push others away?

Though these responses to anger could all be considered *common*, none of them are *constructive*. Handling anger improperly causes a lot of stress for everyone involved. Friends. Family. You. Your kids. The clerk on the other side of the checkout counter. The car that just pulled out in front of you. *Everyone.*

When we get all fired up and emotionally charged, we send our adrenal glands (our fight or flight responses) into high hear. When this happens, we're moody, we don't think clearly, our bodily functions are slowed, and our metabolism is off-balanced. Anger, when handled unhealthily, not only affects everyone around us, it affects our body—and *not* in a good way.

When we look at anger this way, it's easy to see why living in a continual state of stress is so harmful to our health. If this is how *not* to handle anger, how *do* we handle it healthily? Remember, anger itself, isn't the problem. The problem is the way we *respond* to it.

Wise Responses to Anger

Here's the thing about anger. It gets a pretty bad rap, so we tend to try and shut it down. Stuff it in. Shove it away and act like it doesn't exist.

When we hear the word *anger*, we often envision people road-raging it down the highway. We imagine parents screaming at their kids in the store or those who have used us as an outlet for their rage. All of these are really good examples of explosive, uncontrolled anger. Destructive anger. But if handled properly, anger can actually be quite constructive. So the question is, how? How do we move from *destructive* anger to *constructive* anger?

If handled properly, anger can actually be quite constructive. The question is, how? How do we move from destructive anger to constructive anger?

As we've already said, healthy boundaries lead to healthy emotions, even emotions like anger. If we don't know how to live within healthy boundaries, we'll likely find ourselves giving and giving until we absolutely cannot give anymore. As we continue to pour out, we may even start to resent the ones we're pouring into. The longer we linger in this place of fulfilling everyone else's needs, the greater we give unhealthy emotions the opportunity to boil just below the surface. Until finally ... BAM! We erupt in an explosion of anger. This way of processing emotions such as anger or exasperation isn't only unhealthy for you, it's unhealthy for those around you.

When the brake lights go out in our car or we forget to change the oil, our dashboard indicator lights up to let us know. Anger, when applied constructively, works the same way. It warns us when our boundaries are being crossed or our needs are going unmet.

For those of us who've struggled with unhealthy soul ties or codependency, this isn't a signal we should ignore—even if that's usually our response. To cultivate health boundaries, we must first recognize that no one can fulfill our deepest longings for love and intimacy, belonging, acceptance, and approval except *God*. So if we're not spending time in His presence, of course we're going to feel edgy and irritable. Because communion with Him is truly what we were made for.

Healthy communion with *others* comes out of our healthy communion with *God*. Time spent with Him—whether it's in quiet or as we're doing the dishes or washing the car—will absolutely affect the way we do relationships. For it affects the way we see ourselves which always affects the way we see others.

Healthy boundaries and outlets start with a healthy acknowledgment of our feelings. When I say we acknowledge our feelings, I *don't* mean we let them master us. Feelings never make good masters. Healthy feelings follow healthy choices. As we make our emotions *servants*, rather than *masters*, we're well on our way to healthy choices and healthy boundaries.

Acknowledging our feelings means we actually *address* the emotional issues we might not have been willing to look at before. Sorting through our emotions is just like stopping to read what the indicator on our dash is warning us about. We're heeding the warnings in our hearts and finding out why they're there in the first place. We're *not* giving our emotions the opportunity to rule over our lives and lead us where we don't want to go. Because the truth is, sometimes I'm emotional because I didn't sleep well the night before, or I'm hungry, or I feel frazzled about my cram-packed schedule (which is another boundary issue). But other times, I feel emotional because I haven't stopped to address the underlying issue(s) *tied* to my emotions.

Let me give you a brief example. Let's say you and your friend meet every Wednesday for lunch, but each time she (or he) picks where you're going to eat. Initially, it's fine ... but eventually, it starts to wear on you, especially when they reject your suggestions or ignore them altogether. Over time, your frustration turns to anger, and as time continues to drag on, you become *so* angry you don't even know why you were friends in the first place. Now, you can't *wait* to see them because you're totally gonna unleash all your anger on them and tell them everything you've been holding back on saying. The sad thing is, all of this could have been easily avoided and you could have spared yourself *and* your friendship all kinds of frustration.

Once you started feeling frustrated and angry, your emotions were warning you that your boundaries were being crossed. In this case, your thoughts and ideas were being rejected and ignored. Anger was the sign that something was wrong or missing in your relationship with your friend. If you had given yourself time to find out what that was and respectfully addressed the issue with them, you would've sustained your friendship. But because anger was ignored—until it refused to be ignored any longer—your friendship has suffered. Now *you* feel foolish since it seems like you were unable to control your emotions well enough to civilly discuss the issue.

This may seem like a silly example, but this sort of stuff happens, doesn't it? I mean, how many times has anger made a fool of you? It's certainly made a fool of me—more times than I care to count! All because I didn't take the time to find out *why* I was feeling *what* I was feeling.

When you look at anger in this light, can you see how it has alerted you of boundaries being crossed or needs going unmet many times before? Do you find yourself feeling guilty when you're angry or ignoring your anger until you can't ignore it any longer and eventually explode? Do you have a negative outlook on anger because you've been hurt by the anger of others? Are there times you find yourself getting angry and you don't even know why?

I encourage you, friend, when you feel your anger starting to arise, rather than avoiding it, ask yourself a couple of questions. First, is my anger toward this issue valid? Or am I just hungry, sleepy, or feeling overly emotional right now?

Second, how have my sleep patterns been? Am I getting enough sleep for the demands, responsibilities, and issues in my life? Lastly, is my anger geared toward the person, situation, or myself? If you find your anger isn't simply the result of last night's pizza or because you're overly exhausted or emotional or hungry, take the time to examine how or where and in which relationships your boundaries are being crossed or what needs are going unmet.

Your answers may surprise you. Or maybe they've been right under your nose the whole time, but you haven't *taken* the time to notice. You may even find that it's *you* who hasn't been validating your *own* needs, and therefore, you may be the reason you're feeling what you're feeling. If you are the reason behind your anger, ask God to give you the grace you need to lighten your workload, declutter your schedule, or simply take more quiet time to decompress, pray, and connect with His heart. Most importantly, unburden all your anxiety and shame, heaviness and self-hate onto Him and let Him replace it with His mighty love, power, and peace. He'll make the exchange for you as you simply rest in Him, let go, and refuse to take it all back.

Remember, my dear one, you are *not* powerless against what you find. You are a powerful child of God who has *all* the support and strength of Heaven behind you!

Healthy Outlets for Anger

Not only do we need to know *how* to respond to anger wisely, but we also need to know *what* to do with it healthily. An important part of processing our anger is finding healthy outlets for it. The outlets we use for our anger may vary based on what we're upset about, but I've found not having a healthy release for my anger only makes it grow worse. We don't want that.

Unresolved, unreleased anger leads to resentment, and resentment leads to even more issues. That's *not* what we need when we're angry! We need to *decompress*, not *add* to our stress. With this in mind, let's take a look at some healthy ways we can *release* our anger.

Are you someone who gets nervous and jittery when you're angry? You may need to release your anger by going on an invigorating walk or quick jog. You may find that throwing up some weights at your gym is far better for you than throwing down some arguments at your home. For you, doing something physical will likely help you mentally sort through your emotions and their source. Getting your nervous energy out would be a wise route to take *before* you act upon what you're feeling and respond to those involved.

When you feel anger creeping in, do you become anxious and upset, maybe even a bit panicky? Then you may find Christian-based yoga, Pilates, or other deep-breathing exercises beneficial. These practices help clear our airways as well as our emotions as they promote peaceful processes and pauses. Rather than incorporating new aged or mystical ideologies into your yoga or Pilates practice, I encourage you to pray through your poses. Meditate upon a Scripture instead of a mantra. As you work your way around your mat, ask God to work His way around your heart. Breathe deeply and imagine His presence filling and expanding your every cell. Allow this expansion by stilling your emotions and releasing the tension in your muscles and mind so your heart will be ready to receive what He has to lovingly say.

Maybe you get terribly tongue-tied and flustered when frustration knocks on your door. If this sounds like you, you may find journaling particularly helpful. In your journal, you can log all your frustrations and feelings in one safe place.

I find writing helps me sort through my thoughts and emotions. This process reminds me that my emotions don't own me. My emotions are my servants *not* my master. *I* get to tell them what is true, not the other way around. In this way, journaling helps me put self-control into practice. As Proverbs 29:11 says, a foolish person gives full vent to their rage, but a wise person will bite their tongue in self-control until afterwards and bring calm in the end. Rather than foolishly airing out all my emotions in the heat of the moment, writing helps me filter them from God's perspective. Then, I can calmly share what I need to say without losing control because there's more than just *my* feelings that need to be considered.

The nice thing about journaling is we don't have to share what we've written unless we *want* to—when and *if* it's wise and safe to do so. That being said, if you're in an unsafe environment where your words can be used against you, keep your journal in a safe place. Journaling is an intimate exchange where we openly share *our* heart with God and listen for what *His* heart has to say about the issues we're experiencing. If you can't seem to get the words out when you're upset, or if you're not in a safe place to express them, then I'm certain you'll find this therapeutic process helpful to your healing.

Maybe you have the opposite problem. Rather than being tongue-tied, you're quick witted, and your cutting remarks hit their target every time. You might feel good about the apt aim of your words at first, but later on, you're filled with regret over the wounds your words have inflicted. Because we can't take back what we say—even when we want to. Thankfully, we can always pray for restoration to take place within the relationships we've wounded with our words. We can ask God for wisdom to know what steps we need to take toward pursuing peace, and if possible—and *safe*—reconciliation, within those relationships.

Some of those steps will include exploring healthy outlets for your anger. So, when it seems someone is pushing your buttons and you know you're getting to the place where you could very well say some things you'll regret later—*walk away*. Go for a run. Lift weights. Do some yardwork. Shoot some hoops. Sort out what you're feeling on paper. Pray and read the wisdom God gives us in His Word. Just do something *constructive* with the rush of adrenaline you my experience with anger.

I want to be clear; it would be wise to talk to those involved in or affected by the new direction you're choosing to take in how you handle your anger. So please do the smart thing and talk to them *ahead of time*, like *before* you leave. Let those in your circle know you're actively working toward healthier outlets, so if you need to take some time to decompress by walking away, ask them to respect your need for space. You may also want to come to an agreement on how much time you take so the other person is assured that you're not abandoning them.

As you work through healthy outlets for your anger, please remember helpful these tips:

- Overtraining—working out too much—is not a healthy outlet for our anger.

- Overreacting—making more of the situation than is necessary—is not a healthy outlet for our anger.

- Over-criticizing—giving ourselves or others an extra hard time—is not a healthy outlet for our anger.

- Overeating—eating even after we've had enough—is not a healthy outlet for our anger.

- Undereating—not eating as a means of punishing ourselves or those who hurt us—is not a healthy outlet for our anger.

- Over-arguing—hounding someone, following them around, and refusing them the space they need to sort through their feelings—is definitely not a healthy outlet for our anger.

- Under-involvement—ignoring or staying disconnected from life and those we love—is not a healthy outlet for our anger.

- Overindulging—living a life of continual excess—is not a healthy outlet for our anger.

The point in finding healthy outlets for our anger is to protect others and ourselves from the destruction that carelessly venting our anger can bring. But it's also to get us into the place where we can calmly communicate with the ones involved. So let's remember, friend, half of communication is *listening*, and there are far more emotions to consider than our own. When framing our responses to any anger we may feel, we would be wise to follow the words found in James 1:19 and be quick to listen, slow to speak, and slow to get angry.

When we allow the sun to set on our anger, the Bible says we give the enemy an opportunity to manipulate our emotions (see Ephesians 4:26, 27). We don't want that. We don't want it for our lives or our relationship(s) or those we love. So let's be wise and resolve what we can of the issue and refuse to go to bed angry. We can put a pin in the conversation if we must and agree to come back together another time to work toward resolution. When we make a conscious effort to go to sleep in peace, we have sounder sleep. What's more, we safeguard our relationships from resentment and emotional manipulation of the enemy. All really good reasons to work toward resolution *before* we go to bed.

Resentment:
Finding Release by Laying Down Our Rights

I woke up in a cold sweat. My pajamas were stuck to my skin, tightly wrapped all around my arms and legs for the perspiration pouring out of me. Fear was taunting me. Cackling in the darkness as my imagination ran wild with deadly delusions. I didn't know where I was or who was with me. I tried very hard to remember the date or what I'd done the day before, anything to tie me to reality, but it was like every rational answer alluded me.

Breathe. I needed to breathe. Kicking off the restrictive blankets, I slowly breathed deep in through my nose and out of my mouth until my heartrate returned to normal. Finally, I worked up the courage to feel around beside me to see if he was really there. Relief flooded my soul as my hand found an empty space where he used to lay.

Since I finally left Manny, I'd been awoken by the same sort of nightmare several times a week. The memories and emotional trauma from my past mixed with images of what life could have looked like had I not left and haunted me as I slept. The images were always so vivid, so *awful*. I'd wake up full of panic, so out of touch that I actually *expected* him to be in the bed beside me. Each time I had to catch my breath while I built up the courage to feel around me. And each time I found he wasn't there, I was brought back to the present, filled with unspeakable relief.

I sat up, feeling the blood returning to my extremities. I was *so sick* of this. It *had* to stop. I was tired of being traumatized by someone who wasn't even in my life anymore. I took a long drink of water to rehydrate my body and soothe my scratchy throat. I switched the lamp on beside me and sat up straighter, my new little puppy groaning in protest from all my movement. I grabbed my Bible and flipped to the passage my mom taught me to read as a little girl, whenever I was scared. I had most of it memorized, still I wanted to see it with my own eyes. Psalm 91 had become the reassuring resort I ran to when fear tried to be louder than the truth.

My eyes burned with tiredness but still the verses brought comfort. "He who dwells in the secret place of the Most High shall abide under the shadow of the Almighty. I will say of the Lord, 'He is my refuge and my fortress; my God, in Him I will trust.' Surely He shall deliver you ..." (verses 1-3, NKJV). There it was ... I was *delivered*. He promised to deliver me. So why was I experiencing so much torment?

As I sat and meditated upon this promise, my heart started to slow and settle within my chest. My little puppy had since snuggled up beside me and was now snoring in his sleep. The sound was actually quite soothing, tying me to the present. Here in this moment of stillness, I invited God to speak to my heart. Asking Him to show me where I had allowed fear to come in and why my peaceful sleep was being attacked. I was *sick* of waking up with panic, in a cold sweat. I *needed* and was finally *ready* to see whatever He had to show me, even if it was hard to hear. If there was something I was doing to keep me from entering into His promise, I needed to know about it. Blaming other people or things for my problem wasn't helping me and ignorance was obviously not bliss.

In the most tender way, He started talking to me about the ways I'd been blocking His deliverance. By holding onto the hurt and anger of unresolved issues, I had allowed resentment to have access to my heart. And by giving resentment access to my heart, I'd opened the door to torment and trauma. While entertaining what felt like my *right* to be angry, I'd unintentionally opened my heart to *unwelcomed* visitors.

If I wanted the nightmares to stop and the torment and trauma to end, my right to be resentful had to end too. I want to be clear; it's not like I was outrightly holding onto resentment or counting all the reasons I had to hate Manny. To be honest, most of the time I wasn't even thinking about him or aware of my emotions related to him. I was just ready to move on. But in all of my moving on, there was one thing I was for sure—and that was *angry*.

I was plain old angry. It's not like I was angry at *him*, specifically. I found myself angry at *all* men, and to be honest, I was more than angry. I actually *expected* every single guy (besides my dad and my brother) to be a no good, abusive liar (sorry about that guys!).

In my hurt, I shut out all men, saying I would rather stay single for the rest of my life since I could *never* trust any man to be faithful in a relationship. I had completely put my heart out there, time and time again, and look where it got me ... brokenhearted and feeling like a fool. I *refused* to feel like a fool *ever* again.

Unconsciously using anger as a means of self-protection, I put walls up around my heart so no one could hurt it again; not realizing how much I was actually hurting myself in the process. I was so focused on all the reasons I had to be angry that I couldn't see how I was *still* allowing Manny to control my emotions. In my resentment, I wasn't only giving him a right to control my emotions, I was giving fear and trauma a right to torment my mind.

Until now.

Here in this moment of revelation, I was ready to surrender all the anger and hurt in my heart. I had been holding onto things that were only working to *ruin* me. All of a sudden, the thought made me sick to my stomach. I didn't want to hold onto anything my Father knew I shouldn't have. I was ready to stop reliving the painful memories I had with Manny. Ready to give up my right to be angry. Ready to stop expecting every man I'd ever meet to hurt me. I could now clearly see how this had only kept me under his control.

I could completely let go of my past. I didn't have to live with the fear of it happening all over again. I wasn't that girl anymore. A radical transformation was taking place on the inside of me—and a big part of that was learning how to let go. Giving up my right to live from a place of resentment, meant gaining my right to live from a place of His wholeness. I couldn't have both. Jesus hadn't paid the highest price for *half* my heart. If I wanted to be whole, if I wanted to be healed, if I wanted to be delivered and set free, I had to give Him my *whole* heart—He was *wholly* worthy of it.

The truth is, friend, resentment can keep us in a holding pattern until our wrong is resolved—until we have what we often call, *closure*. The thing is, not everyone is going to give us closure. Not everyone is going to apologize, no matter how much we might deserve it. But here's the good news, when we let go of our resentments and hurts with the Lord's help, we can find our own closure.

When we get to the place where we can finally say, enough is enough and we're really ready to move on, God will give us the grace to follow through and step into our new. He's the One who picks up all our pieces and puts us back together again.

No matter how much we might want it to, *resentment* will never lead to *restitution*. It'll never restore what's been broken or pay back what we've lost. In fact, resentment keeps us broken and disconnected. Like refusing to put the finishing pieces into the puzzle, it leaves us incomplete, walking around with holes in our heart. We might think we're protecting ourselves by holding onto our hurt, but we only end up hurting ourselves more in the process.

When God asks us to give up our right to resent those who have harmed us, it's only because He wants to make our heart whole. Handing Him over the parts that hurt us most is the most liberating thing we can do. He takes our broken pieces and with His very own heart, makes ours whole. Wow. That's who our Father is for us, each and every one of us.

Resentment won't ever stop on its own. It'll ruin our lives along with our health. It manifests itself in ways like indigestion, headaches, and body aches. If left to fester, resentment can even lead to destructive disorders and depression. When we welcome resentment, we welcome other *unwelcomed* guests, just as I did. Nightmares, fearful imaginations, and other disorders of panic will work to destroy our peace.

Oh, my friend, it's *so* not worth it. If you struggle with resentment, I get it, I *really* do. I have simply found it's just not worth the tradeoff. I encourage you to take some time with our Father today and allow Him to speak to you about the areas He's asking you to let go of and lay down. Surrender isn't scary, and it doesn't even have to be hard. Surrender is what makes us *come alive* on the inside. Laying down our own rights allow us to pick up His. I'd rather live with the rights *He* gives me any day, living by my own only led to a lot of harm.

When we lay down our right to harbor resentment or hurts from our past, we pick up our rights to live free and full of joy—we pick up our right to *forgive*. You heard me right, forgiveness is actually our *right*. It's as much for *our* sake as it is *theirs*. For when we live from forgiveness, we live from freedom.

CHAPTER ELEVEN

Forgive for Goodness Sake
(Finding Freedom in Forgiveness)

If it weren't for God's grace, you and I wouldn't be
able to live for even one more minute.
—Billy Graham

As I looked around my apartment, I felt a sense of accomplishment arising within me. It was the first time I'd ever officially lived on my own. I was *finally* doing it! Facing my fears and actually feeling secure—another *first* for me. In fact, my life was filling up with all kinds of *firsts*. I was excited!

I sat at my kitchen counter and felt overwhelmed with amazement as I reflected on the transformation that had recently taken place within me. My heart overflowed with gratitude, so thankful I wasn't still stuck in what had tried to overtake me only a few short days ago. I paused as the memory of that day came rushing back to me ...

Everyone had just left, and I was *exhausted*. The hustle and bustle of moving was over at last. All my stuff had been sorted and I was all settled. There wasn't a body in sight. It was just me and my little doggy, Buster Brown, left to face the great big world all by ourselves. That's how it felt in the moment, at least. All of a sudden, a sinking feeling filled my soul. I'd prepared myself for this move as much as possible. Still, I hadn't expected to face such an overwhelming sense of loneliness. It hadn't only caught me by surprise, it caught me completely *off guard*.

Suddenly, I was overcome by a series of *awful* thoughts, they fired in rapid succession relentlessly echoing in my ears. Why was I even alive? What was the point of my existence, anyway? Who really even cared that I was around? Obviously, I wasn't good for myself, let alone anyone else, so what was the point of living? I'd wasted over eight years of my life—that's eight years I could *never* get back! What had I been thinking? What took me so long to *finally* see the light? How could I have been *so stupid?* I don't think I'll *ever* be able to forgive myself for *such* stupidity. I was lonely and it was all my fault. If I had been wiser, I wouldn't be here, stuck starting life all over again.

I'd be living like all my other happily married friends, off having families, living perfect lives. That's where I should have been. Why wasn't I farther ahead in life by now? Oh, that's right, because I made dumb decisions. I should've listened to my instincts and runaway at the altar. Actually, if I was going there, I should've listened to wisdom and left *long* before we were even engaged. I would've been so much farther ahead in life right now. Ugh, what was I thinking?

I felt like such a failure. What was the point in even trying? Everything I touched went to ruin, including my own life. Life would be far better for everyone if I wasn't even around. I was only a burden to my parents; I'd be doing them *and* myself a favor if I just ended it all now.

The thoughts were choking me. Filling my mind with images of how I could take my own life. I walked around my apartment *literally* trying to get away from the images, but no matter where I turned, they were there. I sat down on my bed and took a deep breath. I needed to *breathe*, get some perspective, and someone to talk me off the ledge and back onto stable ground.

Before I changed my mind, I reached out to my prayer-partner friend. If anyone could relate to what I was feeling, she could. We'd had a solid history of holding up each other's arms in battle, waging war together and fighting the good fight of faith for longer than I could remember. I grabbed my phone and shakily dialed her number. My thoughts turned to our friendship as the phone rang. We hadn't seemed as close since I left Manny, but I figured it was just my imagination working overtime and chalked it up to us both being busy. It felt like the phone had been ringing for at least five minutes when she finally answered. As soon as I heard her voice, relief flooded my soul—but it wouldn't last.

She had answered, but unfortunately, she wasn't in a place where she could talk. It simply wasn't a good time. She was sorry, but she had to go. And just like that (*snap*), I was left alone with life-threatening thoughts all over again.

I took another deep breath, maybe no one *really would* care if I was gone. I mean, wasn't this a sign? Would it really be better if I wasn't here? My heart sunk to my stomach with the thought. Suddenly, I felt sick.

I realized I'd been holding my breath and exhaled as I prayed, "Lord, if someone doesn't reach out to me in the next thirty minutes, I'm really doing it this time. It feels like this place would be better off without me. If I'm wrong, I really need you to prove it. I need to know I belong. I need to know You see me and that Your love for me isn't merely a theory, it's *more real* than I am. If even one person reaches out in the next half hour to tell me they care, I'll take it as Your way of telling me the same and that You see my life as precious and full of purpose."

Not even five minutes later, my mom called to tell me they were on the way. She said my dad had suddenly felt an overwhelming sense to see me and tell me how much he loves me. He needed me to know he was here for me, no matter what I needed. His job was to point me back to my Heavenly Father's love, and he was on his way to do just that.

Less than twenty minutes later, they were at my door, arms overflowing with groceries and love. My dad *immediately* dropped his bags and grabbed me, eyes flooding with tears. Somehow, he knew my life had been in danger. He held me close and looked me in the eye, affirming me and reminding me how precious I am to them, my family and friends, but most of all to my Heavenly Father. Right there in my living room, he and my mom held me as tears streamed down our faces. With their arms around me in a warm embrace, they asked God to reveal Himself to me in greater ways than ever before, reminding Him—and more importantly *me*—of His faithful promises and increasing my faith with every word.

They had no idea how timely their arrival was until I shared with them the demonic thoughts that had been attacking my mind all afternoon before they got there. I hadn't been so close to taking my own life since I was seventeen, and *both* times, God sovereignly stepped in and saved me. What a faithful Father we have. His loving intervention is absolutely amazing.

My little doggy whined beside me, interrupting my thoughts and bringing me back to the present. The events from a few days ago faded from my mind as Buster Brown reminded me of my responsibilities: it was time for his breakfast and he was hungry. I walked over to the pantry, got a scoop of his favorite food and dumped it in his bowl. He happily wagged his tail in appreciation. As I closed the pantry door, I found myself shaking my head in amazement. It was hard to believe only a few short days ago I'd been seriously considering taking my life, while today I was filled with so much hope for my future.

I came back around the counter to where my Bible and journal were opened, but I was too overcome with gratitude to sit down. Instead, I started walking around my apartment, raising my hands high in surrender, praising God for saving me from the enemy's plan to overtake me with *their* toxic thoughts of unforgiveness, self-hatred, and suicide. I didn't have to live in that junk any longer. It wasn't *my* identity, it was *theirs*.

My identity was forgiven and free in Christ! For the first time that I could remember, my mind wasn't filled with thoughts of self-hatred and reasons I didn't deserve forgiveness. Regret was no longer my portion, for I was feasting at the table of the redeemed.

Jesus had set me free, now it was my job to *stay* free. Staying free meant letting the peace of God rule in my heart and guard my mind. It meant choosing to forgive myself for my past, as He *already* had. If I wanted to stay free, it meant I could no longer get into conversations with the enemy, rather God's Word would be my only confession. Regardless of what I felt, I would choose to value what God said *over* my feelings, my emotions would catch up; I knew this was a big part of living free and *staying* free.

Staying free meant, when the enemy worked to get access through my thoughts and emotions, my response to him would be decided *ahead* of time: *access denied*. I was starting to understand, peace wasn't only a feeling which came from being in right relationship with God—peace was my *weapon*.

I took a quick glance at the clock. Oh man! I needed to get going if I didn't want to be late for work, and I still had to get ready! Well, at least I was ready on the inside, that's what mattered most anyway. If I was ready on the *inside*, the *outside* was certain to follow.

"You Don't Deserve It"

"You don't deserve forgiveness. You don't deserve God's grace. You don't deserve His mercy. You don't deserve His love. You don't deserve His blessings. You don't even deserve His favor." Want to know how many times I've been hounded by these lies? *Countless*.

And here's the kicker—I *don't* deserve it. *None* of us do. There's nothing we can do to *deserve* what God so generously gives us; this is true. But there's a *higher* truth that says, we don't have to! God's not asking us to *earn* anything. For when we strive to earn His forgiveness and love, we stop trusting Him and start trusting in our own efforts. (*Yuck.*)

The truth is, we could *never* earn what God has freely given. It's far, *far* too expensive. All of history prior to Jesus proves this to be true, and all of history since continues to point us to this truth. At the cross, Jesus took everything *we* deserve upon *Himself*, then He took everything *He* deserves and gave it to *us*. It's the most amazing, uneven exchange in all of history. And He gladly made it for us. The Righteous for the unrighteous. The King for the slave. The Son for the orphan. The Worthy for the unworthy. The Deserving for the undeserving.

Everything we receive in the Kingdom of God has been made available to us because *Christ* made it available. Forgiveness. Grace. Mercy. Righteousness. Favor. Anointing. All of it comes out of the sacrifice Christ paid for us. Not because we earned it. They are gifts and as such, they are only available by *receiving*.

By the sacrifice of His Son, Romans 5:8 says, God *proved* to us His love, for while we were still sinners Christ died for us. God wanted us to be so sure, so *certain* of His love, that He sent His Son into the world to save us, *before* we could ever even attempt to earn it. Christ didn't come to condemn us; He came to save us. By the shed blood of His sacrifice, we are forgiven and we are redeemed (see Ephesians 1:7).

To be *redeemed* means we've been restored to right relationship with God. He sees us as if we've never sinned. That's the power of the blood of Jesus. It restores and redeems every broken thing. Not only is God faithful to redeem and forgive us of our sins, He is faithful to cleanse us of all unrighteousness. Christ's blood cleanses us so thoroughly of sin that we are able to stand before the Father in *full* confidence, knowing we're *fully* forgiven. God goes to great lengths in His Word to carefully confirm His forgiveness toward us. He wants us to be confident that *we* are the forgiven, because *He* is the Forgiver.

The truth is, friend, it's really hard to forgive *ourselves* when we refuse to receive the forgiveness *God* freely gives us. You know, if He doesn't expect us to be perfect, why would we? If He's not asking us to pay for what we've done by living in regret, why would we ask it of ourselves? If He

227

tells us we can walk in the light as He is in the light, why would we refuse?

Forgive for Your Own Sake

As I said a minute ago, when we try to earn what God freely gives, such as His forgiveness and grace, we stop trusting Him and start trusting ourselves. Dear one, when we do this, we set aside the grace of God, as if it were *secondary* to us saving ourselves through our own religious efforts and rule-keeping. Galatians 2:21 says in doing this, we *frustrate* the grace of God, for if we could save ourselves, Christ died in vain—but He *didn't*, because we *can't*.

The first step in forgiving ourselves is receiving the forgiveness God has already made so readily available to us. His forgiveness is always there for the taking. It's not complicated. He doesn't tell us to do penance or live with regret for a certain length of time before we're forgiven. You and me, we're forgiven the minute, the *second* we ask. Yes, even when we're asking for the *millionth* time.

For His *own* sake, God wipes away our sins and remembers them no more. Not only does He fully forgive us, He fully promises to make no mention of our past sin and even to remove the guilt associated with our sin. These promises are beautiful gifts from God, but just like any other gift we're given, they don't do us any good until we *receive* them. Until then, they're really nothing more than ornately decorated boxes. They're pretty to look at, but they don't serve much purpose unless we open them. When we stop making the issues of sin and our past *bigger* in our minds than *God* is, we are well into unwrapping His promises of forgiveness for us.

We've said it before, and now we're saying it again; what we *believe* is what we *empower*. When we believe the lie that there's no way we can be forgiven because what we did was too awful, we empower the liar and allow him to afflict our minds with fear. But when we take God at His Word and believe we're forgiven, simply because *He* said so, we empower the truth, and the truth sets us free.

While I know sometimes we *feel* like we don't deserve forgiveness (and there might even be others around who would agree), this is when we must remember to refuse our emotions the right to rule over us. We must allow the *peace of God* to rule our hearts and minds—not our *emotions*. Peace comes from walking in the truth of what *God* says, and as we walk in the truth, our emotions *will* catch up.

Conviction versus Condemnation

Forgiving ourselves of past mistakes and poor decisions doesn't mean we're dismissing what we did. Giving ourselves permission to move on isn't the same as ignoring the effects of our choices or never having to work through what happened.

Forgiving ourselves means, while we recognize what we did was wrong and not in the best interest of others or ourselves, we choose to let go of past hurts so we can start fresh. And we start fresh by asking forgiveness of those we've hurt and by forgiving ourselves. For we can't fully move on from our follies and faults until we forgive ourselves.

If we never move on, we're far more likely to keep repeating the same mistakes because guilt keeps the pain of what we did *present*. If we don't give our guilt over to God, it will consume us with a sorrow and regret so great that we'll feel powerless against it. So powerless, we'll want to give up and escape our emotions by turning to the *very thing* which put us in that position in the first place.

See the cycle? Remaining in the realm of regret and unforgiveness won't assuage our guilt. If anything, attempting to cope with the guilt and shame of what we've done, only weighs us down with a heavy burden our body, soul, and spirit were never created to carry.

Condemnation always makes us feel shame and ashamed of what we've done. Guilt says we've *done* something wrong. Shame says we *are* something wrong.

Christ's *conviction*, on the other hand, will never make us feel any sort of guilt or shame or embarrassment. On the contrary, the conviction Christ brings makes us feel clean by graciously and kindly revealing those things we need to turn from and give up.

Condemnation, guilt, and shame make us feel *dirty*. The conviction of the Holy Spirit makes us feel *clean*, free, and wakes us up to the rights we have in Him. Conviction says we get a say in what we choose. Condemnation says we're stuck.

The other side of conviction is righteousness. Conviction doesn't just highlight those things we need to run from, it reveals within us a sense of what's righteous—what's good—and helps us turn toward those things. Conviction helps us lay down our burdens. Condemnation keeps those burdens right between our shoulders. Conviction tells us we're forgiven. Condemnation tells us we're unforgiveable.

Conviction produces grateful, humble dependence upon Jesus because He alone is our righteousness. And the more we rest in who *He* is, rather than trying to do or earn everything ourselves, the more we become like Him. Our walk with Him really can be effortless. What's more, He designed it to be a delight!

Unforgiveness directed toward ourselves not only makes it harder for us to forgive *others*, it also makes it harder for others to move on. To make amends and move on, others often need us to hear their heart about the ways they've been hurt (directly or indirectly) by our decisions. But if we're living with unforgiveness, it's hard to hear about how we hurt others, as it feels like it only reinforces the wrongdoings we *already* regret.

When we make the *conscious* decision to walk in forgiveness toward ourselves and others, we'll be willing to lovingly listen, because we're able to sort out who we *were* from who we *are*. And as we hear them out, healing happens—for them and for us.

Please understand, I'm not suggesting we give ear to everyone who wants to rub our past in our faces. Or even that we need to rehash the conversation multiple times or revisit what happened when something triggers a memory. And the select times we *do* choose to revisit the past, we do so not to keep it alive, not to place blame or offend and oppress, not to defend and deny, but to *rejoice* at how far we've come!

The thing about condemnation and conviction is *we* get to choose which one we'll follow. We can't follow both because they're two entirely different paths. Condemnation leads to guilt, strife, and destruction. Conviction leads to forgiveness, peace, and life. Which one will you choose, friend? I've already made my choice and I'm choosing to walk in freedom!

Forgive for Freedom's Sake

If anyone had reason to withhold forgiveness, it was Jesus. The very people He came to save are the very ones who crucified Him. But instead of sending His angels to avenge Him and crush His accusers, He prayed "Father, forgive them, for they do not know what they are doing," in Luke 23:34 (NIV).

Jesus practiced what He preached. He didn't just talk the talk. He walked the walk. All throughout scripture we see Him telling us to forgive others just as God forgives us. He spent so much time on the topic of forgiveness because He knew how essential it would be to everything about us. Including our freedom.

I've heard it said that living in unforgiveness is like drinking poison and expecting the other person to get sick. In other words, it hurts *us* far more than it hurts *them*. Living with unforgiveness is like living with toxic waste. Its poison contaminates every corner of our lives, its corruptions seeps into every relationship.

Knowing this doesn't mean we won't run into an occasion when we feel we have the right to feel offended by others. When we've been wronged, we feel an apology is in order. Right? And we want the *apology* to correspond with the *offense*. I mean, why should we forgive when they haven't even bothered to apologize—or apologize *enough?* The truth is an apology isn't actually required for us to forgive. Don't get me wrong, it's *nice*. It's just not *necessary*.

If we withhold forgiveness until they apologize, we could be holding our breath for a long time. What a waste of perfectly good energy on our part because it's exhausting to hold a grudge, isn't it? And what do we do when those who've hurt us aren't even around to offer an apology? What then? Do we allow them to keep controlling our thoughts and emotions? Because that's exactly what we're doing when we refuse to forgive.

In holding onto unforgiveness, we may think we're hurting the ones who have wronged us, but the truth is, we're hurting *ourselves*. We may think unforgiveness gives us control over them, but the truth is, it actually allows *them* to control *us*. Think about it. When we refuse to forgive someone, what are we keeping at the forefront of our mind? All the ways they did us wrong. Right? Here's the thing, holding onto all that hurt only keeps it *current*, which means we're allowing them and their choices to hurt us all over again. Day in and day out. In *no* way does this help us or give us the upper hand.

If we really want to show ourselves strong, we'll forgive them. Because forgiveness doesn't make us weak—forgiveness reveals our strength. Forgiveness says, while I realize that what you did was wrong and it hurt me, for my own sake and the sake of those I love, I intentionally choose to forgive you. The key word here being *choose*. Forgiveness isn't a feeling; it's a *conscious choice*. We would do well to remember that.

Choosing to forgive frees us from *their* choices. It also *frees* us from making the same choices *they* did. Harboring unforgiveness toward someone makes us susceptible to hurting others the way *they* hurt *us*. You see, when we're constantly consumed with what they did, even if we're focusing on it to make sure we don't become like them, we're *still* entertaining the thoughts of how they hurt us on a regular basis.

Remember when we discussed being careful about what we entertain because it affects our reality and what we attract? Well, the more we're consumed with how they did us wrong, the greater our propensity is to wrong others in similar ways. For what we think in our hearts will be revealed through our lives (see Luke 6:45).

This is why Jesus warned us to not judge. For the in same manner we judge, we will be judged. But in the same way we show mercy, we'll be shown mercy, and mercy *always* triumphs over judgment. Christ proved this at the cross.

Choosing to walk in forgiveness is choosing to walk in obedience. Jesus told us, as we freely receive, we are enabled to freely give. So, since we have freely received His forgiveness, we are enabled to freely give forgiveness. What's more, the more aware we become of how much we've been forgiven, the more empowered we are to love others (see Luke 7:47). That's beautiful.

Ephesians 4:32 commands us to forgive one another as God, through Christ forgives us. With this (or any other) command comes the grace to obey. In whatever God calls us to—whether in Word or whisper—the empowering *grace* to obey comes the moment we *choose* to obey. Grace over-flows within us as we give Him our yes.

So even when we don't *feel* like forgiving, but we *choose* to because God said we should, the grace to follow through with this choice comes in our surrender. We don't work it up. We can't. We may *initially* choose to forgive someone based on our willpower, but the choice to *remain* walking in forgiveness won't come from willpower alone. It comes when we simply give God our "yes."

Freedom from Torment through Forgiveness

Forgiveness is in *no* way the same as making excuses for what someone said or did. But sometimes we worry that when we *do* forgive, it's like saying what they did is okay. No biggie. When really, it *was*. And sometimes we feel like if we forgive, it somehow gets them off the hook. Like now they don't need to be responsible for what they did.

What then? And what if they just go and do it all over again?

My friend, I can't tell you what's in *their* heart, but I can encourage you to guard what's in *yours*. Honestly, when someone continues to make the same unwise decisions over and over again, something's clearly not okay on the inside of them. They're probably going through some tough stuff we don't know about. Ultimately, what they really need is an encounter with the One who knows and loves them best. Because when people don't know they're loved and worth loving, they don't act very loveable.

As we pray for the love of Jesus to encounter them in real and irrefutable ways, we actually change the airways (the culture and communication lines) around them. Their atmosphere becomes pregnant with the promises of God's love, and their eyes can be open to options they might not have noticed before.

This is what forgiveness does. It frees us from resentment. It frees us up to pray and proclaim God's promises. Not only for our lives and the lives of those we love but even for the lives of those who've hurt us.

I realize it's really easy to pass judgment on people who have offended us, but they do not need our *judgment*; they need our *prayers*. And to be honest, *we* need to pray for them as much as *they* need our prayers. Because praying for others who have hurt or offended us keeps our hearts from becoming hardened. We want soft, tender hearts, not hard hearts; for a tender heart is receptive to God. A soft heart receives. A hard heart rejects. Jesus told us to pray for our enemies and bless those who hurt us, not only because it's a great way to reflect the Father's love, but because it protects our hearts from becoming hard.

I feel I need to be *crystal clear* in what I'm saying here, as there may be some of you reading this today who are in abusive relationships. This is *not* me telling you that you bless those who abuse you by subjecting yourself to further abuse. You don't bless others by being their doormat, you're actually doing the exact opposite. Enabling and forgiving are *not* the same things. We'll talk more about that in a minute.

It's totally possible to forgive someone from a safe distance. You can even forgive someone who's no longer around or alive because there is no geographical distance or time in the spiritual realm. This means your prayers for those who hurt you are as effective from a *safe distance* as they are *up close*. You don't have to be in the same house for your prayers to work effectively on their behalf. I *really* want you to get this because *I* didn't and ended up putting a lot of pressure on myself to stay in an unsafe environment because of it.

Please, if you are in an unsafe situation, don't make the same mistakes I did and put your safety and sanity at unnecessary risk. It is not weak or unwise to put a safe distance between you and your abuser, especially if you, your children, or loved ones are in danger. Staying in an unsafe, abusive environment isn't the brave thing to do. The brave thing is to get some safe distance, and from that safe place, seek sound wisdom and help, and prayerfully set wise boundaries for you and your family. You must remember, you're doing this as much for their sake as you are yours. We'll talk more about healthy boundaries in just a bit.

As we said, forgiveness frees us up to pray and proclaim God's goodness over us, and even over those who've hurt us. The devil doesn't want us walking in forgiveness or decreeing God's goodness over *anyone*, for this disrupts *his* airways (communication lines). Disrupting his communication lines causes a shift in the spirit. As things shift in the spirit, we'll see a shift in the environment inside us, around us, and even in the world.

The enemy would rather have us repeating what *he* says about others because it keeps *us* in bondage and torment (see Matthew 18:21–35). What's more, walking in outright unforgiveness allows the enemy access to our life. It gives him the opportunity to come in with accusation and offense, both which bring torture and torment to our souls. Remember, demons work by feeding us *their* thoughts. They want us to think *their* thoughts are our own. For this reason, we must diligently filter our thoughts and stubbornly cast down every imagination that rises up against the knowledge of God. (For more about this, revisit chapter six where we discussed this issue at greater length.)

Forgiveness frees us from the imprisonment of the enemy. Jesus came to set the captives free. *He* overcame the enemy and now holds the keys to death and hell, satan can no longer dangle them over us!

I feel like somebody reading this really needs to know Jesus *isn't* our prison guard. He's not our abuser or our accuser. He's our Deliverer, our Rescuer, and our Redeemer! He came to give us life more abundantly, not withhold life from us. Since He came to set free the captives and release the prisoners, we don't have to live in bondage to unforgiveness any longer. We can call upon His name and He'll set us free, but it's up to us to stay free. Refusing to entertain offenses and unforgiveness is a big part of that.

While it's up to us to stay free by intentionally filtering what we ruminate, the grace to filter our thoughts comes from Jesus. For everything is from Him, and through Him, and to Him (see Romans 11:36). I want to remind you of this because I don't want you carrying around all kinds of false responsibility. We align ourselves with *Him*, and He provides and sustains our healing and freedom. It really is that profoundly simple because He really is that profoundly good.

The Last Time

It was a warm summer evening, and the golden oranges and deep purples splashed across the sky said the sun was getting ready to set. The sweet smell of flowers was floating on the breeze as my doggy (who wasn't so little anymore) and I were on our return route home. We'd just finished running around downtown, passing by storefronts, parks, and people, and were now winding back through the adjoining neighborhoods of our quaint little city.

Running gave me time to think and marvel at how far my life had come. It'd been over a year now since I'd left Manny, and I'd never been so excited in all my life to actually *live* it. I'd never felt so comfortable in my own skin and was enjoying exploring God's love and giving Him all of me. I never knew surrender could be so freeing and feel so good! It was like I felt *alive* for the first time.

I checked my posture as I ran and took a deep breath in through my nose, making sure to keep a consistent pace. My mind wandered back to the encounter I'd had with the Lord a few months before. I had been so absolutely amazed by His pursuit of me and how He counted me worthy of His attention and affection. Wow! He was totally winning my heart with His love. I had found my emotions so overcome by His kindness in this encounter that I began crying uncontrollable tears of joy. I was so swept away by His goodness, my heart felt like it would explode with adoration for all He was and all He was doing.

There, in that encounter, I gave Him my *whole* heart. Even the part that still hoped to find a man who would see me through *His* eyes. In that place of surrender, I cried out with all sincerity, "God, I don't even need a romantic relationship. *You* so thoroughly satisfy me and touch my heart in ways no man ever could. If this is what life looks like for the *rest* of my life—just You and me—*bring it on!* I'm so excited to live it with You! Whatever it looks like. Wherever it leads."

The sound of the wind blowing through the trees brought me back to the present, and I exhaled through my mouth, reminding myself to land lightly and stay loose as I went along. The corners of my lips turned up into a smile, and I shook my head in amazement at the new memory arising in my mind. I couldn't help but laugh at the thought of how God led me to a new Bible study the very next week, and there, I met a man I felt an instant connection with within my heart. I remember going home that night, getting on my knees, and praying, "Lord, I don't want this unless *You're* in it. I don't want to force a anything *ever* again. So, if this isn't *You*, take this man and *any emotion* I may feel toward him out of my life. I only want what *You* want for me."

I chuckled at the thought that we were now a month into our "taking it slow and only as the Lord leads" relationship. I'd been genuinely content with just Jesus and here He was giving me even more. I shook my head and laughed again as a lightness lifted my heart. How like Him to be even better than I expected!

One of the things that felt really good about this relationship was knowing that, while this guy was great, the One I couldn't live without, the One I *really* needed was Jesus. It felt so wonderful to be living in healthy relationship with someone I wasn't obsessing about. Whatever this was, it was in *God's* hands. Together, we were giving Him total control over where we were going. That was the only way we could have a healthy relationship. Wherever it led us ...

(Turns out, it led to our getting married ... But that's a story for another time and another book!)

My not-so-little doggy, Buster Brown, and I rounded the corner and slowed down our pace as we approached the last block. But he knew what was coming and perked up with extra energy in his step. I gave his leash some slack as I came to my racer's pose. I could see his muscles twitching underneath his coat as he excitedly waited for me to give the order. With our feet right behind the old crack in the sidewalk—the one we used as our starting line—Buster looked up at me with anticipation, his tail wagging his whole body. "Ready. Get set. Go!" Off we ran, racing each other home. I sprinted with all my might, my muscles screaming in protest for the miles we'd just finished, but no matter how fast I ran, it was always the same. He was faster! Ugh. Lost again!

Buster stood proudly in the driveway, chest out, head held high. He seemed quite pleased with himself, the dominate champion of our grand competition. He was one happy boy knowing his water and treats were on the way. "Good job, buddy! Way to go!" I cheered, giving him his after-run rub down as he victoriously wagged his tail in triumph. "Now, let's get some dinner."

The evening went on as usual. Dinner was over, and we were dancing around the kitchen, cleaning up. Well, I cleaned; Buster wagged his whole body to the beat of the music, barking at my dance moves as I spun my mop around the kitchen floor and sung into it like a microphone. I was just finishing up my award-winning performance when I heard a knock at my front door, which wasn't anything out of the ordinary. Sometimes friends would occasionally drop in unannounced for a quick visit.

But as I answered the door, what I saw sent chills running down my spine. I felt like I'd been punched in the gut and nausea instantly overwhelmed me. Manny was standing in my entryway with his hands in his pockets, gazing at the ground. He looked up as I opened the door and blurted out,

"What are *you* doing here?" This was *completely* unexpected. *Way* out of the blue.

I knew he'd found out where I lived awhile back but since he hadn't tried to contact me, I assumed he'd finally moved on, for which I was *really* grateful. He mumbled something about having trouble with his *baby momma* and began blurting out all the drama that was going on between them. Something about threats and restraining orders, and the police getting involved. I wasn't really following since my focus was mainly on how *utterly* relieved I was to be out of all that mess.

My response was short. "Okay, so what does this have to do with *me?*" He seemed to be expecting me to feel sorry for him, like I would have before. But he was dealing with a whole new person now, the girl I used to be didn't exist anymore. "Well, I just wanted you to know how much I miss you. I'll never love anyone the way I love you, Hope. Is there any chance you'd be willing to try and work things out between us? I don't want to be with her; I want to be with you." The nausea was getting worse.

I took a deep breath to try and calm down before I con-tinued. Because my initial response was to shout at him that he was *crazy* to expect me to come back after he'd treated me so terribly, and apparently, he was *still* with the other woman. But I wasn't about to let him control my emotions this time. I knew now that I got to choose how I reacted to his responses. It was time to take everything I'd been learning in theory and put it into practice. I was *not* going to be emotionally manipulated anymore. We were not going to start this crazy cycle up again if I had a say in it—*and I did.*

At the same time, I felt compassion arising within me for his situation, as I watched him sitting there hunched over with a heavy burden between his shoulders, so shaken by his life's choices. But I felt *no* obligation to make him happy or fix his life. I'd already learned that I couldn't control his choices. *I* wasn't the answer he was seeking. What he wanted—the love he was look for—was *God's* love. The darkness, which had once been so intriguing to him, was now tormenting him. He didn't need *me*; he needed the *Savior* to save and deliver him.

I looked at him and replied with kindness but firmness in my voice, I needed him to really get it this time, "I'm not what you need, Manny. *I* can't save you. I know now, I never could. There's only *One* who can, as we've talked about so many times before. But *I* can't make the decision to receive Christ as your Savior, *for* you. That's entirely up to you. *You* have to make that choice.

"I *can* tell you this though, we'll *never* be together again. What I felt for you feels like a million years ago and honestly, I've moved on. I met someone else, and he's *good* to me, and I'm really growing to love him."

He shook his head as he stood up to go, telling me that wasn't exactly the answer he was hoping to hear, but it also wasn't unexpected. He hoped I'd be happy in life and was sorry for how things turned out. "I never wanted to become like my dad, and now I'm just like him," he sighed with regret in his voice. I walked to the door and held it open for him, "You know, you have a say in that. You're not victim to your dad's fate. There's no written rule that says you have to be like him. Jesus loves you. He'll bring the love and change you seek. Call upon Him, and He'll set you free. He really will."

He walked out the door and turned around, taking one last look at me as he inhaled deeply through his nose and just stood there for a moment. Finally, blinking back tears, he nodded his head and shrugged his shoulders, "Well, I guess this is really goodbye, then." I leaned against the door jam and crossed my arms around myself. My heart ached for him, but not in the way it used to; the desire to run into his arms and make it all better was no longer within me. For that, I was truly grateful. "I guess it is," I nodded as I watched him head down the walkway toward his car. "Never forget, God loves you, and He's always on your side. He'll help you find the answers. You get a say in the person you choose to become. So, choose wisely for you and your child." He attempted a smile as he looked over the hood of his car and waved. Then, he got in and left. It would be the last I ever saw of him.

As I turned to close the door and go back inside, I was filled with such wonder at God's goodness. Months before, that scene would have wrecked me. Now, I was smiling, filled with overwhelming joy and hope. For my future, yes, but for what awaited me right now too. I was truly content. I *now* knew if I had God, I had *everything*.

Forgiveness versus Reconciliation

It took more years than I cared to count, but I finally knew that just because I felt compassion for Manny, didn't mean I was supposed to go running right back into his arms. I'd already tried that. Several times. It never turned out well. I was realizing that *reconciliation* and *compassion* were two totally different things. Simply because Manny showed up saying he was sorry and wanted to work things out, didn't mean he was at a place where he actually *could*. Neither did it mean that I *should*.

Does that mean reconciliation is *always* out of the question for *everyone*? Definitely not. It wasn't the right road for us, for a lot of really good reasons. In all the times we tried before, I had no idea what boundaries were, let alone how to set and maintain them. And reconciliation can't work without healthy boundaries. It hadn't really been reasonable of me to expect a different result when I hadn't really had a significant change in the way I interacted in our relationship, and neither had he.

Each time I went back to him, I only enabled his behavior. Allowing him to manipulate my emotions and responses by giving into his controlling ways. All while trying to come up with some ways to insert my own level of control. Each time he promised he would change, he ended up reverting back to his old behavior because he wasn't trying to change for himself. He was trying to change for me. And it doesn't work that way. There's simply not enough staying power when we try to change for others. True change is only truly effective when we truly do it for ourselves.

Each time he wanted to get back together, he promised to be a dedicated, loyal husband, the leader of our home. But every time we tried to reconcile, his true colors came out—and he wasn't really ready to give up his bachelor lifestyle. He said he was ready to be faithful to me, but when push came to shove, he simply wasn't able to follow through with his word.

He'd been torn between two worlds, and by the way it sounded from our last conversation, he *still* was. So *no*, I *wasn't* willing to try again. I already knew where it would lead, he had let me know without even realizing it.

Like I said before, this *doesn't* mean reconciliation is out of the question for everyone. My story won't be the same as yours, and thank goodness it's not because the world would be an awfully boring place if we were all the same.

At the same time, it would be really wise for us to set some groundwork for what reconciliation *is* and what it *isn't*. I've found quite a bit of confusion can revolve around this subject when we don't have a healthy framework for it.

While forgiveness can sometimes *lead* to reconciliation, forgiveness doesn't *automatically equal* reconciliation. Reconciliation cannot successfully be achieved without wise, healthy boundaries first being in place. The boundaries you set should consider your safety and wellbeing, the safety and wellbeing of your children and loved ones, as well as that of the other party involved.

Without healthy boundaries, we easily slip into enabling, and this is no more beneficial to them than it is healthy or safe for us. That means, setting and maintaining healthy boundaries is as much for *their* sake as it is our *own*.

Safe boundaries become sound parameters. Parameters establish the barriers and gates of our relationships with people and things. Gates *allow* access. They say, okay, you're healthy and safe, you are welcome in to do life with me. Gates are entryways that allow others access to the places of our heart that we, with the direction of the Lord, decide. We are not subject to the relationships in our lives. God has beautifully given us a say in them through our *choice*.

Barriers *refuse* access. When we're in an abusive relationship, it's really easy to remain in it because we feel bad for them or bad about ourselves. So, what we need to do is build a barrier, a safety wall, by refusing those lies and the thoughts and emotions *attached* to those lies, access and adjust our relationships accordingly.

That may look like ending the relationship all together or reiterating our boundaries in a way that they can be clearly understood. And if the person in question understands and just doesn't care or respect us enough to respect our boundaries, then we need to respect *ourselves* enough to do something about it. Because God *does*—He loves and respects His children enough to give us choice. We don't look like Jesus by letting everyone walk all over us, friend.

That's a huge misconception that spreads through the church like cancer. And it can be just as destructive.

These parameters help us identify who and what is healthy, and who and what is not. The more we set and maintain healthy boundaries, the more we become aware of the atmosphere around us and our internal environment will actually start to alert us when someone or something isn't safe. This is true of our relationships as well as our choices and interactions in everyday life.

One of the biggest mistakes I made throughout all those years was ignoring this internal alarm. It was an alarm sounded by the Spirit, but I was afraid I was merely being mean or judgmental. Friend, please hear me. There's a *world* of difference between judgment and discernment.

Looking back, I wasn't *judging* Manny for feeling like he might not have been good for me. I was using *wisdom* and *discernment*. I would've been judging him if I knew nothing about him and *then* made that assumption based on fleshly feelings. But I knew all I needed to know to make this call. I only wish I would've listened to that voice of wisdom.

Just as a word of warning, not listening to our instincts can get us into a lot of trouble. I'm not giving anyone permission to be skeptical of others or paranoid either. I'm giving you permission to be *wise*. Actually, the One who has given us permission—and the call—to be wise was Jesus. To be innocent, yet wise (see Matthew 10:16). These two go well together.

So, when you're thinking of setting boundaries, remember, it's not selfish; it's *safe* and it's *wise*. Boundaries actually free us up to have healthy interactions with others. Boundaries remind us, it's not *love* to let others control us. It's not *love* to let them walk all over us. It's not *love* to let them beat us around or manipulate us into believing we deserve what they give us. These reasons and more are why healthy boundaries help us discern whether reconciliation is something that is possible.

To be clear, forgiveness is a given; reconciliation is not. It's really important for us to know the difference. God commands us to forgive, which means, He also gives us the grace to do so. Are we expected to not have feelings about forgiving those who've hurt us? No. Forgiveness doesn't take our emotions out of the picture. Forgiving God's way means we *choose* to forgive in spite of our emotions (see Matthew 6:15).

As we explore our new nature and grow in experiential relationship with Jesus, forgiveness and reconciliation become a part of our growth experience. But the wisdom to know *if* and *when* to reconcile becomes just as much a part of our growth experience as the reconciliation itself.

Let me be crystal clear, reconciliation doesn't mean we pick up a relationship right where it left off or act like nothing happened. That's not reconciliation. That's ignoring and enabling recurring issues which got us there in the first place.

Sometimes it's simply not safe to restore certain relationships. Especially the ones which put us or our loved ones at risk or continue to have the same destructive results. At the very least, it's unsafe for these relationships to be restored *until* and *unless* the other person gets help and becomes renewed in the way they operate within the relationship and life in general.

We would be wise, friend, to forgive *and* set healthy boundaries at the same time—not to threaten forgiveness—but promote positive interaction, preserve sanity, and protect everyone's safety. Healthy boundaries not only help us decide if reconciliation is the wise and right thing to do at the time, they also help us recognize the difference between forgiving and enabling.

For example, should you *forgive* your adult child for repeatedly stealing from you for drugs? Yes, absolutely. Should you, in their current drug-induced state, entrust them with your entire life savings? No! This is definitely not a wise decision. Not for you, but even more, not for them. Would you ask a mugger to hold your purse for you? Of course not! At least I'd hope not. God told us to be *forgiving*—not *foolish*.

There's a definitive difference between *forgiveness* and *trust*. Forgiveness is *granted*. Trust is *earned*. We're called to forgive, indefinitely. But trust, once broken, must be rebuilt. And the more it's broken, the more carefully it needs to be repaired. But thankfully, it's not impossible—nothing is with God.

Too often we lump forgiveness and trust into the same category. But the two are totally distinct from each other. Forgiveness is up to *us*. How much we can trust is up to *them*. Forgiveness provides us with proper perspective and rightly reminds us who's responsible for other people's decisions. (Here's a helpful hint: It's not me and it's not you, we're responsible for *our* choices, not *theirs*.) And though forgiveness helps us heal and move on, it also helps us break the bad habit of enabling—so we *can* get on with the moving on.

Trying to solve their problems, like they're our own, isn't part of the solution. It's part of the problem. When we allow others to mop up their messes, we're actually allowing them the opportunity to learn valuable life lessons that can only come from making amends for our mistakes. The truth is, *we* can't fix their life. Only *God* can. He'll step in the *second* they ask Him.

And the truth is, He's always reaching out to them with His influence: His heart; His love; His comfort; His goodness; His guidance (see Psalm 23:2, 3). For these are how He influences us. So if we're always trying to fix everything for others, we could actually be interfering with His perfect influence. *We* don't know where they'll find Him, but *God* does.

So, one of the best things we can do is fully surrender them to Jesus. He loves them *far* more than we ever could. They're the reason He came into this world—to seek and save the lost. We talked about that in chapter one, remember? He came so we'd no longer be lost. He came so we'd be *found*. God is great at finding things.

Instead of interfering or enabling, I think it would be wise if we simply asked Him what we should do. Because God isn't only great at finding things, He's great at restoring things that have been broken. Broken hearts. Broken lives. Broken relationships. Broken minds.

What's more, He's great at knowing if and when a relationship is safe and ready for reconciliation. God is great at finding things, restoring what's broken, and He's *perfect* in the way He leads us. When we let *Him* lead, He'll never lead us wrong. He'll never lead us where He won't go. So let's go with Him.

In my case, He led me to Himself. He led me away from the toxic soul tie I'd had with Manny so I could find abundant life and freedom in Him. But that wouldn't have happened if I hadn't let Him lead. I would've sunk into even deeper destruction if I hadn't finally made the choice to simply trust and follow. And what was it that helped me make that choice? His influence. His heart.

But I know of other couples whose relationships have been restored better than before because they let the Lord lead them into reconciliation. And what helped them make that choice? His influence. His heart.

See how important it is to take a step back (or maybe several) and just follow Jesus? We often look at the exterior and make decisions based upon what we can see. But God sees what is *unseen*. What is invisible to our eyes is *clearly* visible to His. He doesn't look at how people or things appear to be, He looks at the heart. So we would be wise to let the One who sees it all, lead us all. For He'll only ever lead us to His heart, and His heart holds what's best for us. All of us.

The truth is, regardless of whether the relationship is reconcilable, forgiveness is absolutely possible. And according to God, forgiveness is *required*. For our own sake as well as theirs.

Forgiveness is powerful, and it's packed with a powerful message. We partner with Jesus when we forgive. Representing *Him* and *His* message for everyone to come. Come and be reconciled to the One who gave it *all* to reconcile us to Himself.

Epilogue

The Process
(His Pursuit in Our Process)

Oh my goodness, my dear, sweet friend, I have *so* enjoyed my time with you! What a beautiful journey this has been, and you've been *such* a great listener along the way! I've learned so much throughout this season. I've received revelations for me, revelations for you, and I've stepped deeper into the heart of God. I hope you have too!

I was just telling my hunky husband, Alan, it's amazing what we can do when we just give Jesus our "yes." I had so many people tell me I should write a book around my story, but I never really had the confidence to do so. And then, when I *did* try, I was so overwhelmed by all the lies that said I couldn't do it, I'd never succeed, I wasn't qualified. It took me *several* years to see that those lies only had the power to cripple my confidence when *I* entertained them.

Throughout the early years of my writing, I'd come up with all kinds of excuses not to write because it felt like I was fighting a major battle every time I did. Finally, after years of stalling and making excuses, the Lord brought me to a place where I remembered it wasn't my battle to fight. It was His, and He'd *already* won it for me! I just had to rest in Him and receive the precious gift of grace He paid the highest price to give. And as I leaned into Him, He led me in ways to activate my faith.

I excitedly started writing more from the secret place of His heart and less out of striving. As I made this my practice, the faith for what I was doing arose on the inside of me. For when we hide in His heart, faith naturally arises from that secret place. Finally, I was ready to start pursuing the publishing process when I suddenly suffered a traumatic brain injury from an accident where I was hit in the head. This injury put me in a place where I had to learn how to walk and talk all over again. All the sudden, my writing and the publishing process came to a screeching halt. I could barely put one *foot* in front of the other, let alone one *word*.

The road to recovery was an extremely *lo-o-ng* one and I'd be lying if I said it wasn't hard. The impact produced ongoing, overwhelming migraines along with auditory and visual impairments. While I longed to write and finish what I'd started, for quite some time I was unable to read or write because my eyes were unable to focus and words would move all over the page.

After several months of therapy, I decided to try and pick up my writing again. It was super slow going, but with the help of Holy Spirit, I was doing it! He's the One who empowered me through the whole process. (I'm eternally grateful and humble, He's so amazing, my friend, *so amazing!*) I learned so much about myself through this process and what's more, I learned God's love truly doesn't come out of what I do for Him. I love God *because* He first loved me. His love is not only my empowering, energizing force, it's what enables me to love Him and others as well as myself.

A lot changed about me through this injury, but I'd say the most predominate change was my faith. I used to think that what I *did* defined me, now I know what truly defines me is *who* and *Whose* I am. I am my Heavenly Father's daughter. It's a who *I* am because of who *He* is. I am the bride of Christ. It's who *I* am because of who *He* is. I am a friend of the Holy Spirit. It's who *I* am because of who *He* is. I am saved, free, delivered, healed, and made whole (regardless of what my body or emotions or others try to tell me) *this* is who I am because of who *He* is.

I never had as much bold, Christ-centered confidence as I do now. And it came out of my injury—out of the time He led me to decree and declare His promises of love, healing, and goodness over myself *in spite* of the state of my circumstances and body. I'm telling you what, friend—His love makes us *resilient* and *tenacious*. I realize I was stubborn before, but *now* I'm stubborn for the Kingdom of God! I *refuse* to change the subject or move off what is truth—*no matter what!* For His truth is higher and superior to anything we experience, this side of Heaven.

All that to say, when I *did* start writing again and reviewing what I had previously written, I realized my very message had changed. I was bolder now. More passionate. More vulnerable. It was the message He was asking me to write all along. I just needed to believe I could. I needed to believe that *He* could—and He wanted to, through me. Because it's a partnership. We co-labor with Him and it's our greatest joy in life.

Is there more to this story? You know it. But it's a story for another time and another book. The takeaway today is—what the enemy means for our destruction, God always, *always* turns around for our good. Jesus is King! He is above every other name and at His name, *everything* must bow. It will. And we'll see it bow as we wrap ourselves in His love and let Him carry us in His heart to our victory.

Ever since my injury, my message is so much about *rest*, the beautiful and blessed rest of God. I used to think I had to work to meet His approval and step into His good graces, but now I know simply being with Him and resting in Him is what He wanted for me and from me the whole time. I share more about my story and the love we encounter by making ourselves fully available to Jesus at my blog www. hopezins.com. Feel free to check it out, friend!

Do I have more to share with you? More journeys to take? More mountains to scale and valleys to explore? You'd better believe it! While we're on this side of Heaven, we're all perfectly in process, and He will always perfectly pursue us in the process. So, we're just getting started on our excursions together! Until next time, let me leave you with this: You are *beautiful*, Jesus loves you, and so do I!

For those of you who haven't yet asked Jesus to be your Best Friend, your constant Guide, your loving Lord, I encourage you to revisit chapter two and turn to the section titled "Our Best Friend." This section can easily be turned into a prayer simply by reading the words and personalizing them. In fact, it was written with this in mind, for it was written with *you* in mind. If you've been searching for that "something" to fulfill you, that something is actually *Someone,* and His name is Jesus.

As I say in that section, entering into relationship with Jesus will be the *best* decision you'll ever make—or it'll be your saddest miss. I can lead you to this choice, but I can't make it for you. You alone have the power and, yes, the responsibility to *choose*. When we take the time to stop and listen to the message of love that God is whispering to us, we'll choose wisely every time. Because His love will *never* lead us wrong.

I love you guys! Thanks so much for listening to my heart! I would love to hear from you too! Feel free to reach out to me via my blog, www.hopezins.com. I look forward to chatting again soon!

If the message in this book has blessed you, pass it on! Don't keep it to yourself! There are more hurting people out there that need to hear the message of God's love and hope than we know. So pass it on! Whether through this book or your own story, spread the goodness of God's love around and pretty soon the sparks will become a flaming fire in your life and in the lives of others!

God bless you, my friend, and never forget, He loves you with an *everlasting* love!

Appendix

Scriptures Applied
(In Order of Mention)

So, a few days ago, I got a message from my dear friend, Andrea, and she suggested that I make an index of all the Scriptures I've used throughout my book. Because, like her, there may be many of you who are beginning to read the Bible and learning how to *apply* and *personalize* it to your lives for the first time. (Which is really exciting! Yea for you, my friend!) My immediate thought was, *Oh my goodness, this is such a genius idea!* I loved it as soon as I heard it! So, thanks to Andrea's suggestion and her Holy Spirit-led idea, I've included the verses I've used throughout this book.

I hope this helps you apply and personalize Scripture in a whole new way! Have fun exploring the power of God's Word. The more you use it, the more you'll see just how powerful it truly is!

Please note, any Scriptures I may have used in multiple locations I've only included once in this Appendix. The only exception is where I used multiple versions of a Scripture for emphasis. I've included several different versions of Scripture in this Appendix for your enjoyment and reference. If I included a Scripture within the book text, I did not include it in this list since it has already been provided. Please note, all Scriptures are provided in order of mention throughout the book.

I pray these Bible verses come alive to you as you read, explore, and personalize them. For God's Word *is* alive, and He has *personally* provided it just for you, my dear friend!

- Zephaniah 3:17 (NIV): The LORD your God is with you, the Mighty Warrior who saves. He will take great delight in you; in his love he will no longer rebuke you, but will rejoice over you with singing.

- Hebrews 9:27 (NKJV): And as it is appointed for men to die once, but after this the judgment.

- Job 14:15 (NLT): You have decided the length of our lives. You know how many months we will live, and we are not given a minute longer.

- Ephesians 2:10 (NASB emphasis added): For we are His *workmanship*, created in Christ Jesus for good works, which God prepared beforehand so that we would walk in them.

- Ephesians 2:10 (NLT emphasis added): For we are God's *masterpiece*. He has created us anew in Christ Jesus, so we can do the good things he planned for us long ago.

- Psalm 139:19 (NLT): You made all the delicate, inner parts of my body and knit me together in my mother's womb.

- Genesis 1:26 (KJV): And God said, "Let us make man in our image, after our likeness: and let them have dominion over the fish of the sea, and over the fowl of the air, and over the cattle, and over all the earth, and over every creeping thing that creepeth upon the earth."

- Hebrews 13:5 (NLT): For God has said, "I will never fail you. I will never abandon you."

- Romans 8:38, 39 (NIV): For I am convinced that neither death nor life, neither angels nor demons, neither the present nor the future, nor any powers, neither height nor depth, nor anything else in all creation, will be able to separate us from the love of God that is in Christ Jesus our Lord.

- 1 John 3:20 (NKJV): For if our heart condemns us, God is greater than our heart, and knows all things.

- John 3:16 (NLT): For this is how God loved the world: He gave his one and only Son, so that everyone who believes in him will not perish but have eternal life.

- Romans 8:32 (NASB): He who did not spare His own Son, but delivered Him over for us all, how will He not also with Him freely give us all things?

- Philippians 2:5-8 (NLT): You must have the same attitude that Christ Jesus had. Though he was God, he did not think of equality with God as something to cling to. Instead, he gave up his divine privileges; he took the humble position of a slave and was born as a human being. When he appeared in human form, he humbled himself in obedience to God and died a criminal's death on a cross.

- Hebrews 4:15 (TPT): He understands humanity, for as a Man, our magnificent King-Priest was tempted in every way just as we are, and conquered sin.

- John 16:33 (NLT): I have told you all this so that you may have peace in me. Here on earth you will have many trials and sorrows. But take heart, because I have overcome the world.

- John 5:19 (NKJV): Then Jesus answered and said to them, "Most assuredly, I say to you, the Son can do nothing of Himself, but what He sees the Father do; for whatever He does, the Son also does in like manner."

- John 12:49 (NIV): For I did not speak on my own, but the Father who sent me commanded me to say all that I have spoken.

- Matthew 8:16 (NKJV): When evening had come, they brought to Him many who were demon-possessed. And He cast out the spirits with a word, and healed all who were sick.

- Luke 6:19 (NKJV): And the whole multitude sought to touch Him, for power went out from Him and healed them all.

- Acts 10:38 (NASB): You know of Jesus of Nazareth, how God anointed Him with the Holy Spirit and with power, and how He went about doing good and healing all who were oppressed by the devil, for God was with Him.

- Hebrews 1:3 (TPT): The Son is the dazzling radiance of God's splendor, the exact expression of God's true nature—his mirror image! He holds the universe together and expands it by the mighty power of his spoken word. He accomplished for us the complete cleansing of sins, and then took his seat on the highest throne at the right hand of the majestic One.

- John 21:25 (NASB): And there are also many other things which Jesus did, which if they were written in detail, I suppose that even the world itself would not contain the books that would be written.

- Matthew 20:28 (NIV): Just as the Son of Man did not come to be served, but to serve, and to give his life as a ransom for many.

- Isaiah 53:5 (NLT): But he was pierced for our rebellion, crushed for our sins. He was beaten so we could be whole. He was whipped so we could be healed.

- 1 Peter 2:24 (NLT): He personally carried our sins in his body on the cross so that we can be dead to sin and live for what is right. By his wounds you are healed.

- Romans 8:34, 37 (TPT): Who then is left to condemn us? Certainly not Jesus, the Anointed One! For he gave his life for us, and even more than that, he has conquered death and is now risen, exalted, and enthroned by God at his right hand. So how could he possibly condemn us since he is continually praying for our triumph? Yet even in the midst of all these things, we triumph over them all, for God has made us to be more than conquerors, and his demonstrated love is our glorious victory over everything!

- Isaiah 53:3 (NKJV): He is despised and rejected by men, a Man of sorrows and acquainted with grief. and we hid, as it were, our faces from Him; He was despised, and we did not esteem Him.

- Isaiah 61:1-3 (NKJV): The Spirit of the Lord God is upon Me, because the Lord has anointed Me to preach good tidings to the poor; He has sent Me to heal the brokenhearted, to proclaim liberty to the captives, and the opening of the prison to those who are bound; to proclaim the acceptable year of the Lord, and the day of vengeance of our God; to comfort all who mourn, to console those who mourn in Zion, to give them beauty for ashes, the oil of joy for mourning, the garment of praise for the spirit of heaviness; that they may be called trees of righteousness, the planting of the Lord, that He may be glorified.

- 2 Corinthians 8:9 (NIV): For you know the grace of our Lord Jesus Christ, that though he was rich, yet for your sake he became poor, so that you through his poverty might become rich.

- Galatians 3:13 (TPT): Yet, Christ paid the full price to set us free from the curse of the law. He absorbed it completely as he became a curse in our place. For it is written: 'Everyone who is hung upon a tree is doubly cursed.' Jesus, our Messiah, was cursed in our place and in so doing, dissolved the curse from our lives, so that all the blessings of Abraham can be poured out upon even non-Jewish believers. And now God gives us the promise of the wonderful Holy Spirit who lives within us when we believe in him.

- Galatians 5:1 (TPT): Let me be clear, the Anointed One [Jesus] has set us free—not partially, but completely and wonderfully free! We must always cherish this truth and stubbornly refuse to go back into the bondage of our past.

- John 11:25 (NKJV): Jesus said to her, "I am the resurrection and the life. He who believes in Me, though he may die, he shall live."

- John 3:16 (NKJV): For God so loved the world that He gave His only begotten Son, that whoever believes in Him should not perish but have ever-lasting life.

- 1 Corinthians 15:57 (NLT): But thank God! He gives us victory over sin and death through our Lord Jesus Christ.

- 1 Corinthians 15:55-57 (NLT): O death, where is your victory? O death, where is your sting? For sin is the sting that results in death, and the law gives sin its power. But thank God! He gives us victory over sin and death through our Lord Jesus Christ.

- 2 Corinthians 5: 18-21 (NASB): Now all these things are from God, who reconciled us to Himself through Christ and gave us the ministry of reconciliation, namely, that God was in Christ reconciling the world to Himself, not counting their trespasses against them, and He has committed to us the word of reconciliation. Therefore, we are ambassadors for Christ, as though God were making an appeal through us; we beg you on behalf of Christ, be reconciled to God. He made Him who knew no sin to be sin on our behalf, so that we might become the righteousness of God in Him.

- Luke 19:10 (NKJV): for the Son of Man has come to seek and to save that which was lost.

- Luke 19:10 (NLT): For the Son of Man came to seek and save those who are lost.

- John 1:12 (NASB): But as many as received Him, to them He gave the right to become children of God, even to those who believe in His name.

- Matthew 26:53 (NIV): Do you think I cannot call on my Father, and he will at once put at my disposal more than twelve legions of angels?

- Romans 12:2 (NKJV): And do not be conformed to this world, but be transformed by the renewing of your mind, that you may prove what is that good and acceptable and perfect will of God.

- Jeremiah 29:11 (NIV): "For I know the plans I have for you," declares the LORD, "plans to prosper you and not to harm you, plans to give you hope and a future."

- John 10:10 (NASB): The thief comes only to steal and kill and destroy; I came that they may have life, and have it abundantly.

- Ephesians 1:5, 6 (TPT): For it was always in his perfect plan to adopt us as his delightful children, through our union with Jesus, the Anointed One, so that his tremendous love that cascades over us would glorify his grace—for the same love he has for his Beloved One, Jesus, he has for us. And this unfolding plan brings him great pleasure!

- Jeremiah 17:7 (NLT): But blessed are those who trust in the LORD and have made the LORD their hope and confidence.

- Matthew 7:9-11 (NLT): You parents—if your children ask for a loaf of bread, do you give them a stone instead? Or if they ask for a fish, do you give them a snake? Of course not! So if you sinful people know how to give good gifts to your children, how much more will your heavenly Father give good gifts to those who ask him.

- Matthew 10:16 (AMP): Listen carefully: I am sending you out like sheep among wolves; so be wise as serpents, and innocent as doves [have no self-serving agenda].

- 1 Corinthians 14:33 (NKJV): For God is not the author of confusion but of peace, as in all the churches of the saints.

- Hebrews 11:3 (NKJV): By faith we understand that the entire universe was formed at God's command, that what we now see did not come from anything that can be seen.

- Genesis 1:3 (NLT): Then God said, "Let there be light," and there was light.

- Proverbs 11:10 (NASB): When it goes well with the righteous, the city rejoices, And when the wicked perish, there is joyful shouting.

- Proverbs 29:2 (NKJV): When the righteous are in authority, the people rejoice; But when a wicked man rules, the people groan.

- Luke 15:31 (NASB): And he said to him, "Son, you have always been with me, and all that is mine is yours."

- John 16:13-15 (MSG): ...when the Friend comes, the Spirit of the Truth, he will take you by the hand and guide you into all the truth there is. He won't draw attention to himself, but will make sense out of what is about to happen and, indeed, out of all that I have done and said. He will honor me; he will take from me and deliver it to you. Everything the Father has is also mine. That is why I've said, "He takes from me and delivers to you."

- Luke 1:37 (NASB): For nothing will be impossible with God.

- Romans 8:11 (TPT): Yes, God raised Jesus to life! And since God's Spirit of Resurrection lives in you, he will also raise your dying body to life by the same Spirit that breathes life into you!

- Genesis 22:16 (NIV): ...I swear by myself, declares the LORD...

- Isaiah 45:23 (NKJV): I have sworn by Myself; the word has gone out of My mouth in righteousness, And shall not return, that to Me every knee shall bow, every tongue shall take an oath.

- Hebrews 6:13 (NASB): For when God made the promise to Abraham, since He could swear by no one greater, He swore by Himself.

- 2 Timothy 2:13 (NASB): If we are faithless, He remains faithful, for He cannot deny Himself.

- Isaiah 55:11 (NASB): So shall My word be that goes forth from My mouth; It shall not return to Me void, But it shall accomplish what I please, And it shall prosper in the thing for which I sent it.

- Colossians 1:19, 20 (NIV): For God was pleased to have all his fullness dwell in him, and through him to reconcile to himself all things, whether things on earth or things in heaven, by making peace through his blood, shed on the cross.

- 1 Peter 1:3 (NIV): Praise be to the God and Father of our Lord Jesus Christ! In his great mercy he has given us new birth into a living hope through the resurrection of Jesus Christ from the dead.

- Nehemiah 8:10, 12 (NIV): Nehemiah said, "Go and enjoy choice food and sweet drinks, and send some to those who have nothing prepared. This day is holy to our Lord. Do not grieve, for the joy of the Lord is your strength... Then all the people went away to eat and drink, to send portions of food and to celebrate with great joy, because they now understood the words that had been made known to them.

- 1 John 4:7, 8, 19 (NKJV): Dear friends, let us love one another, for love comes from God. Everyone who loves has been born of God and knows God. Whoever does not love does not know God, because God is love.

- 1 John 4:19 (NKJV): We love Him because He first loved us.

- Psalm 36:7-8 (NKJV): How precious is Your lovingkindness, O God! Therefore the children of men put their trust under the shadow of Your wings. They are abundantly satisfied with the fullness of Your house, and You give them drink from the river of Your pleasures.

- John 17:20 (NLT): I am praying not only for these disciples but also for all who will ever believe in me through their message.

- Ephesians 2:19 (TPT): So, you are not foreigners or guests, but rather you are the children of the city of the holy ones, with all the rights as family members of the household of God.

- Galatians 6:10 (TPT): Take advantage of every opportunity to be a blessing to others, especially to our brothers and sisters in the family of faith!

- John 13:35 (NIV): By this everyone will know that you are my disciples, if you love one another.

- 1 Corinthians 13:1-2 (TPT): If I were to speak with eloquence in earth's many languages, and in the heavenly tongues of angels, yet I didn't express myself with love, my words would be reduced to the hollow sound of nothing more than a clanging cymbal.

- John 8:2-11 (TPT): Then at dawn Jesus appeared in the temple courts again, and soon all the people gathered around to listen to his words, so he sat down and taught them. Then in the middle of his teaching, the religious scholars and the Pharisees broke through the crowd and brought a woman who had been caught in the act of committing adultery and made her stand in the middle of everyone. Then they said to Jesus, "Teacher, we caught this woman in the very act of adultery. Doesn't Moses' law command us to stone to death a woman like this? Tell us, what do you say we should do with her?" They were only testing Jesus because they hoped to trap him with his own words and accuse him of breaking the laws of Moses. But Jesus didn't answer them. Instead he simply bent down and wrote in the dust with his finger. Angry, they kept insisting that he answer their question, so Jesus stood up and looked at them and said, "Let's have the man who has never had a sinful desire throw the first stone at her." And then he bent over again and wrote some more words in the dust. Upon hearing that, her accusers slowly left the crowd one at a time, beginning with the oldest to the youngest, with a convicted conscience. Until finally, Jesus was left alone with the woman still standing there in front of him. So he stood back up and said to her, "Dear woman, where are your accusers? Is there no one here to condemn you?" Looking around, she replied, "I see no one, Lord." Jesus said, "Then I certainly don't condemn you either. Go, and from now on, be free from a life of sin."

- Luke 19:1-10 (NIV): Jesus entered Jericho and was passing through. A man was there by the name of Zacchaeus; he was a chief tax collector and was wealthy. He wanted to see who Jesus was, but because he was short he could not see over the crowd. So he ran ahead and climbed a sycamore-fig tree to see him, since Jesus was coming that way. When Jesus reached the spot, he looked up and said to him, "Zacchaeus, come down immediately. I must stay at your house today." So he came down at once and welcomed him gladly. All the people saw this and began to mutter, "He has gone to be the guest of a sinner." But Zacchaeus stood up and said to the Lord, "Look, Lord! Here and now I give half of my possessions to the poor, and if I have cheated anybody out of anything, I will pay back four times the amount." Jesus said to him, "Today salvation has come to this house, because this man, too, is a son of Abraham. For the Son of Man came to seek and to save the lost."

- Luke 7:36-50 (NLT): One of the Pharisees asked Jesus to have dinner with him, so Jesus went to his home and sat down to eat. When a certain immoral woman from that city heard he was eating there, she brought a beautiful alabaster jar filled with expensive perfume. Then she knelt behind him at his feet, weeping. Her tears fell on his feet, and she wiped them off with her hair. Then she kept kissing his feet and putting perfume on them. When the Pharisee who had invited him saw this, he said to himself, "If this man were a prophet, he would know what kind of woman is touching him. She's a sinner!" Then Jesus answered his thoughts. "Simon," he said

to the Pharisee, "I have something to say to you."
"Go ahead, Teacher," Simon replied. Then Jesus
told him this story: "A man loaned money to two
people—500 pieces of silver to one and 50 pieces to
the other. But neither of them could repay him, so
he kindly forgave them both, canceling their debts.
Who do you suppose loved him more after that?"
Simon answered, "I suppose the one for whom he
canceled the larger debt." "That's right," Jesus said.
Then he turned to the woman and said to Simon,
"Look at this woman kneeling here. When I entered
your home, you didn't offer me water to wash the
dust from my feet, but she has washed them with her
tears and wiped them with her hair. You didn't greet
me with a kiss, but from the time I first came in,
she has not stopped kissing my feet. You neglected
the courtesy of olive oil to anoint my head, but she
has anointed my feet with rare perfume. I tell you,
her sins—and they are many—have been forgiven,
so she has shown me much love. But a person who
is forgiven little shows only little love." Then Jesus
said to the woman, 'Your sins are forgiven.' The
men at the table said among themselves, "Who is
this man, that he goes around forgiving sins?" And
Jesus said to the woman, "Your faith has saved you;
go in peace."

- John 4:4-26 (NIV): Now he had to go through
Samaria. So he came to a town in Samaria called
Sychar, near the plot of ground Jacob had given to his
son Joseph. Jacob's well was there, and Jesus, tired
as he was from the journey, sat down by the well. It
was about noon. When a Samaritan woman came to
draw water, Jesus said to her, "Will you give me a

drink?" (His disciples had gone into the town to buy food.) The Samaritan woman said to him, "You are a Jew and I am a Samaritan woman. How can you ask me for a drink?" (For Jews do not associate with Samaritans.) Jesus answered her, "If you knew the gift of God and who it is that asks you for a drink, you would have asked him and he would have given you living water." "Sir," the woman said, "you have nothing to draw with and the well is deep. Where can you get this living water? Are you greater than our father Jacob, who gave us the well and drank from it himself, as did also his sons and his livestock?" Jesus answered, "Everyone who drinks this water will be thirsty again, but whoever drinks the water I give them will never thirst. Indeed, the water I give them will become in them a spring of water welling up to eternal life." The woman said to him, "Sir, give me this water so that I won't get thirsty and have to keep coming here to draw water." He told her, "Go, call your husband and come back." "I have no husband," she replied. Jesus said to her, "You are right when you say you have no husband. The fact is, you have had five husbands, and the man you now have is not your husband. What you have just said is quite true." "Sir," the woman said, "I can see that you are a prophet. Our ancestors worshiped on this mountain, but you Jews claim that the place where we must worship is in Jerusalem." "Woman," Jesus replied, "believe me, a time is coming when you will worship the Father neither on this mountain nor in Jerusalem. You Samaritans worship what you do not know; we worship what we do know, for salvation is from the Jews. Yet a time is coming and has now come when the true worshipers will worship the Father in the Spirit and in truth, for they are the kind of worshipers the Father seeks. God is spirit, and his worshipers must worship in the Spirit and in truth." The woman said, "I know that Messiah" (called Christ) "is coming. When he comes, he will explain everything to us." Then Jesus declared, "I, the one speaking to you—I am he."

- John 3:1-3 (NKJV): There was a man of the Pharisees named Nicodemus, a ruler of the Jews. This man came to Jesus by night and said to Him, "Rabbi, we know that You are a teacher come from God; for no one can do these signs that You do unless God is with him." Jesus answered and said to him, "Most assuredly, I say to you, unless one is born again, he cannot see the kingdom of God."

- Mark 16:9 (NASB): Now after He had risen early on the first day of the week, He first appeared to Mary Magdalene, from whom He had cast out seven demons.

- Galatians 3:13, 14 (TPT): Yet, Christ paid the full price to set us free from the curse of the law. He absorbed it completely as he became a curse in our place. For it is written: 'Everyone who is hung upon a tree is doubly cursed.' Jesus, our Messiah, was cursed in our place and in so doing, dissolved the curse from our lives, so that all the blessings of Abraham can be poured out upon even non-Jewish believers. And now God gives us the promise of the wonderful Holy Spirit who lives within us when we believe in him.

- John 1:1, 14 In the beginning was the Word, and the Word was with God, and the Word was God... And the Word became flesh and dwelt among us, and we beheld His glory, the glory as of the only begotten of the Father, full of grace and truth.

- John 10:4, 5 (NLT): After he has gathered his own flock, he walks ahead of them, and they follow him because they know his voice. They won't follow a stranger; they will run from him because they don't know his voice.

- John 10:26 (NLT): My sheep listen to my voice; I know them, and they follow me.

- 1 Corinthians 5:17 (NKJV): Therefore, if anyone is in Christ, he is a new creation; old things have passed away; behold, all things have become new.

- John 1:4, 5 (NLT): The Word [Jesus] gave life to everything that was created, and his life brought light to everyone. The light shines in the darkness, and the darkness can never extinguish it.

- John 8:12 (NASB): Then Jesus again spoke to them, saying, "I am the Light of the world; he who follows Me will not walk in the darkness, but will have the Light of life."

- Matthew 5:45 (NIV) …He causes his sun to rise on the evil and the good, and sends rain on the righteous and the unrighteous.

- Matthew 5:14-16 (NKJV): You are the light of the world. A city that is set on a hill cannot be hidden. Nor do they light a lamp and put it under a basket, but on a lampstand, and it gives light to all who are in the house. Let your light so shine before men, that they may see your good works and glorify your Father in heaven.

- Mark 12:28-31 (NKJV): Then one of the scribes came, and having heard them reasoning together, perceiving that He had answered them well, asked Him, "Which is the first commandment of all?" Jesus answered him, "The first of all the commandments is: 'Hear, O Israel, the Lord our God, the Lord is one. And you shall love the Lord your God with all your heart, with all your soul, with all your mind, and with all your strength.' This is the first commandment. And the second, like it, is this: 'You shall love your neighbor as yourself.' There is no other commandment greater than these."

- Romans 5:8 (TPT): But Christ proved God's passionate love for us by dying in our place while we were still lost and ungodly!

- Proverbs 4:23 (NKJV): Keep your heart with all diligence, for out of it spring the issues of life.

- Luke 12:32 (NLT): So don't be afraid, little flock. For it gives your Father great happiness to give you the Kingdom.

- Ecclesiastes 3:11 (NIV): He has made everything beautiful in its time. He has also set eternity in the human heart; yet no one can fathom what God has done from beginning to end.

- Proverbs 4:20-22 (NIV): My son, pay attention to what I say; turn your ear to my words. Do not let them out of your sight, keep them within your heart; for they are life to those who find them and health to one's whole body.

- Hebrews 11:6 (NKJV): But without faith it is impossible to please Him, for he who comes to God must believe that He is, and that He is a rewarder of those who diligently seek Him.

- Genesis 1:27 (NASB): God created man in His own image, in the image of God He created him; male and female He created them.

- Matthew 28:18-20 (NKJV): And Jesus came and spoke to them, saying, "All authority has been given to Me in heaven and on earth. Go therefore and make disciples of all the nations, baptizing them in the name of the Father and of the Son and of the Holy Spirit, teaching them to observe all things that I have commanded you; and lo, I am with you always, even to the end of the age." Amen.

- Genesis 1:28 (NKJV): Then God blessed them, and God said to them, "Be fruitful and multiply; fill the earth and subdue it; have dominion over the fish of the sea, over the birds of the air, and over every living thing that moves on the earth."

- Romans 8:22 (NIV): We know that the whole creation has been groaning as in the pains of childbirth right up to the present time.

- Colossians 2:15 (NIV): And having disarmed the powers and authorities, he made a public spectacle of them, triumphing over them by the cross.

- Philippians 4:8 (NASB): Finally, brethren, whatever is true, whatever is honorable, whatever is right, whatever is pure, whatever is lovely, whatever is of good repute, if there is any excellence and if anything worthy of praise, dwell on these things.

- Colossians 3:23 (NASB): Whatever you do, do your work heartily, as for the Lord rather than for men.

- 1 Corinthians 15:10 (TPT): But God's amazing grace has made me who I am! And his grace to me was not fruitless. In fact, I worked harder than all the rest, yet not in my own strength but God's, for his empowering grace is poured out upon me.

- 1 Corinthians 1:2 (NASB): To the church of God which is at Corinth, to those who have been sanctified in Christ Jesus, saints by calling, with all who in every place call on the name of our Lord Jesus Christ, their Lord and ours.

- Ephesians 2:8 (NKJV): For by grace you have been saved through faith, and that not of yourselves; it is the gift of God.

- Matthew 6:9-10 (NKJV): In this manner, therefore, pray: Our Father in heaven, hallowed be Your name. Your kingdom come. Your will be done on earth as it is in heaven.

- Romans 12:6 (NKJV): Having then gifts differing according to the grace that is given to us, let us use them: if prophecy, let us prophesy in proportion to our faith.

- 1 Peter 4:10 (NKJV): As each one has received a gift, minister it to one another, as good stewards of the manifold grace of God.

- Acts 4:33 (NKJV): And with great power the apostles gave witness to the resurrection of the Lord Jesus. And great grace was upon them all.

- Acts 5:41 (TPT): The apostles left there rejoicing, thrilled that God had considered them worthy to suffer disgrace for the name of Jesus.

- Luke 2:52 (NKJV): And Jesus increased in wisdom and stature, and in favor with God and men.

- Psalm 118:17 (NASB) I will not die, but live, and tell of the works of the LORD.

- 1 John 4:7-11 (NKJV): Beloved, let us love one another, for love is of God; and everyone who loves is born of God and knows God. He who does not love does not know God, for God is love. In this the love of God was manifested toward us, that God has sent His only begotten Son into the world, that we might live through Him. In this is love, not that we loved God, but that He loved us and sent His Son to be the propitiation for our sins. Beloved, if God so loved us, we also ought to love one another.

- 2 Corinthians 10:4, 5 (NKJV): For the weapons of our warfare are not carnal but mighty in God for pulling down strongholds, casting down arguments and every high thing that exalts itself against the knowledge of God, bringing every thought into captivity to the obedience of Christ.

- Revelation 1:14 (TPT): His head and his hair were white like wool—white as glistening snow. And his eyes were like flames of fire!

- John 17:21-23 (TPT): I pray for them all to be joined together as one even as you and I, Father, are joined together as one. I pray for them to become one with us so that the world will recognize that you sent me. For the very glory you have given to me I have given them so that they will be joined together as one and experience the same unity that we enjoy. You live fully in me and now I live fully in them so that they will experience perfect unity, and the world will be convinced that you have sent me, for they will see that you love each one of them with the same passionate love that you have for me.

- John 4:23 (NKJV): But the hour is coming, and now is, when the true worshipers will worship the Father in spirit and truth; for the Father is seeking such to worship Him.

- 1 Corinthians 12:31—1 Corinthians 13:3 (NIV): Now eagerly desire the greater gifts. And yet I will show you the most excellent way. If I speak in the tongues of men or of angels, but do not have love, I am only a resounding gong or a clanging cymbal. If I have the gift of prophecy and can fathom all mysteries and all knowledge, and if I have a faith that can move mountains, but do not have love, I am nothing. If I give all I possess to the poor and give over my body to hardship that I may boast, but do not have love, I gain nothing.

- Psalm 34:8 (NLV): O taste and see that the Lord is good. How happy is the man who trusts in Him!

- 1 Corinthians 2:10 (NIV): These are the things God has revealed to us by his Spirit. The Spirit searches all things, even the deep things of God.

- Acts 17:28 (NKJV): For in Him we live and move and have our being, as also some of your own poets have said, 'For we are also His offspring.'

- Romans 5:1, 2 (TPT) Our faith in Jesus transfers God's righteousness to us and he now declares us flawless in his eyes. This means we can now enjoy true and lasting peace with God, all because of what our Lord Jesus, the Anointed One, has done for us. 2 Our faith guarantees us permanent access into this marvelous kindness that has given us a perfect relationship with God. What incredible joy bursts forth within us as we keep on celebrating our hope of experiencing God's glory!

- Hebrews 12:2 (NASB): Fixing our eyes on Jesus, the author and perfecter of faith, who for the joy set before Him endured the cross, despising the shame, and has sat down at the right hand of the throne of God.

- James 5:16 (NASB): Therefore, confess your sins to one another, and pray for one another so that you may be healed. The effective prayer of a righteous man can accomplish much.

- Proverbs 28:13 (TPT): If you cover up your sin you'll never do well. But if you confess your sins and forsake them, you will be kissed by mercy.

- Psalm 32:1-5 (NKJV): Blessed is he whose transgression is forgiven, whose sin is covered. Blessed is the man to whom the Lord does not impute iniquity, and in whose spirit there is no deceit. When I kept silent, my bones grew old through my groaning all the day long. For day and night Your hand was heavy upon me; my vitality was turned into the drought of summer. Selah. I acknowledged my sin to You, and my iniquity I have not hidden. I said, "I will confess my transgressions to the Lord," and You forgave the iniquity of my sin. Selah.

- Song of Songs 1:7 (TPT, emphasis added): Won't you tell me, lover of my soul, where do you feed your flock? Where do you lead your beloved ones to rest in the heat of the day? *For I wish to be wrapped all around you* as I wander among the flocks of your shepherds. It is you I long for, with no veil between us!

- John 3:3-5 (NKJV): Jesus answered and said to him, "Most assuredly, I say to you, unless one is born [a]again, he cannot see the kingdom of God."

Nicodemus said to Him, "How can a man be born when he is old? Can he enter a second time into his mother's womb and be born?" Jesus answered, "Most assuredly, I say to you, unless one is born of water and the Spirit, he cannot enter the kingdom of God.

- Romans 6:11 (NASB): Even so consider yourselves to be dead to sin, but alive to God in Christ Jesus.

- 1 Corinthians 1:18 (NKJV): For the message of the cross is foolishness to those who are perishing, but to us who are being saved it is the power of God.

- Revelation 19:10 (TPT): At this I fell facedown at the angel's feet to worship him, but he stopped me and said, "Don't do this! For I am only a fellow servant with you and one of your brothers and sisters who cling to what Jesus testifies. Worship God. The testimony of Jesus is the spirit of prophecy."

- Matthew 8:3 (NASB): Jesus stretched out His hand and touched him, saying, "I am willing; be cleansed." And immediately his leprosy was cleansed.

- 2 Kings 5:1-19 (NLT): The king of Aram had great admiration for Naaman, the commander of his army, because through him the Lord had given Aram great victories. But though Naaman was a mighty warrior, he suffered from leprosy. At this time Aramean raiders had invaded the land of Israel, and among their captives was a young girl who had been given to Naaman's wife as a maid. One day the girl said to her mistress, "I wish my master would go to see the prophet in Samaria. He would heal him of his leprosy." So Naaman told the king what the young girl from Israel had said. "Go and visit the prophet," the king of Aram told him. "I will send a letter of introduction for you to take to the king of Israel."

So Naaman started out, carrying as gifts 750 pounds of silver, 150 pounds of gold, and ten sets of clothing. The letter to the king of Israel said: "With this letter I present my servant Naaman. I want you to heal him of his leprosy." When the king of Israel read the letter, he tore his clothes in dismay and said, "Am I God, that I can give life and take it away? Why is this man asking me to heal someone with leprosy? I can see that he's just trying to pick a fight with me." But when Elisha, the man of God, heard that the king of Israel had torn his clothes in dismay, he sent this message to him: "Why are you so upset? Send Naaman to me, and he will learn that there is a true prophet here in Israel." So Naaman went with his horses and chariots and waited at the door of Elisha's house. 10 But Elisha sent a messenger out to him with this message: "Go and wash yourself seven times in the Jordan River. Then your skin will be restored, and you will be healed of your leprosy." But Naaman became angry and stalked away. "I thought he would certainly come out to meet me!" he said. "I expected him to wave his hand over the leprosy and call on the name of the Lord his God and heal me! Aren't the rivers of Damascus, the Abana and the Pharpar, better than any of the rivers of Israel? Why shouldn't I wash in them and be healed?" So Naaman turned and went away in a rage. But his officers tried to reason with him and said, "Sir, if the prophet had told you to do something very difficult, wouldn't you have done it? So you should certainly obey him when he says simply, 'Go and wash and be cured!'" So Naaman went down to the Jordan River and dipped himself seven times, as the man of God had instructed him.

And his skin became as healthy as the skin of a young child, and he was healed! Then Naaman and his entire party went back to find the man of God. They stood before him, and Naaman said, "Now I know that there is no God in all the world except in Israel. So please accept a gift from your servant." But Elisha replied, "As surely as the Lord lives, whom I serve, I will not accept any gifts." And though Naaman urged him to take the gift, Elisha refused. Then Naaman said, "All right, but please allow me to load two of my mules with earth from this place, and I will take it back home with me. From now on I will never again offer burnt offerings or sacrifices to any other god except the Lord. However, may the Lord pardon me in this one thing: When my master the king goes into the temple of the god Rimmon to worship there and leans on my arm, may the Lord pardon me when I bow, too." "Go in peace," Elisha said. So Naaman started home again.

- Mark 8:22-25 (NKJV): Then He came to Bethsaida; and they brought a blind man to Him, and begged Him to touch him. So He took the blind man by the hand and led him out of the town. And when He had spit on his eyes and put His hands on him, He asked him if he saw anything. And he looked up and said, "I see men like trees, walking." Then He put His hands on his eyes again and made him look up. And he was restored and saw everyone clearly.

- Luke 8:43-48 (NASB): And a woman who had a hemorrhage for twelve years, and could not be healed by anyone, came up behind Him and touched the fringe of His cloak, and immediately her hemorrhage stopped. And Jesus said, "Who is the one who

282

touched Me?" And while they were all denying it, Peter said, "Master, the people are crowding and pressing in on You." But Jesus said, "Someone did touch Me, for I was aware that power had gone out of Me." When the woman saw that she had not escaped notice, she came trembling and fell down before Him, and declared in the presence of all the people the reason why she had touched Him, and how she had been immediately healed. And He said to her, "Daughter, your faith has made you well; go in peace."

- Luke 18:1-8 (NASB): Now He was telling them a parable to show that at all times they ought to pray and not to lose heart, saying, "In a certain city there was a judge who did not fear God and did not respect man. There was a widow in that city, and she kept coming to him, saying, 'Give me legal protection from my opponent.' For a while he was unwilling; but afterward he said to himself, 'Even though I do not fear God nor respect man, yet because this widow bothers me, I will give her legal protection, otherwise by continually coming she will wear me out.'" And the Lord said, "Hear what the unrighteous judge said; now, will not God bring about justice for His elect who cry to Him day and night, and will He delay long over them? I tell you that He will bring about justice for them quickly. However, when the Son of Man comes, will He find faith on the earth?"

- 1 Samuel 30:6-8 (NLT): David was now in great danger because all his men were very bitter about losing their sons and daughters, and they began to talk of stoning him. But David found strength in the Lord his God. Then he said to Abiathar the priest,

"Bring me the ephod!" So Abiathar brought it. Then David asked the Lord, "Should I chase after this band of raiders? Will I catch them?" And the Lord told him, "Yes, go after them. You will surely recover everything that was taken from you!"

- Mark 4:25 (TPT): For those who listen with open hearts will receive more revelation. But those who don't listen with open hearts will lose what little they think they have!"

- 1 Kings 3:10-14 (NKJV): The speech pleased the Lord, that Solomon had asked this thing. Then God said to him: "Because you have asked this thing, and have not asked long life for yourself, nor have asked riches for yourself, nor have asked the life of your enemies, but have asked for yourself understanding to discern justice, behold, I have done according to your words; see, I have given you a wise and understanding heart, so that there has not been anyone like you before you, nor shall any like you arise after you. And I have also given you what you have not asked: both riches and honor, so that there shall not be anyone like you among the kings all your days. So if you walk in My ways, to keep My statutes and My commandments, as your father David walked, then I will lengthen your days."

- Exodus 33:15, 16 (NASB): Then he said to Him, "If Your presence does not go with us, do not lead us up from here. For how then can it be known that I have found favor in Your sight, I and Your people? Is it not by Your going with us, so that we, I and Your people, may be distinguished from all the other people who are upon the face of the earth?"

- Exodus 33:18, 19 (NASB, emphasis added): Then Moses said, "I pray You, show me Your glory!" And He said, "*I Myself will make all My goodness pass before you*, and will proclaim the name of the Lord before you; and I will be gracious to whom I will be gracious, and will show compassion on whom I will show compassion."

- Job 22:28 (NASB): You will also decree a thing, and it will be established for you; and light will shine on your ways.

- Proverbs 18:21(NKJV): Death and life are in the power of the tongue, and those who love it will eat its fruit.

- Genesis 1:31 (NKJV): Then God saw everything that He had made, and indeed it was very good. So the evening and the morning were the sixth day.

- Proverbs 23:7 (NKJV): For as he thinks in his heart, so is he...

- Matthew 18:3 (TPT): Learn this well: Unless you dramatically change your way of thinking and become teachable, and learn about heaven's realm with the wide-eyed wonder of a child, you will never be able to enter in.

- Proverbs 29:18 (KJV): Where there is no vision, the people perish...

- Matthew 16:24 (TPT): Then Jesus said to his disciples, "If you truly want to follow me, you should at once completely reject and disown your own life. And you must be willing to share my cross and experience it as your own, as you continually surrender to my ways. For if you choose self-sacrifice and lose your lives for my glory, you will continually discover true life. But if you choose to keep your lives for yourselves, you will forfeit what you try to keep.

- Proverbs 29:11 (TPT): You can recognize fools by the way they give full vent to their rage and let their words fly! But the wise bite their tongue and hold back all they could say.

- James 1:19 (NIV): My dear brothers and sisters, take note of this: Everyone should be quick to listen, slow to speak and slow to become angry.

- Ephesians 4:26, 27 (TPT): But don't let the passion of your emotions lead you to sin! Don't let anger control you or be fuel for revenge, not for even a day. Don't give the slanderous accuser, the devil, an opportunity to manipulate you!

- Ephesians 4:26, 27 (NIV): In your anger do not sin: Do not let the sun go down while you are still angry, and do not give the devil a foothold.

- Romans 8:5 (BSB): But God proves His love for us in this: While we were still sinners, Christ died for us.

- Ephesians 1:7 (NKJV): In Him we have redemption through His blood, the forgiveness of sins, according to the riches of His grace.

- Galatians 2:21 (KJV): I do not frustrate the grace of God: for if righteousness come by the law, then Christ is dead in vain.

- Luke 6:45 (NKJV): A good man out of the good treasure of his heart brings forth good; and an evil man out of the evil treasure of his heart brings forth evil. For out of the abundance of the heart his mouth speaks.

- Luke 7:47 (NASB): For this reason I say to you, her sins, which are many, have been forgiven, for she loved much; but the one who is forgiven little, loves little.

- Ephesians 4:32 (NASB): Be kind to one another, tender-hearted, forgiving each other, just as God in Christ also has forgiven you.

- Matthew 18:21-35 (NKJV): Then Peter came to Him and said, "Lord, how often shall my brother sin against me, and I forgive him? Up to seven times?" Jesus said to him, "I do not say to you, up to seven times, but up to seventy times seven. Therefore the kingdom of heaven is like a certain king who wanted to settle accounts with his servants. And when he had begun to settle accounts, one was brought to him who owed him ten thousand talents. But as he was not able to pay, his master commanded that he be sold, with his wife and children and all that he had, and that payment be made. The servant therefore fell down before him, saying, 'Master, have patience with me, and I will pay you all.' Then the master of that servant was moved with compassion, released him, and forgave him the debt. "But that servant went out and found one of his fellow servants who owed him a hundred denarii; and he laid hands on him and took him by the throat, saying, 'Pay me what you owe!' So his fellow servant fell down at his feet and begged him, saying, 'Have patience with me, and I will pay you all.' And he would not, but went and threw him into prison till he should pay the debt. So when his fellow servants saw what had been done, they were very grieved, and came and told their master all that had been done. Then his master, after he had called him, said to him, 'You wicked servant! I forgave you all that debt because you begged me. Should you not also have had compassion on your fellow servant, just as I had pity on you?' And his master was angry, and delivered him to the torturers until he should pay all that was due to him. "So My heavenly Father also will do to you if each of you, from his heart, does not forgive his brother his trespasses."

- Romans 11:36 (NASB): For from Him, and through Him, and to Him are all things. To Him be the glory forever. Amen.

- Matthew 6:15 (TPT): But if you withhold forgiveness from others, your Father withholds forgiveness from you.

- Psalm 23:2, 3 (TPT): He offers a resting place for me in his luxurious love. His tracks take me to an oasis of peace, the quiet brook of bliss. That's where he restores and revives my life. He opens before me pathways to God's pleasure and leads me along in his footsteps of righteousness so that I can bring honor to his name.

About Hope Zins

Hope Zins is an author, speaker, and prophetic revivalist who is passionate about helping people recognize and embrace their God-given value. Her message of Christ-centered confidence and hope encourages others to discover the Father's love and delight in who He uniquely created them to be. By applying God's promises through His Word and voice, she invites her audience to explore the secret places of His heart and step into the *much more* He has in store for those who simply ask Him.

Hope incorporates her personal experience of living in abuse and self-harm into her writing. She invites her readers into her own vulnerable and gritty journey of discovering how she stopped living like a victim and started living like a victor. Her unfiltered examples, honest humor, and encouraging message show her readers that while she can relate to their struggle, her suggestions and solutions have come from a place of personal triumph and testimony.

Hope currently resides in Dayton, Ohio, with her husband, Alan and their little doggy, Nibbles. Hope and Alan both have had near-death experiences and are now passionate about living fully alive and wide awake for Jesus, hearts overflowing with gratitude and joy for each day. Their greatest desire is to reach souls with the message of the love of Jesus and to see the Father's Kingdom come and will be done on earth as it is in Heaven through the manifest power of the Holy Spirit through yielded lives.

To find out more about Hope Zins, visit her website, www.hopezins.com. To book Hope for your next event, please contact her at info@hopezins.com.